TROPICS OF VIENNA

AUSTRIAN AND HABSBURG STUDIES
General Editor: Howard Louthan, Center for Austrian Studies, University of Minnesota

Volume 1
Austrian Women in the Nineteenth and Twentieth Centuries: Cross-Disciplinary Perspectives
Edited by David F. Good, Margarete Grandner, and Mary Jo Maynes

Volume 2
From World War to Waldheim: Culture and Politics in Austria and the United States
Edited by David F. Good and Ruth Wodak

Volume 3
Rethinking Vienna 1900
Edited by Steven Beller

Volume 4
The Great Tradition and Its Legacy: The Evolution of Dramatic and Musical Theater in Austria and Central Europe
Edited by Michael Cherlin, Halina Filipowicz, and Richard L. Rudolph

Volume 5
Creating the Other: Ethnic Conflict and Nationalism in Habsburg Central Europe
Edited by Nancy M. Wingfield

Volume 6
Constructing Nationalities in East Central Europe
Edited by Pieter M. Judson and Marsha L. Rozenblit

Volume 7
The Environment and Sustainable Development in the New Central Europe
Edited by Zbigniew Bochniarz and Gary B. Cohen

Volume 8
Crime, Jews and News: Vienna 1890–1914
Edited by Daniel Mark Vyleta

Volume 9
The Limits of Loyalty: Imperial Symbolism, Popular Allegiances, and State Patriotism in the Late Habsburg Monarchy
Edited by Laurence Cole and Daniel L. Unowsky

Volume 10
Embodiments of Power: Building Baroque Cities in Europe
Edited by Gary B. Cohen and Franz A. J. Szabo

Volume 11
Diversity and Dissent: Negotiating Religious Differences in Central Europe, 1500–1800
Edited by Howard Louthan, Gary B. Cohen, and Franz A. J. Szabo

Volume 12
"Vienna Is Different": Jewish Writers in Austria from the Fin de Siècle to the Present
Hillary Hope Herzog

Volume 13
Sexual Knowledge: Feeling, Fact and Social Reform in Vienna, 1900–1934
Britta McEwen

Volume 14
Journeys Into Madness: Mapping Mental Illness in the Austro-Hungarian Empire
Edited by Gemma Blackshaw and Sabine Wieber

Volume 15
Territorial Revisionism and the Allies of Germany in the Second World War: Goals, Expectations, Practices
Edited by Marina Cattaruzza, Stefan Dyroff, and Dieter Langewiesche

Volume 16
The Viennese Café and Fin-de-Siècle Culture
Edited by Charlotte Ashby, Tag Gronberg, and Simon Shaw-Miller

Volume 17
Understanding Multiculturalism: The Habsburg Central European Experience
Edited by Johannes Feichtinger and Gary B. Cohen

Volume 18
Sacrifice and Rebirth: The Legacy of the Last Habsburg War
Edited by Mark Cornwall and John Paul Newman

Volume 19
Tropics of Vienna: Colonial Utopias of the Habsburg Empire
Ulrich E. Bach

TROPICS OF VIENNA

Colonial Utopias of the Habsburg Empire

Ulrich E. Bach

berghahn
NEW YORK · OXFORD
www.berghahnbooks.com

First published in 2016 by
Berghahn Books
www.berghahnbooks.com

© 2016, 2021 Ulrich E. Bach
First paperback edition published in 2021

All rights reserved. Except for the quotation of short passages for the purposes of criticism and review, no part of this book may be reproduced in any form or by any means, electronic or mechanical, including photocopying, recording, or any information storage and retrieval system now known or to be invented, without written permission of the publisher.

Library of Congress Cataloging-in-Publication Data

Names: Bach, Ulrich E., author.
Title: Tropics of Vienna: Colonial Utopias of the Habsburg Empire / Ulrich E. Bach.
Description: New York: Berghahn Books, 2016. | Series: Austrian and Habsburg studies; volume 19 | Includes bibliographical references and index.
Identifiers: LCCN 2015045612| ISBN 9781785331329 (hardback: alkaline paper) | ISBN 9781785331336 (e-book)
Subjects: LCSH: Austrian literature--Austria--Vienna--History and criticism. | Austrian literature--19th century--History and criticism. | Utopias in literature. | Colonies in literature. | Vienna (Austria)--Intellectual life--19th century.
Classification: LCC PT3828.V5 B327 2016 | DDC 830.9/943613--dc23 LC record available at http://lccn.loc.gov/2015045612

British Library Cataloguing in Publication Data
A catalogue record for this book is available from the British Library

ISBN 978-1-78533-132-9 hardback
ISBN 978-1-80073-014-4 paperback
ISBN 978-1-78533-133-6 ebook

Contents

Acknowledgments	vi
Introduction	1
1. Leopold von Sacher-Masoch: Utopian Periphery	13
2. Lazar von Hellenbach: Utopia or Theosophy	39
3. Theodor Hertzka: Seeking Emptiness	68
4. Theodor Herzl: Vienna in Palestine	84
5. Robert Müller: Anti-Exoticism, and Joseph Roth: Finis Austriae	111
Index	137

Acknowledgments

Every book has a turning point that its author can look back on and recognize as the moment when it was clear the book would become a reality. This moment occurred to me one afternoon in the Wienbibliothek im Rathaus, when I finally followed up on Jost Hermand's dismissive description of Lazar von Hellenbach's *Insel Mellonta* (1883). Hermand sees the complex novel as a mere utopian island adventure that takes up the conventional shipwreck motif. *Insel Mellonta* was for me what the Austrian writer Norbert Gstrein has providentially coined as "das Glück des Recherierenden" (researcher's luck), and it marked the turning point that shaped the entire book. *Tropics of Vienna: Colonial Utopias of the Habsburg Empire* began with an interest in colonialism, narrative utopias, and fin-de-siècle Vienna. By the time the chapter on Theodor Hertzka's *Freiland* (1890) was completed, I came across the colonial utopias of Leopold von Sacher-Masoch and Theodor Herzl. In this respect, the 'discovery' of *Insel Mellonta* in the Wienbibliothek helped me to establish a discourse on colonial utopias in the last decades of the nineteenth century.

Over the years, many have supported my scholarly endeavors and I would like to take this opportunity to express my gratitude to all of them. To start with Vienna: Ernst Fischer encouraged me even before I came to the United States to pursue an academic career, and offered invaluable advice about the various possible ways to structure the book at a meeting in Albany, New York. Also closely connected to Vienna, my gratitude goes to Ursula Reber and Clemens Ruthner for publishing an early version of the von Hellenbach chapter.

I want to thank explicitly Andrew Hewitt, who has been a most insightful reader. Among many other ideas, he encouraged me to explore the "inner" colonialism in Leopold von Sacher-Masoch's novellas in Chapter 1. At the initial stages of writing this book in Los Angeles, Jeff Prager, Jimmy Fisher and Rita Coufal always gave discerning criticism and advice. In fact, it was Jeff who inspired me to pursue my interest in narrative utopias in the first place. Also, my dear friends Charlton Payne and Jack Cumming carefully read drafts of every chapter.

In Palo Alto, Seth Lerer, Jessie Labov, Anna North, Na'ama Rokem and George Bloom helped to reformulate the von Sacher-Masoch chapter. More recently, my former colleague Tanya Weimar edited the Hertzka chapter, and Robert Fischer, the chair of the Modern Language Department at Texas State University approved a stipend for the editing of the entire manuscript. Patricia "Casey" Sutcliffe, a marvelous editor at the German Historical Institute in Washington, DC, successfully purged my Teutonic syntax whenever it was needed, and provided me with many last minute insights. Also, I would like to thank the editors Adam Capitanio, Molly Mosher, Chris Chappell, and Nigel Smith of Berghahn Books, and the anonymous peer reviewers, whose collective criticism contributed to the quality of the book.

I would like to dedicate the book to Paula Park, for encouraging me throughout the publication process, and to thank her for preparing the entire manuscript with me in the course of last summer. Without her help, this book would be fictitious. I also want to dedicate the book to my son Nicholas Bach, who has been an inspiration for the book from the beginning.

Athens, Ohio, April 2015

Introduction

> The conquest of the air was being prepared here too, but not too intensively. A ship would now and then be sent off to South America or East Asia, but not too often. There was no ambition for world markets or world power. One was at the very center of Europe, where the world's old axes cross, words such as colony and overseas sounded like something quite untried and remote.
> —Robert Musil, *Der Mann ohne Eigenschaften*[1]

The Habsburg monarchy, in Robert Musil's passage in *Mann ohne Eigenschaften* (1930–43), is an ideal but unacknowledged empire in an almost timeless space. *Kakanien*, Musil's term for the *kaiserlich-königlich* (k. & k., imperial-royal) Austro-Hungarian monarchy, represents a distant dreamlike world, complete in and of itself, which unhurriedly moves through time. By describing a seemingly peaceful Slovakian village as "cowered between two small hills as if the earth had parted its lips to warm its child between them,"[2] Musil's eroticized metaphor not only looks patronizingly towards the lower lands on the Habsburg periphery but literally creates a colonial space within the boundaries of the empire. Stretching from the Adriatic Sea to the endless Ukrainian cornfields of Central Europe, the Habsburg realm—unlike Germany and France—possessed colonies within its own borders. Musil advances the view that Austria, as the peaceful center of Europe, has no need to compete in the colonial race with England, France, or Germany. The borders of the multiethnic state did not need to be crossed in pursuit of experiencing the foreign. The multicultural capital, Vienna, served many as the domain of the "inland foreigners," whose seemingly threatening embodiment lay nearby.[3] Ernst Bloch states that the perfect social utopia is characterized by the holding of individual freedom in balance through a state-sponsored order.[4] Seen in light of this interpretation, Musil's reminiscences about the Austrian army and administration come very close to the timeless model of an ideal state that provides for peace and order in the state, yet also gives sufficient freedom to citizens in the Habsburg state.

Austria, arguably, never undertook colonization in the form of overseas settlements. But contrary to the historical reality in Central Europe, Austrian colonial utopian narratives from the end of the nineteenth century are saturated with conscious and unconscious aspirations for an alternative social and spatial organization. This colonial discourse relates to the construction of an imaginary space, and takes precedence over any specific or overt program of dominating other ethnicities.[5] As Musil's portrayal of "Kakanien" suggests, the Habsburg Empire was itself in the position of the "other," foreign or even uncanny when compared to the European colonial powers. However, the Austrian colonial utopian narratives contradict the ideology of the Habsburg myth, which portrayed Austria and her beloved emperor as harmonious, and too peaceful and unambitious to participate in vicious European colonialism.[6]

While the colonial utopias in this book tend to develop different rhetorical and narrative strategies, every text seeks to find solutions to the dire economic situation, fierce ethnic conflicts, and contested gender relations in the Viennese metropolis by creating visionary spaces in Africa and the Near or Far East. On the one hand, these colonial utopian narratives challenge the image of Austria as peacefully couched between Germany and Russia by projecting Austrian colonial fantasies abroad. On the other hand, these liberal utopian writers develop their own "transnational" discourse in which they rethink Europe precisely at a time when other European intellectuals were mired in the concept of "the nation" as something "transhistorical."[7]

In *Enlightenment or Empire* (1998), Russell A. Berman proposes a similar discourse on German colonialism in the wake of the Enlightenment. Berman presents two seemingly opposite strategies of addressing difference: Captain Cook's and Georg Forster's simultaneous, yet distinct, descriptions of their first contact with South Sea Islanders. For Berman, the contrast between the two modes—Cook's fact-oriented geometric cartography and Forster's humanistic, aesthetically informed philosophical universalism—is emblematic of the differences between an interested English and a *disinterested* German position within the colonial project. Cook's technocratic prose represents a form of instrumental rationality, whereas Forster's emphatic humanism reflects a possibility of emancipatory reason.[8] I argue that the Austrian colonial imagination was, likewise, invested in liberal humanism emerging from the dire socioeconomic experiences in contemporary Vienna. Through their experiences as marginalized intellectuals within Austrian society, the utopian writers claimed to have a more empathetic and more humane colonial policy toward other fringe groups. This allegedly special position implies a critique of the instrumental rationality in British colonial policy. In this respect, Theodor Hertzka's imaginary colonization of Africa is proposed as a project of global enlightenment. But rather than merely an Austrian colonial imagination, Berman insists that actual experience was necessary to assess the nature of the colonial encounter; accordingly, he advocates paying close attention to the written records of German travelers abroad.

Since all of the Austrian colonial narratives create visionary vacant spaces, one of the crucial topics this book will explore is the interrelation of the prevalent colonial discourse on race and utopian visions of space. Conquering space goes hand in hand with imaginary as well as scientific explorations of the world, with the representation of Austrian colonialism functioning as a symbol of human progress, but also denoting the continual proliferation of Western capitalism.[9]

Arguing against Berman's position that reason in German colonialism helped to emancipate people, Susanne Zantop attempts to reveal Germany's colonial legacy and imagination. In her book, *Colonial Fantasies* (1997), she elaborates on a kind of colonialism without colonies in the formation of German national identity. Interpreting historical, anthropological, literary, and popular texts, Zantop explores the imaginary colonial encounters between "Germans" and "natives" in late eighteenth- and early nineteenth-century literature, and shows how these colonial fantasies acted as a rehearsal for actual colonial ventures in Africa, South America, and the Pacific. Berman, on the other hand, questions whether such "hermeneutic or critical analyses of literary works are giving way to what are basically historiographical or even social scientific claims regarding empirical actions."[10] He proposes that instead of prompting empirical colonialism, the extensive literature about colonial South America rather propelled German mass emigration to the Americas in the nineteenth century.

Opposing Berman's insistence on actual experiences, Zantop claims that it was "precisely the lack of actual colonialism . . . [that] created a pervasive desire for colonial possessions and a sense of entitlement to such possessions in the mind of many Germans."[11] That is to say, her collection of primary texts aims to set the stage for the appearance of German imperialism toward the end of the nineteenth century, whereas the present book seeks to illustrate that the aesthetic and political aims of the Austrian colonial imagination were very different than vying for an overseas empire. While building on Zantop's conceptual premises about the importance of colonial fantasies, in my analysis of a much smaller sample of Austrian utopias, I come to considerably different conclusions.

In the late 1990s, Zantop and Berman were among the few scholars who opened up the field of postcolonialism for German studies. The relative absence of postcolonial literature written by former colonial subjects in the language of the colonizers had delayed the discussion substantially in the wake of influential scholars such as Edward Said, Benedict Anderson, and Anne McClintock. The absence of overseas possessions made the Austrian situation even more complex. Still, several studies have focused on the relevance of postcolonial theory to the Habsburg Empire in the new millennium.[12] For Clemens Ruthner, the goal of applying this theory in this context could signify a paradigm shift, or at least a meaningful contribution to the globalization of Austrian studies, and in this way could inspire us to rethink the arbitrary boundaries of national literatures.[13] In this respect, postcolonial theory, in its applicability to a historically, politically, and linguistically unique situation in Central Europe, has certainly turned into an asset within the last decade.

One study that follows this line of argument critically is Robert Lemon's *Imperial Messages* (2011). With the aid of literary works by writers such as Hugo von Hofmannsthal, Robert Musil, and Franz Kafka, Lemon seeks to "demonstrate that far from promulgating Western imperialism, these texts subvert received notions of national and cultural identity and thus problematize the very practice of orientalism."[14] Lemon shows how Austrian fin-de-siècle fiction challenged perceived power structures. Departing from Said's Manichean Occident/Orient paradigm, Lemon also questions whether German-speaking Austrians exercised colonial rule everywhere in the eastern part of the Habsburg Empire. The notion of colonial exploitation, after all, is difficult to reconcile "with the fact that just before the First World War the regions of Bohemia and Moravia enjoyed a higher per capita income than all but one of the provinces of Austria proper."[15] Although the authors of his study frequently deploy orientalist motives, they "engage in self-critique rather than advance imperial hegemony."[16] In summary, Lemon's book addresses the shortcomings of Saidian postcolonial theory, pointing out its failure to attend to the specific situation of Austrian history and literature. Like the works analyzed in *Imperial Messages*, the utopian narratives examined in *Tropics of Vienna* question the received notions of Austria's national and cultural identity. But while Lemon focuses on moments of self-criticism by three modernist Austrian authors, the fin-de-siècle writers of my study—even though they belonged to the same social class—still propagate possibilities for social change in their narrative utopias.

*

Wolfgang Müller-Funk argues that the distribution of dystopian and utopian Austrian novels written shortly before and after World War I is lopsided. Between 1870 and 1920, the dystopias presented in Alfred Kubin's *Die Andere Seite* (1909), Franz Kafka's *Das Schloss* (1926), and Joseph Roth's *Hotel Savoy* (1924) were highly acclaimed, while—with the exception of Herzl's *Altneuland* (1902) and Müller's *Tropen* (1915)—Müller-Funk cannot recall "any noteworthy utopian novels."[17] The reason for his failure to notice the utopias by Hertzka, von Sacher-Masoch, and von Hellenbach might be found in the ambivalence of their genres. They constitute a special kind of representation; neither merely literary texts, nor just social theory, these narratives are, according to Phillip Wegner, "an in-between form that mediates and binds together these other representational acts."[18] In accordance with Louis Marin's thesis, utopias are organized around a neutral discursive space that creates narrative energy and performative force.[19] Hence, the present set of Austrian colonial utopias can be read as configurations or cognitive mappings of cultural space or history in the making. Keeping Marin's concept of utopia's neutrality, or "in-between space"[20] in mind, we can interpret the fundamental notion of the otherness of space—prevalent in all Austrian colonial utopias—as unconsciously compensating for anti-Semitism in Vienna by projecting a positive wish-concept at an exotic distance. But as we will see in Herzl's Palestine, or Hertzka's Kenya, merely imagining vacant spaces does not necessarily take geopolitical realities into account. Instead, as Hans Christoph Buch reveals in his Frankfurt poetic lectures *Die Nähe und die Ferne* (1991), the underlying mechanism of most exotic (and utopian) narratives is projection: the relationship between the "foreign" and the "familiar" is dialectical, hence things near and things far collapse into each other.[21] To illustrate such a dialectical movement, this book shows that through a process of inversions, hybridizations, and transgressions, Austrian colonial utopias conjure up an idealized image of Vienna projected onto a vacant colonial space. The present study also corresponds thematically to Ian Reifowitz's *Imagining an Austrian Nation* (2003), an intellectual history that pivots around Joseph Samuel Bloch, a Jewish civic leader and the publisher of the *Österreichische Wochenschrift* (1884–1920). Reifowitz describes Bloch as an ardent advocate of a supraethnic Austrian patriotism at a time of soaring nationalism. A public intellectual, Bloch favored a federal model that sought to generate patriotism for the monarchy with the help of ethnic diversity. Suffice it to say, Bloch's early version of *Verfassungspatriotismus*[22] aimed to reform the institutions from within, and he opposed any Zionist solutions to counter contemporary anti-Semitism.[23] Similar to Reifowitz's study, *Tropics of Vienna* discusses political, ideological, and gender issues relevant at the time in light of the ways they are addressed in the utopias it analyzes. Unlike Joseph Samuel Bloch's plea for real civic reformation, the authors addressed in this study envision *fictional* social formations outside the confines of the Habsburg Empire.

Tropics of Vienna is neither a history of imperial politics nor a discussion of Austria's economy or its cultural institutions in the aftermath of the great recession in 1873 (*Gründerkrise*). Instead the book examines a set of narrative utopias that point to an imaginary imperialism. *Tropics of Vienna* outlines a conceptual framework within which the late nineteenth-century authors worked before the onset of modernism. In this respect, *Tropics of Vienna* not only assesses the aesthetic achievements of the individual utopias but draws attention to the narratives' articulation of moments of imaginary cultural collisions. The aim is to carve out a synchronic historical slice to compare and contrast colonial utopias all written by Viennese intellectuals between 1870 and 1900 with an outlook on how this discourse developed in the twentieth century. These writers shared comparable cultural backgrounds and similar professional inclinations (e.g., publishing and politics). I have applied psychoanalytically informed insights without attempting to "analyze" the authors themselves or Viennese culture at large, especially concerning the relevant gender and sexuality issues. Still, it was important to tease out moments in which the texts produce rather than reflect the colonial and utopian discourse of their time. In this sense, as Wegner puts it, the Austrian colonial utopias can be read as "more akin to travelers' itineraries, or an architectural sketch, tracing an exploratory trajectory, a narrative line that, as it unfolds, quite literally engenders something new in the world."[24] It is the imaginary colonial space that ultimately encourages the reader to play with alternatives, trying out variations and permutations imaginatively before possibilities became fixed by history itself.

*

Unlike Germany in the 1880s, the Austro-Hungarian Empire did not participate in overseas imperialism. In fact, the Austro-Hungarian Empire was the only European power that did not possess colonies and, at least officially, did not seek to obtain any.[25] As a corollary, the Habsburg monarchy is rarely mentioned in the extensive literature on the subject of nineteenth-century imperialism. Nevertheless, following the spirit of the time, Austria-Hungary did pursue expansionist projects, primarily in Southeastern Europe (Bosnia-Herzegovina).[26] The Habsburg Empire's role in Central Europe was exceedingly complex and contradictory. Alexander Honold describes its geopolitical situation in the following terms:

> To be sure, contained within the *Kakanian* multiethnic structure, there were quite a few nations and ethnicities that experienced the Habsburg regime as the apparatus of political, economic, and cultural oppression, which was not so different from that experienced in colonial relationships; the well-known phrase 'ethnic prison' alludes to this. Yet, this system of supranational affiliations was not in a position to effectively suppress partisan nationalism and insurgencies, and therefore had to adjust far more to fundamental opposition than was the case for other imperial powers.[27]

Considering the supranational structure of the Habsburg Empire, the foray into the Balkans cannot easily be compared to the colonialism of other European powers, although conditions on the periphery of the Habsburg Empire resembled in some respects the oppressiveness of a colonial setting. This line of argument will be elaborated in Chapter 1 through a reading of Leopold von Sacher-Masoch's novella *Der Kapitulant* (1870), and his colonial utopia *Paradies am Dniester* (1877), both of which are set in the periphery of the Austro-Hungarian Empire. Von Sacher-Masoch, the controversial author of the erotic novella *Venus in Furs* (1877), is little known for his distinctive political utopianism. In contrast to von Sacher-Masoch's usual portrayal of fierce ethnic conflicts as a form of natural determinism within the paracolonial space of Eastern Europe, the conflict in his utopian story *Paradies am Dniester*, I argue, is a prerequisite for his discussion of a utopian pan-Slavic community in Eastern Europe. With *Paradies*, von Sacher-Masoch propounds a colonial utopia, suspended in fantasy by being displaced within the insurmountable spatial limitations of Europe. Although the utopia addresses the practical political problems of his time, and although von Sacher-Masoch sets his narratives in Eastern Europe, he is motivated by a utopian conception of a new order that covers all of Europe. He disassociates the characters in his novella from a limited and limiting reality to allow them to act out in an imagined space what is not possible in reality, so that the fictional conversation substitutes for the real. In his utopia *Paradies am Dniester*, he creates a discourse on utopian space that delivers its message by being suspended in fantasy, thus denying the spatial realities and political limitations of Eastern Europe.

Chapter 2 focuses on the utopian narrative *Insel Mellonta* (1883) by the philosophically inclined politician Lazar Baron von Hellenbach, which he wrote shortly after von Sacher-Masoch's stories were published. In *Insel Mellonta*, a highly educated German aristocrat is shipwrecked and stranded in the Indian Ocean near a coral island, where natives come to his rescue. The ensuing story of an idyllic, dreamlike existence in the South Sea is interrupted by a volcanic eruption that causes the island to disappear into the ocean. What is more, the entire island society turns out to be merely the protagonist's dream. At first glance, von Hellenbach's socially emancipated *Insel Mellonta* appears to be a classic liberal utopia, but its intricate narrative structure undermines this simple categorization as von Hellenbach merely "utilizes" the utopian genre to bring his theosophical philosophy to a broader audience. Like the other Austrian utopias, von Hellenbach's narrative is steeped in the contemporary debates about colonialism and thrives on inversions, hybridizations, and transgressions of the dominant discourse. *Insel Mellonta* illustrates the extent to which the utopian narrative, even without the "real" experience of the encounter between Polynesians and Europeans, was informed by the real conflicts of the heterogeneous population within the multiethnic Habsburg Empire.

Similar to von Hellenbach, Theodor Hertzka, who will be discussed in Chapter 3, sought to revitalize Central Europe through a projected utopian encounter with exotic cultures in the empty space of East Africa. Hertzka's utopia *Freiland* (1890) emphasizes enlightened universal values and rationality, and proposes to suspend the opposition of town and country through basic democratic land reforms and revised zoning laws. Hertzka aims to create a cheerful society inhabited by young and healthy homeowners coming together to form a productive community. His vision of a new civilization in Africa coincides with nationalism and the surge of anti-Semitism in Vienna. But as I will show, Hertzka goes beyond mere cultural critique of fin-de-siècle Vienna and applies scientific reasoning to social problems to put forth a viable transnational alternative in Africa through radical land reforms and the establishment of a globalized economy.

Theodor Herzl, the topic of Chapter 4, once contemptuously remarked that he regarded Hertzka's *Freiland* as a tall tale.[28] This statement is surprising when one compares Herzl's Zionist utopia *Altneuland* (1902) to *Freiland*, with which it shares many themes. Yet while *Freiland* enjoyed popularity only at the time of its publication, *Altneuland* would become the world-renowned manifesto of

Zionism. In this chapter, I examine how Herzl combines the cosmopolitanism of the German Enlightenment with the secular nationalism inspired by Johann Gottfried Herder and Adolf Fischhof.[29] *Altneuland* diverts the "Jewish question" away from social and religious issues toward the concept of the "Jewish nation" in an imagined empty space of Palestine.[30] *Altneuland* depicts the future Jewish state as a communal utopia. He envisions a new cooperative society rising in the Land of Israel that utilizes science and technology to develop the land. He includes detailed ideas for the future state's political structure, immigration policies, fundraising, diplomatic relations, social laws, and the relationship between religion and the state. The main goal of Herzl's utopia becomes the founding of a new and autonomous state in Palestine. Herzl's vision for the Jewish people represents a homecoming to another (contested) space after a long period of diasporic movements. Underscoring formal, narrative, and semiotic qualities of Herzl's *Altneuland*, my analysis of the novel sees his Zionist vision as a reflection of fin-de-siècle Vienna. The idea for the novel congealed while he was working as a journalist in Spain, England, and Paris. His sojourns abroad helped him to give voice to the sense of alienation he had experienced as a Jew in Vienna. In other words, I will argue that Herzl's Zionist project in Palestine emerges as a sublation of his experiences abroad.

Chapter 5 serves as an epilogue that gives an outlook on the development of Austrian colonial utopias in the first decades of the twentieth century. First, I discuss Robert Müller's modernist novel *Tropen: Der Mythos der Reise* (1915), which envisions the global fusion of the human races. I contend that Müller's self-reflexive exoticism not only sheds a critical light on categories, such as "alterity" and "difference," but also complicates the common understanding of exoticism as a distressed imagination that produces wishful images to compensate for an alienated view of one's self and reality. Müller's vision of amalgamation arises from his sensitivity to the confrontational tensions among and within the ethnic groups, and his awareness of the "exotic" strangeness of the various nationalities comprising that heterogeneous Habsburg Empire. Since the ambivalent incorporation of foreign cultures is an aesthetic feature of these literary Austrian colonial utopias, Müller's redefining exoticism in *Tropen* can be seen as a modernist appropriation of Austrian colonial discourse.

The second half of Chapter 5 discusses the work of Joseph Roth, one of Austria's most revered interwar novelists, and his critical views of the Habsburg legacy. It might seem counterintuitive to look to Roth in a study on Austrian colonial utopias, considering that he is known as a twentieth-century *realist* writer. Nevertheless, like no other author of his generation, it is evident that Roth reflects on the dissolution of the Habsburg Empire in the aftermath of World War I in his historical novels *Radetzkymarsch* (1932) and *Kapuzinergruft* (1938). For him, the essence of Habsburg is not the center but the periphery, a place he populates with subaltern protagonists trying to tackle the windmills of modernity and never quite coming to terms with the loss of the empire. Moreover, in a lucid and sobering fashion, his seminal essay "Juden auf der Wanderschaft" (1927) addresses Hertzka's and Herzl's utopian concepts. Roth undertakes to "demystify" Habsburg nostalgia as he does not see Zionism or a facile acceptance of East European Jews within a Western host culture as a viable solution to their plight. As a keen historian, Roth does not make his fiction a nostalgic utopia, as some of his critics have claimed, nor does he portray Galicia as a place of perennial social injustice. I maintain that instead of embellishing the past, Roth's writings mediate historical truths about the empire's marginal communities through fiction. That is to say, Roth's fiction is neither a backward-oriented utopia nor an insipid portrait of Eastern Europe as a place of despotism and social injustice. Rather than embellishing the past, he claims that his writings turn reality into "a higher form of truth" to convey the history of the empire's marginal communities in a mythical way. Put differently, Roth engages allegorically with history; he does not merely yearn for a paradise lost, but delivers a critique of contemporary culture in his writings.

Notes

1. "Man bereitete die Eroberung der Lüfte vor, auch hier; aber nicht zu intensiv. Man ließ hie [*sic*] und da ein Schiff nach Südamerika oder Ostasien fahren; aber nicht zu oft. Man hatte keinen Weltwirtschafts- und Weltmachtehrgeiz; man saß im Mittelpunkt Europas, wo die alten Weltachsen sich schneiden; die Worte Kolonie und Übersee hörte man an wie etwas noch ganz Unerprobtes und Fernes." Robert Musil, *Der Mann ohne Eigenschaften*, ed. Adolf Frisé, vol. 1 (Reinbek, 2005), 33. [All translations are mine, unless otherwise indicated.]
2. "das Dorf zwischen zwei kleinen Hügeln kauerte, als hätte die Erde ein wenig die Lippen geöffnet, um ihr Kind dazwischen zu wärmen." Musil, *Mann ohne Eigenschaften*, vol. 1, 33.
3. Alexander Honold, "Peter Altenbergs *Ashantee*: Eine impressionistische cross-over Phantasie im Kontext der exotischen Völkerschauen," in *Grenzüberschreitungen um 1900: Österreichische Literatur im Übergang*, ed. Thomas Eicher and Peter Sowa (Oberhausen, 2001), 137.
4. See Ernst Bloch, "Freiheit und Ordnung: Abriss der Sozialutopien", *Das Prinzip Hoffnung*, 3 vols. (Frankfurt, 1959), 2:551.
5. See Russell A. Berman, *Enlightenment or Empire: Colonial Discourse in German Culture* (Lincoln, 1998), 3.
6. See Claudio Magris, *Der habsburgische Mythos in der österreichischen Literatur* (Vienna, 2000). For Magris the characteristic element of the Habsburg myth is the "patriarchal and paternal closeness between the ruler and his subjects, who are deeply enamored of and devoted to their monarch," 44.
7. According to Ernest Gellner, the predominant European discourse on "nation" and "nationalism" in the nineteenth century was "about entry to, participation in, identification with, a literate high culture which . . . is to be compatible with the kind of division

of labour, the type or mode of production, on which this society is based." Ernest Gellner, *Nations and Nationalism* (Oxford, 1983), 95.
8. See Berman, *Enlightenment or Empire*, 21.
9. Nina Berman criticizes Russell Berman's book *Enlightenment or Empire* for its sweeping critique of postcolonial and poststructuralist theory, which is coupled with a passionate defense of the Enlightenment: "Berman insists on the importance of 'reason—and by extension, of science, progress, and normative universalism.' His refutation of postcolonial and poststructuralist criticism is reductive at best: he barely engages with specific critics or with the range of critics that make up the field. Many, if not most of them, see their critique as solidly standing in the emancipatory tradition of the Enlightenment, and, in the line of Theodor W. Adorno and Max Horkheimer's 1944 publication *Dialectic of Enlightenment*, they have indeed elaborated on the internal contradictions of the Enlightenment." Nina Berman, *Impossible Missions? German Economic, Military and Humanitarian Efforts in Africa* (Lincoln, 2004), 11.
10. Russell A. Berman, "Review of Susanne Zantop's 'Colonial Fantasies: Conquest, Family, and the Nation in Pre-colonial Germany 1770–1870,'" *Modern Philology* 98, no. 1 (August 2000): 110.
11. Susanne Zantop, *Colonial Fantasies: Conquest, Family, and the Nation in Pre-colonial Germany 1770–1870* (Durham, 1997), 7.
12. See Johannes Feichtinger, "Habsburg (Post-) Colonial: Anmerkungen zur Inneren Kolonisierung in Zentraleuropa," in *Habsburg Postcolonial: Machtstrukturen und kollektives Gedächtnis*, ed. Moritz Csáky et al. (Innsbruck, 2003); *Kakanien Revisited: Das Eigene und das Fremde (in) der österreichisch-ungarischen Monarchie*, ed. Wolfgang Müller-Funk, Peter Plener, and Clemens Ruthner (Tübingen, 2002); *Understanding Multiculturalism: The Habsburg Central European Experience*, ed. Johannes Feichtinger and Gary Cohen (New York, 2014); and the Interdisciplinary Central European Studies and Networking, under <http://www.kakanien.ac.at>.
13. See Clemens Ruthner, "K. (u.) k. postcolonial? Für eine neue Lesart der österreichischen (und benachbarter) Literatur(en)," *Kakanien Revisited* 10 (2001): 6.
14. Robert Lemon, *Imperial Messages: Orientalism as Self-Critique in the Habsburg Fin-de-Siècle* (Woodbridge, 2011), 1.
15. Ibid., 3.
16. Ibid.
17. Wolfgang Müller-Funk, "Dystopien im Kontext des Habsburgischen Mythos: Joseph Roth, Ludwig Winder," in *Vom Zweck des Systems: Beiträge zur Geschichte literarischer Utopien*, ed. Árpád Bernáth, Endre Hárs, Peter Plener (Tübingen, 2006), 108.
18. Phillip E. Wegner, *Imaginary Communities: Utopia, the Nation, and the Spatial Histories of Modernity* (Berkeley, 2002), xviii.
19. See Louis Marin, "Frontiers of Utopia: Past and Present," *Critical Inquiry* 19, no. 3 (Spring 1993): 404.
20. Louis Marin, *Utopics: The Semiological Play of Textual Spaces*, trans. Robert A. Vollrath (Atlantic Highlands, 1984), xiii.
21. See Hans Christoph Buch, *Die Nähe und die Ferne: Bausteine zu einer Poetik des kolonialen Blicks* (Frankfurt, 1991), 11.
22. *Verfassungspatriotismus* is a key term for post-national theories and has been influential in the development of the European Union. The concept is associated with the political scientists Dolf Sternberger and Jürgen Habermas.

23. "Bloch rejected the idea that Jews should disappear as a collective entity, although he did display some ideological similarities with his liberal, German-acculturated Jewish counterparts (aka Herzl)." Ian Reifowitz, *Imagining an Austrian Nation: Joseph Samuel Bloch and the Search for a Multiethnic Austrian Identity, 1846–1919* (New York, 2003), 94.
24. Wegner, *Imaginary Communities*, xix.
25. To be sure, Austrian explorers, collectors, and voyagers such as Oscar Baumann, Ludwig Ritter von Höhnel, and Dr Emin Pascha traveled to distant continents in the nineteenth century, thereby giving ample proof of the immense Austrian interest in the exploration of foreign territories. See Wilfried Seipel, ed., *Die Entdeckung der Welt, Die Welt der Entdeckungen: Österreichische Forscher, Sammler und Abenteuerer* (Milano, 2001).
26. See Robin Okey, *Taming Balkan Nationalism: The Habsburg "Civilizing Mission" in Bosnia 1878–1914* (Oxford, 2007); and Clemens Ruthner, "Habsburg's Little Orient: A Post/colonial Reading of Austrian and German Cultural Narratives on Bosnia-Herzegovina, 1878–1918," *Kakanien Revisited* 5 (2008).
27. Alexander Honold, "Kakanien Kolonial: Auf der Suche nach Welt-Österreich," in *Kakanien Revisited*, ed. Müller-Funk, Plener, and Ruthner, 105.
28. Tellingly, Herzl makes his contemptuous remark about Hertzka's *Freiland* in the preface of *Der Judenstaat* (1896).
29. Adolf Fischhof (1816–1893) was an Austrian writer and politician of Jewish descent. Fischhof advocated both a federal organization of the Habsburg Empire and a high degree of autonomy for the respective national minorities. See Adolph (sic) Fischhof, *Oesterreich und Bürgschaften seines Bestandes* (Vienna, 1869).
30. In a letter to Lord Rothschild of 22 August 1902, Herzl shows that he thought of Zionism as a modern nationalist movement by raising the following question: "In our own time Greeks, Rumanians, Serbs, Bulgarians have established themselves—so why shouldn't we be able to?" Theodor Herzl, *The Complete Diaries of Theodor Herzl*, vol. 4, trans. Harry Zohn, ed. Raphael Patai (New York, 1960), 1347.

Works Cited

Berman, Nina. *Impossible Missions? German Economic, Military and Humanitarian Efforts in Africa*. Lincoln: University Press of Nebraska, 2004.

Berman, Russell A. *Enlightenment or Empire: Colonial Discourse in German Culture*. Lincoln, NE and London: University of Nebraska Press, 1998.

———. "Review of Susanne Zantop's 'Colonial Fantasies: Conquest, Family, and the Nation in Precolonial Germany 1770–1870.'" *Modern Philology* 98, no. 1 (August 2000): 110–13.

Bloch, Ernst. "Freiheit und Ordnung: Abriss der Sozialutopien." In *Das Prinzip Hoffnung*. 3 vols. Frankfurt: Suhrkamp, 1959.

Buch, Hans Christoph. *Die Nähe und die Ferne: Bausteine zu einer Poetik des kolonialen Blicks* Frankfurt: Suhrkamp, 1991.

Feichtinger, Johannes. "Habsburg (Post-) Colonial: Anmerkungen zur Inneren Kolonisierung in Zentraleuropa." In *Habsburg Postcolonial: Machtstrukturen und kollektives Gedächtnis*, edited by Moritz Csáky et al. 13–31. Innsbruck: Studienverlag, 2003.

Feichtinger, Johannes, and Gary Cohen. *Understanding Multiculturalism: The Habsburg Central European Experience*. New York: Berghahn Books, 2014.

Fischhof, Adolph. *Oesterreich und Bürgschaften seines Bestandes*. Vienna: Wallishausser, 1869.
Gellner, Ernest. *Nations and Nationalism*. Oxford: Oxford University Press, 1983.
Herzl, Theodor. *The Complete Diaries of Theodor Herzl*. Edited by Raphael Patai and translated by Harry Zohn. 5 vols. New York: Herzl Press, 1960.
Honold, Alexander. "Kakanien Kolonial: Auf der Suche nach Welt-Österreich." In *Kakanien Revisted: Das Eigene und das Fremde (in) der österreichisch-ungarischen Monarchie*, edited by Wolfgang Müller-Funk, Peter Plener, and Clemens Ruthner, 104–20. Tübingen: A. Francke, 2002.
———. "Peter Altenbergs *Ashantee*: Eine impressionistische cross-over Phantasie im Kontext der exotischen Völkerschauen." In *Grenzüberschreitungen um 1900: Österreichische Literatur im Übergang*, edited by Thomas Eicher and Peter Sowa, 135–57. Oberhausen: Athena, 2001.
Lemon, Robert. *Imperial Messages: Orientalism as Self-Critique in the Habsburg Fin-de-Siècle*. Woodbridge: Boydell & Brewer, 2011.
Magris, Claudio. *Der habsburgische Mythos in der österreichischen Literatur*. Vienna: P. Zsolnay, 2000.
Marin, Louis. "Frontiers of Utopia: Past and Present," *Critical Inquiry* 19, no. 3 (Spring 1993): 397–420.
———. *Utopics: The Semiological Play of Textual Spaces*. Translated by Robert A. Vollrath. Atlantic Highlands, NJ: Humanities International Press, 1984.
Müller-Funk, Wolfgang. "Dystopien im Kontext des habsburgischen Mythos: Joseph Roth, Ludwig Winder." In *Vom Zweck des Systems: Beiträge zur Geschichte literarischer Utopien*, edited by Árpád Bernáth, Endre Hárs, and Peter Plener, 107–24. Tübingen: Franke, 2006.
Müller-Funk, Wolfgang, Peter Plener, and Clemens Ruthner, ed. *Kakanien Revisited: Das Eigene und das Fremde (in) der österreichisch-ungarischen Monarchie*. Tübingen: A. Francke, 2002.
Musil, Robert. *Der Mann ohne Eigenschaften*. Edited by Adolf Frise. 2 vols. 20th edition. Reinbek: Rowohlt, 2005.
Okey, Robin. *Taming Balkan Nationalism: The Habsburg "Civilizing Mission" in Bosnia 1878–1914*. Oxford: Oxford University Press, 2007.
Reifowitz, Ian. *Imagining an Austrian Nation: Joseph Samuel Bloch and the Search for a Multiethnic Austrian Identity, 1846–1919*. New York: Columbia University Press, 2003.
Ruthner, Clemens. "Habsburg's Little Orient: A Post/colonial Reading of Austrian and German Cultural Narratives on Bosnia-Herzegovina, 1878–1918," *Kakanien Revisited* 5 (2008): 1–18.
———. "K. (u.) k. postcolonial? Für eine neue Lesart der österreichischen (und benachbarter) Literatur(en)." *Kakanien Revisted* 10 (2001): 1–6.
Seipel, Wilfried, ed. *Die Entdeckung der Welt, Die Welt der Entdeckungen: Österreichische Forscher, Sammler und Abenteuerer*. Milano: Skira, 2001.
Wegner, Phillip E. *Imaginary Communities: Utopia, the Nation, and the Spatial Histories of Modernity*. Berkeley: University Press of California, 2002.
Zantop, Susanne. *Colonial Fantasies: Conquest, Family, and the Nation in Pre-colonial Germany 1770–1870*. Durham, NC: Duke University Press, 1997.

Chapter 1

LEOPOLD VON SACHER-MASOCH
Utopian Periphery

The poet boldly flies ahead, and the critic limps laboriously behind. The critic represents the ideas and principles of today, the poet those of the future; consequently, they are destined to conflict with each other continuously in the land of the present.

—Leopold von Sacher-Masoch, *Über den Werth der Kritik*[1]

Leopold von Sacher-Masoch

Leopold von Sacher-Masoch, the controversial author of *Venus im Pelz* (1870) and countless other erotic novellas, is little known for his political utopianism. In what follows, I seek to read von Sacher-Masoch not only as a writer with a distinctive vision of a multicultural, property-free, communal empire, in contrast to the Habsburg state's self-serving image as a politically stable Central European country, but also as a "colonial" writer, focused on the Austrian Empire's ethnic diversity and gender conflicts. As von Sacher-Masoch envisions it, the German language would serve as a common denominator to allow the various nations in the Habsburg Empire to communicate with each other more effectively. Accordingly, much of his work espouses a paradoxical German-language pan-Slavism: "We will represent Austria as a political nationality in which the natural nationalities can be united, each with the full recognition of its rights and freedoms."[2] Despite the provocative political implications of his "Germanic" pan-Slavism, his exciting, page-turning novellas, set at the colonial borders of the Habsburg Empire, have usually been interpreted in relation to sexual transgressions and dominating female figures, of which *Venus im Pelz* is merely the most prominent example.

More recently, Michael Gratzke, Barbara Mennel, and other critics have explored the relationship between von Sacher-Masoch's sexual politics and his political aesthetics in their groundbreaking analyses.[3] However, they barely consider his radically utopian political program.[4] For instance, Albrecht Koschorke argues in his influential literary biography *Sacher-Masoch: Die Inszenierung einer Perversion* (1988) that the most truthful revelation of von Sacher-Masoch's determinism lies in his protagonists' nihilism, asceticism, and renunciation. Koschorke judges him to be depraved when he writes: "[Sacher-Masoch's] impetus toward a fundamental social criticism unexpectedly descends into a demonstration of the world's and humanity's fallen nature. Even the title, *Vermächtnis Kains* [Cain's Legacy], lends a religious consecration to his diagnosed vileness."[5] And shortly before, in the same context, Koschorke affirms:

> Even if the philosophical position that Sacher-Masoch sketches out includes many elements that were exceptionally advanced in his day, even if traces of Stirner's *Der Einzige und sein Eigenthum* cross paths in his work with ideas of a Slavic proto-Communism—some wanted to perceive here a spiritual kinship with Tolstoy—still the degree of intellectual penetration of the depicted deplorable state of affairs remains extraordinarily minimal.[6]

Hence, Koschorke sees von Sacher-Masoch's social criticism and political convictions as no more than ornamentation to the insidious aestheticism of cruelty in his gory stories. This reading has been addressed by literary scholars such as John K. Noyes, Kai Kauffmann, and Torben Lohmüller.[7] Their research has shown, for example, that von Sacher-Masoch's politics are "always coextensive with private, and particularly, sexual power relations"[8] or, as Lohmüller argues, that von Sacher-Masoch commonly displaces anxiety and seduction as modes of hegemony, placing them at a temporal or spatial distance.[9] Hence, one can interpret his seminal novellas as positing an enactment of gender reversals and sexual negotiation that allows the author and his readers to explore the boundaries of permissiveness within the societal order at the borders of the Habsburg Empire. Whereas his masochistic protagonists seek to obtain pleasure by disavowing and suspending reality, his empathetic description of multiethnic society in Galicia portrays the sadistic institutional power tormenting peasants and minorities such as Jews. The suspension in fantasy allows von Sacher-Masoch not only to invert sexual power relationships but also to stylize the periphery as a repository of deeply held fears of emasculation. As Noyes puts it in his book *Mastery of Submission: Inventions of Masochism* (1997):

> Exotic sexuality in Sacher-Masoch's writing was intended as an identification with the minority experiences of Slavic life. . . . Or, to put it in terms that may be more familiar within the "masochism" debate, it allowed the author to take on a position of relative powerlessness and at the same time retain power over this position.[10]

That is to say, these masochist fantasies of the cultural elites were in fact subjective performances that allow them to identify with their degraded victims without changing the existing power relationships. Arguing with Frantz Fanon, Noyes shows how European male masochism in the colonies was encouraged by supremacist feelings and sadistic aggression toward black men, while at the same time the democratic culture at home stigmatized these feelings: "Fanon uses the concept of European male masochism to think through the casual relations between latent and manifest homosexuality, Negrophobia, and racism in the colonial situation."[11] Accordingly, Noyes sees in von Sacher-Masoch's characters a "quest for an alternative masculinity as a social statement of dissent aimed at doctrines of cultural supremacy."[12] Yet again, since von Sacher-Masoch's characters simultaneously identify with the colonized Eastern Europeans and with the colonial power of the Habsburg Empire, the sexually charged colonial narratives also underscore the periphery as a locus for reinvigorating the center of the empire itself.

The bleak determinism and ever-present sexual transgressions in *Vermächtnis Kains* criticize the oppressive nature of class, race, and gender clashes in the Eastern European borderlands. The liminal space of Galicia is prone to raw encounters between the colonizers and their subjects. As Russell A. Berman observes, *Don Juan of Kolomea*, one of von Sacher-Masoch's best-known novellas, shows that he was consciously writing colonial literature for his West European readers:

> 'We drove out of the provincial capital Kolomea into the countryside.' With this beginning of the *Don Juan of Kolomea* (1864), Sacher-Masoch announces the colonial question by attaching a footnote to the name of the city, thereby providing some geographic authenticity for his German and other West European readers, who are presumably not familiar with the map of the expansive East: 'A province and provincial capital in eastern Galicia. Kolomea derives from Colonia because the city is built on the classical ground of a former Roman settlement.' The topic of the novella then is the Don Juan of the colonies or Don Juan as colonial—the full constellation of race, gender, and power.[13]

If Berman positions von Sacher-Masoch in a colonial discourse, I would like to distinguish between two different colonial discourses: on the one hand there is overseas colonial discourse, as in the colonial novella *Afrikas Semiramis* (1901), which takes place overseas in Angola; and on the other hand there is an Eastern European colonial discourse; the vast majority of his novellas are set in Eastern Europe and portray the Habsburg monarchy as a "colonial" power with its colonies within the empire rather than overseas.[14] Because the countries within the Habsburg Empire were economically, socially, and culturally developed to quite differing degrees, mechanisms of "internal colonization" can be seen in that the Austro-German elite functioned as colonizers, and the diverse Eastern European minorities were treated by Austro-German elites as the colonial "other." This is an example of what Michael Hechter termed "Internal Colonialism," which generally describes political, economic, and cultural inequalities between regions within a society, and the uneven effects of state development on various regions and the exploitation of minority groups within the wider society. The relationship between colonizer and colony is unequal and exploitative in both colonialism and internal colonialism. An internal colony typically produces wealth for the benefit of those areas most closely associated with the state, usually metropolitan centers. The members of the internal colonies may be distinguished as different by a cultural variable such as ethnicity, language, or religion. They are then excluded from prestigious social and political positions, which are dominated by members of the ruling class.[15]

While we may question the applicability of postcolonial theory to a historically, politically and linguistically unique situation in Central Europe, we may still profit from using theoretical tools to explore Eastern Europe as a terrain marked by fierce ethnic power struggles. More recently, several studies have focused on the relevance of postcolonial theory to the Habsburg Empire. Following Clemens Ruthner, the goal of such an endeavor would be nothing less than a critical revision of the representation of the k. & k. monarchy:

> This might even effect a paradigm shift, at least it will render a meaningful contribution to a globalization of philologies with a cultural studies emphasis. It would also help these disciplines to rethink their narrow and arbitrary national boundaries, and it could even fulfill an old dream, namely to take a first step towards a supranational literary history of the Habsburg Empire.[16]

If this model creates discursively binary power relations, von Sacher-Masoch's stories invert them and traverse the dichotomy between center and periphery. Rather than an internal colony, the Eastern European borderlands of the Habsburg Empire could be considered a paracolonial space, spatially distant from the center and yet exerting influence on it. Furthermore, these paracolonial novellas reflect more than the monarchy's ethnic diversity; they also envision a unique Habsburg utopia, since they suggest an inextricable link between private, inverted gender roles and public, ethnic conflicts in the paracolonial setting of Eastern Europe. Von Sacher-Masoch's texts can serve as a model for the use of fantasy and utopia as a structural device to illustrate the psychological and social conflicts of colonial borderlands.

*

Born in 1836, Leopold von Sacher-Masoch grew up in a noble family in government service in East Galicia; at home he studied Ukrainian and French, while the family spoke Polish and German. Beginning in 1844, he attended the German Gymnasium in Lemberg, Galicia.[17] His father was the chief of the local police, and although his family was a member of the elite of the Habsburg monarchy as it existed on the fringes of the empire, in his autobiography *Souvenirs* (1985) von Sacher-Masoch emphasizes the multiethnic origins of his family:

> My father's family is originally Spanish. . . . My grandfather was a government official in the administration of Galicia, and drew to himself in that role so much confidence and love that the Galician nobility accepted him into their ranks and awarded him with indigeneity. . . . My mother, Caroline Edle von Masoch, was the last survivor of an old Slavic family. My father therefore, as was the custom in noble families, united her name with his with the approval of the Austrian emperor, and since that time the family has been known as Sacher-Masoch.[18]

When his father was relocated to Prague in 1848, the year of revolutions, von Sacher-Masoch started to study humanities at Charles University. He completed his doctorate and taught for nearly ten years at Graz University, without receiving sufficient recognition for his literary historical writings. At the same time, his early novellas found enough attention that he decided to become a full-time writer. Through a series of complicated and costly love affairs, which serve both as a source and an inspiration for his literary creativity, he got into debt and was forced to write a great deal and to change locations frequently.[19] Although he only returned to Galicia for two short stays, the Eastern European periphery of the Habsburg Empire forms the locus for the majority of his novellas. If one accepts the descriptions of his Galician childhood, then von Sacher-Masoch learns—while still in the care of his Ukrainian nursemaid—of the "magnificent, melancholy songs, as they are sung by the ordinary Russian peasants [and] the heart-rending melodies that are equal to them in force and poetry."[20] Kauffmann offers the opinion that von Sacher-Masoch's autobiography produces a romantic exoticism through its mythological synthesis of the Spanish-Habsburg military, Slavic nobility, and Ukrainian peasant class: "The Slavic people appear as primitive material, which first attains a civilized form through the German-speaking representatives of Austrian literature and administration. In this way, Austria's cultural leadership and political control within the Habsburg Empire is assured and justified."[21] Thus, Kauffmann sees von Sacher-Masoch's poetic works as a tribute to the hegemonic Habsburg ideology. Still, von Sacher-Masoch's "counterfactual" writings deal with real existing conflicts among the multiethnic Habsburgs, and questions the myth that produces the poetic space for transcending existing power relationships.

According to Karl Mannheim, ideology and utopia both share an essence (*Seinswirklichkeit*) that is incongruent with the historical situation in which they exist, and both evoke images transcending those of the present reality.[22] While utopia with its vision of a better society is meant to shatter and overcome the situation in the world, ideological wish-pictures serve to maintain the status quo. The perception of the terms utopia and ideology depends on each subject's position: a member of the ruling class is inclined to judge utopian thought as unrealizable imaginings, whereas someone outside of the circle of power is more likely to view ideology as an incongruent mode of deception by a society in which he or she has no sense of participation. Even though von Sacher-Masoch did not belong to an ethnically or socially underprivileged group of the Habsburg Empire, he perceived himself as an outsider to the dominant society. In this respect, Kauffmann's ideological criticism overlooks the important utopian function of von Sacher-Masoch's ethnographical novellas. To realize the utopian aim of a multiethnic Habsburg state, the individual, psychologically motivated depictions of conflicts first have to transcend the status quo.

Von Sacher-Masoch's political convictions entailed the concept of Central European ethnic cooperation. He believed that the various Eastern European peoples could preserve equal political status under the umbrella of Habsburg rule. In 1866, after Austria's exclusion from the German Federation, von Sacher-Masoch became the editor of the literary periodical *Gartenlaube für Österreich* (Austrian Arbor), whose editorial goal was to promote Habsburg imperial self-sufficiency in the face of mighty Prussia through simultaneous reporting that was regional and cosmopolitan. Alongside regular columns from correspondents in Vienna, Paris, London, and St. Petersburg, the journal offered novellas in serial form by Adalbert Stifter, Karl von Thaler, and von Sacher-Masoch, most of which dealt with themes from the periphery of the monarchy: *Die Zigeuner Österreichs und der Süddonauländer* (The Gypsies and the Southern Danubian Lands), *Eine Wolfsjagd in Siebenbürgen* (Wolf Hunt in Siebenbürgen), and *Schneesturm in Galizien* (Snowstorm in Galicia). Von Sacher-Masoch describes his editorial program as follows:

> The mission of the *Gartenlaube für Österreich* is therefore to rise above partisanship, to be just to all ethnicities and to reveal to each ethnic group the merits of the others, instead of ruthlessly uncovering the reciprocal flaws of each to craft tragic humor into a contemptible polemic. Above all, it will be the task of our journal to cultivate the fallow fields in our fatherland: belletristic literature and popular science.[23]

It was von Sacher-Masoch's declared aim not only to vehemently oppose the growing dominance of the Prussian state with its militaristic, materialistic, and anti-Semitic orientation, but also "to mediate among the various ethnic groups in the monarchy, and to familiarize them with each other."[24] And shortly afterwards: "Love for the homeland, for the people, gave birth to the journal; the sympathy of the homeland, of the people, must keep it fresh and spring-like! From now on it is the task of every genuine patriot to cast his gaze inward, for the best way to learn to love one's fatherland is to get to know it exactly."[25] According to this mission statement, the editors hoped that Austria's forced isolation from Prussia would spark a movement toward a new all-inclusive Austrian patriotism. But the metaphors evoking this home community suggest exclusion instead: an inward-looking people (*Volk*) and homeland (*Heimat*) give birth to this leaflet (*Blatt*), and it is also the people who have to keep the homeland fresh and green.

Far from being all-inclusive, von Sacher-Masoch's language seemingly vies with patriotic metaphors in the wake of the loss of the Austro-Prussian War.

The journal was intended to provide a forum for presenting the entire literary spectrum of the multiethnic Habsburg state: "Since our journal is genuinely Austrian, it will present a cosmopolitan outlook that speaks not just to Austria, or to all of Germany, but indeed it will have a thoroughly innovative and characteristic message for Europe."[26] This somewhat diffuse statement not only reveals von Sacher-Masoch's business acumen but also underscores his paradoxical concept of a German-language pan-Slavism. Rather than condemning German as the language of Habsburg hegemony, he views it as a common denominator, a cosmopolitan vehicle for communication among people of different ethnicities. Von Sacher-Masoch depicts Austria as a nation that is more than the sum of the ethnic groups within the monarchy. Amalgamating two entities—the consensus-driven, calculated, civilized Austrian nation and the genuinely atavistic Slavic community—von Sacher-Masoch imagines unifying multiple Eastern European ethnicities into one Habsburg "nation" while retaining their rights and freedoms. In a way, his utopian agenda provides Austria with what Michael Hardt and Antonio Negri describe as "the multitude [that] is neither an identity (like the people) nor uniform (like the masses), [but given] the internal differences of the multitude [they] must discover the common that allows them to communicate and act together."[27] Thus, von Sacher-Masoch resolves the contradiction between inclusion and exclusion, creating an exclusive imperial identity that still incorporates its colonial components.

Von Sacher-Masoch's adoption of the German language as a universal cultural medium found little acceptance among his contemporaries in Austria. What elevates *Österreichische Gartenlaube* out of the sphere of harmless boredom and into a higher and politically more dangerous sphere is, for the conservative political commentator Hieronymus Lorm, "the Slavic parasite and renegade attitude in Austria, which is supported by the name of the main contributor [von Sacher-Masoch] on the title page."[28] Von Sacher-Masoch was excoriated from two sides: on the one hand, *Die Presse* branded von Sacher-Masoch as a "Slavic" leech and traitor sinning against the German language, while, on the other hand, the Slavic intellectuals in the provinces, hoping for territorial self-determination, rejected his use of the German language because they saw it as subjugation to the hegemonic aspirations of the Germans. Von Sacher-Masoch replied to the chauvinistic censure of Viennese press with a firm tone and stylish irony:

> They [the journalists] are so laughable to see in our Austria program a danger for Austria. Since Austria is not Austria, they say; the Czechs, Hungarians, Russians, Poles, Romanians, Serbs, Croats, Slovenians, Italians aren't Austria; we are Austria, actually not even the Germans, but Vienna, and within Vienna above all the publishers of the outmoded *Presse*.[29]

In 1870, however, Viennese critic Ferdinand Kürnberger perceived in von Sacher-Masoch and his productive sensuality the chance for a new start for contemporary German literature, and greeted his prose as a "first, fleeting ray of dawn."[30] Hence, Kürnberger enthusiastically promoted von Sacher-Masoch's nonconformist writings in the introduction to the novella *Don Juan von Kolomea*. Although Kürnberger shied away from improperly conceding the dignity of Austria's old literary culture "to a half-alien foreigner,"[31] he orientalized von Sacher-Masoch by repeatedly referring to his Slavic naturalness (*Natürlichkeit*) and his exotic sensuality, which, in his view, wafted like "fresh adolescent sensitivity over virgin fields of the fantastical."[32] If Western orientalist discourse, as Edward Said claims, produces not only exotic despotism, cruelty, and sensuality but also irrational, childlike difference, then Kürnberger successfully molded von Sacher-Masoch into an "oriental" writer for the German-speaking public. Tellingly, contemporary Austrian writer Karl Emil Franzos published his collected stories about East European Jews under the title *Aus Halb-Asien* (1883) in the same vein. But while Kürnberger's criticism infantilized von Sacher-Masoch, it also made him a potential fount of new energy for Europe. In some respects, Kürnberger merely broadened von Sacher-Masoch's own dichotomy between the tired civilization of Western Europe and the pristine vitality of the Slavic East.

The following passages may explain what Kürnberger had in mind. At the end of von Sacher-Masoch's novella *Der Hajdamak*, the first-person narrator, Sacher, stands on a peak of the Carpathian mountain range and spells out a program for the Eastern renewal of the burnt-out European civilization: "Over there is tired Europe, weathered like rock that crumbles under our feet and falls into the abyss. . . . Here in contrast are the young, fresh nations on the rise, . . . looking toward the future without fear and without doubt."[33] Kürnberger's treatment of von Sacher-Masoch thus reveals the central paradox of Western orientalism: the orientalized subject becomes both the childlike other and the source of renewal, even the heir to empire. In this vein, Kürnberger foresees an "authentic future Canaan"[34] latent in these Eastern lands, related by custom and conduct, but neither geographically nor politically part of the German federation, in which a sense of shared humanity can be drawn from the shared "pan-Slavic common identity."[35] In light of this interpretation, it is not surprising that the Viennese critic wanted to enlist von Sacher-Masoch in his decidedly German-Austrian project:

> How would it be if—instead of the Great Russian Turgeniev—we had a Ukrainian [*Kleinrussen*] from East Galicia, that is to say an Austrian, that is to say a German? What if in Austria—which has up to now so inadequately fulfilled its mission of Germanization—what if, in times when the nationalities in Austria are in open rebellion against all things German, a Slavic-born author from the banks of the Prut sent an excellent German novella to the banks of the Main and the Neckar? . . . That could

mean that German literature had conquered totally new Eastern longitudes, and had annexed totally new and fresh primitive peoples [*Naturvölker*], who did not yet write German but who, in the course of history, had begun to do so more and more.[36]

With this vision of cultural annexation, it is fitting that Kürnberger refers to von Sacher-Masoch since they both suppose that improvement of the Austrian state concept will come from the East. Von Sacher-Masoch and Kürnberger write in the tradition of a cyclically recurring idea of a revitalization of Austria or Germany through the infusion of a new spirit and creativity from Eastern culture. A generation later, in the midst of modernism in Vienna and Berlin, one finds intimations of a divine redemption from the East in Hugo von Hofmannsthal's essay "Die österreichische Idee" (1917), which posits that Austrian leadership in Central Europe counterbalances the political reality of the German-dominated alliance during World War I. As Berman adds, "the notion that an amelioration might come from the East anticipates the arguments both in Max Weber's *Protestantische Ethik und der Geist des Kapitalismus* (1904) and in Thomas Mann's *Tod in Venedig* (1913), where Aschenbach dreams of a new God arriving from Asia."[37] According to Kauffmann, the Austrian idea was frequently recycled as an alternative to a "Prussian confederation or to Great-German annexations."[38] In light of this, the Austrian idea and its inherent nationalistic, geopolitical, and racist implications become more and more central to our understanding of the contending cultural and intellectual currents of the time.

To further understand Kürnberger's problematic support of von Sacher-Masoch's prose, one should consider W. G. Sebald's geopolitical critique, and Berman's more favorable interpretation of the same passage. Referring to von Sacher-Masoch's *Jüdisches Leben* (1892), Sebald sees Kürnberger's introduction not merely as a cultural program but also as a dangerous geopolitical one:

> An unholy avenue of thought, and yet in it is most clearly expressed what is just then taking place. For, even in the ghetto story written in the German language, there is a component of the ideal process of Germanization, which had so little political realization in Eastern Europe in the course of the bourgeois century, disappointing the growing number of geopoliticians in the process, that the vision was put into practice by force some generations later.[39]

In other words, Kürnberger's vision alarms Sebald by showing how von Sacher-Masoch's German-language novellas could be read as part of an aggressive Germanization process. Berman, however, pushes Sebald's critique of the German desire to dominate and expand into Eastern Europe a little further. He sees Kürnberger's argument as a degradation of Western civilization resulting in a (rhetorical) elevation of marginal cultures, when he writes: "[I]t is this primitivist inversion that characterizes the predominant trope of German colonial discourse: an inversion of power in the cultural sphere not unlike the symbolic staging of submission in von Sacher-Masoch's fiction."[40] In the context of German-Austrian imperialism, Berman's reference to von Sacher-Masoch is significant: if sadism follows the logic of institutional dominance and the oppressor's pleasure in the victim's feeble resistance, then in contractual masochism it would be the victim, the one who authorizes his own humiliation, who is paradoxically in charge of the scenario. Accordingly, in von Sacher-Masoch's narrative representation of gender relationships, his apparently weak male characters are in control of the situation. More importantly, by referring to von Sacher-Masoch, Berman inverts the stable power dichotomy between colonizers and colonized. For Berman, the colony is precisely the site of destabilization, where cultural hierarchies lose their credibility, and values lose their integrity. Thus, it is at the periphery of the empire, in a paracolonial space, that a mixed race emerges and change ferments, the distillate of which alters the intellectual metropolitan culture.

While Sebald sounds a cautionary note about the unadulterated Germanic politics of cultural hegemony found in Kürnberger's introduction, Berman sees in the same text a positive function for Germanic colonialism as a mechanism for mixing and rejuvenation. Consequently, I would like to pursue the question of whether and to what extent a colonial utopian program can be read from the gender conflicts depicted in von Sacher-Masoch's paracolonial novellas. Since von Sacher-Masoch's erotic tales with dominating, fur-coated women and submissive, servile men show only one side of his manifold creativity, it is time to take a closer look at his self-pronounced magnum opus *Das Vermächtnis Kains*.

That von Sacher-Masoch regarded his great, uncompleted novella cycle, *Cain's Legacy*, as his principal work is not unfounded. It comprises six books, each addressing one theme: love, possession, the state, war, work, and death. In a letter to his publisher, J. G. Cotta, von Sacher-Masoch described the structure as follows: "Each of these [above mentioned themes] will be addressed in a particular part within six novellas, of which five illuminate the issue itself in its manifold nuances, while the sixth always contains the response, the solution and reconciliation."[41] Although he intended for the cycle to represent the totality of the human condition, the author was able to complete only the first two themes (love and possession) in their entirety, and a couple of dispersed novels such as *Iluj* and *Judenraffael* belonging to other themes (the state and death). The first cycle includes aesthetically sophisticated novels like *Venus im Pelz*, in which a man seemingly lets himself be tormented by a woman; *Don Juan von Kolomea*, in which a man gets revenge on a woman by leading an amoral lifestyle; and *Der Kapitulant*, in which a woman betrays a man through egoism and pursuit of pleasure. As Koschorke notes, notwithstanding its aesthetic brilliance, the "novella, as a flash illumination of a singular and strange occurrence, is unsuited for the construction of such a cosmology. What von Sacher-Masoch brings about exhausts itself, therefore, in a striking phenomenologically oriented juxtaposition of exemplary cases."[42] In tune with Koschorke's argument, the following textual analysis is not concerned with von Sacher-Masoch's failed intention to represent a poetic totality but undertakes a critical reading to discern his colonial and utopian impetus.

The prologue to the entire cycle, "Der Wanderer," epitomizes both his colonial and utopian leanings in a troubling Slavic character, "an authentic national figure of the great Slavic world to the east," who "belongs to the company of monks, who dismisses marriage as a mortal sin, and to whom only a 'free life together between the sexes' is permitted."[43] For von Sacher-Masoch, the wanderer, fleeing the demands of the world to actively seek a putative release from the existing social order, embodies the anarchistic ascetic. This type, in addition to his religious, ascetic pathos, certainly presents social-Darwinist perspectives by portraying humans as "the most reasonable, bloodthirsty, and cruel of all beasts."[44] But at the same time, von Sacher-Masoch's wanderer is troubled and in search of his identity, divorced from nation, family, and any other roots.[45] His self-inflicted departure from a sedentary, predictable life in search of a German pan-Slavic national identity is caused by multiple losses in the form of cultural and territorial ties. In this sense, the nihilistic Slavic wanderer voices Schopenhauer's pessimistic view of humanity:

> The nations, the states are big humans, and identical to the smaller humans in their lust for booty and blood. Indeed, he who wants to do no harm cannot exist. Nature has directed that we should live from the death of others, but as soon as we accept the right to exploit lesser organisms only as a necessity arising in the instinct for self-preservation, then we can go beyond to the justification for humans to harness animals to the plow or to slaughter them, to the justification for the strong to exploit the weak, for the gifted to exploit the less gifted, for the stronger white race to exploit the coloreds, for the more capable, more educated, or those peoples lucky to be more developed to exploit the less developed.[46]

The wanderer recounts nothing less than a natural history of colonialism. However, he wants to transcend this natural order and withdraw from human society. The wanderer portrays mankind *as it is* and later in the resolution *as it should be*. This dialectical move is mirrored by the structure of the novella cycle in general: five materialistically grounded novellas, reflecting the realities of human conduct, are followed by one idealistic story, which represents the alternative. All aspects of public life, according to von Sacher-Masoch, need for the exploitative, social-Darwinist structure to be generally reconstituted if Europeans are to be allowed to pursue happiness. Unlike Kürnberger with his Germanizing fantasies, von Sacher-Masoch speaks clearly against any form of power politics, and he sees the answer in a pan-European democracy with unlimited equality for all citizens. He strongly rejects the autocratic rule of the nobility, as well as war, which falls as a burden first of all on the deprived populace. At a time when nationalist discourses prevailed, the utopist von Sacher-Masoch looked forward instead, anticipating transborder alliances like the European Union that would not come into being for another century.

Thus, von Sacher-Masoch vacillates in his writings between a Darwinian and a religious view of humanity. The so-called author of perversion does not see the goal of his poetics in sexual union but in its disavowal. For only the disavowal of egoism, sexuality, and possessions brings deliverance from nature-ordained human suffering. In place of these things, he calls for an art that "finds its purpose not in equaling the ancients in beauty and brightness, in the transformation of sensuality and of nature, but instead in transcending these. To heal, one must first lay the wound open; to give victory to the spiritual, the sensual nature must be developed to its full demonic potential."[47] In the suffering ascetic, for whom eroticism is personified in the revealing yet withdrawn and reticent woman, von Sacher-Masoch sees the redeemer of humanity, who eventually will move beyond the prudish forces of nature and will—on an intellectually higher plane—subjugate them. Renunciation for von Sacher-Masoch implies no passive resignation to the status quo, but instead calls for a growing acceptance of the limits imposed by life itself, limits arising from the nature of space and time, or, to be more precise, from the conflicts of gender, ethnicity, and class in the paracolonial setting. When we bear this precondition in mind, it is scarcely surprising that von Sacher-Masoch's two existing resolution-novellas in *Vermächtnis Kains* (*Märchen vom Glück*[48] and *Paradies am Dniester*), with their idealization and visionary optimism, can only be fully appreciated in conjunction with the stories renouncing various aspects of human nature. Noyes sheds light on the intrinsic connection between the novellas reflecting the human condition and von Sacher-Masoch's stories of resolution: "[T]he models of synthesis that he offers remain weak and unconvincing in comparison to the conflict he sees inherent in the human condition. In keeping with his time, he sees salvation in a mixture of work ethic, ascetic self-denial, and a strong sense of duty."[49]

Accordingly, for von Sacher-Masoch renunciation is not a *Triebverzicht* [renunciation of a drive] to appease a bad conscience, as Sigmund Freud describes it, but a means to transcendence, because it allows human beings to overcome the limitations of rationality, which serves their innate passions for power and sexuality.[50] For von Sacher-Masoch, human beings are at the same time both rational and cruel beasts, and their dangerous erotic passions and political zeal can only be restrained through renunciation.

Der Kapitulant (1870)

The novella *Der Kapitulant* enacts a gender power reversal in the borderland of Galicia. This setting allows the author and his readers to explore the boundaries of permissiveness within the Habsburg social order. The periphery of the empire functions in this as a projection screen for innovative sociopolitical ideas, and the distance opens up possibilities for social revitalization. In *Kapitulant*, one of the six novellas that constitute the cycle *Liebe* (love) in *Vermächtnis Kains*, we learn about the destiny of the introverted peasant Balaban, who loses his fiancée Katharina to their master but subsequently rationalizes her infidelity to himself as an inevitable consequence of women's nature, thereafter compensating for the loss by leading a life of quiet renunciation. Here we can see what Michael T. O'Pecko describes as a typical paradigm for von Sacher-Masoch's tales: "a couple, one of whom is a gifted woman whose sex prevents her from completely realizing her abilities in a male-dominated society and the other of whom is a weak,"[51] underprivileged man whose passivity has become a barrier to his entry into the practical and sensual sides of life. The man's modesty finally succeeds in provoking the woman into giving him a thrashing, which accompanies a crisis in his life, forcing him to re-evaluate his behavior. A parting of the ways usually brings about the resolution in his novellas, when the man's transformation proves insufficient to raise him to his partner's level.

The frame story of *Kapitulant* is a wintertime sleigh ride that provides the narrator with an opportunity to depict the broad plains of Galicia in their splendid glory:

> As we flew down the bare mountainside with ringing, bright bells, the plain spread out before us, immeasurable, incomprehensible, infinite. The winter coat of ermine lent it the greatest majesty. It was completely covered by it. Only the bare trunks of the low willows, a few long-armed meadow springs, and in the distance a few forlorn sooty huts, left black marks on the furry white surface of the snow.[52]

This eroticized description of nature elevates the snow to a fetish, giving the reader a sense of a wintertime Galicia cloaked in white, sensuous ermine. It is such depictions that ignite Kürnberger's passions, as when he writes of von Sacher-Masoch's prose: "We would see rise up from the prairies of the Weichsel and the forests of the Dniester new earthbound German writers, who do not write books out of books, but who create books from nature."[53] In Kürnberger's reading, the vastness of the Eastern European borderlands brings the people back to their natural condition. Kürnberger attributes the greater vitality of Slavic peoples in von Sacher-Masoch's prose to unleashed forces of nature in Eastern Europe—pristine rivers, snowcapped mountains, and immense fields. As narrative technique, the landscape description of the frame story anchors the work to what is to come and depicts the climate in which the displayed human destiny can first be fulfilled.

The pastoral structure ends when the narrator comes across the peasant (and later *Kapitulant*) Balaban. The term *Kapitulant* (re-enlistee) refers to someone who has signed up voluntarily for a double or triple term of military service. But, at the same time, it suggests a person who has given up on himself, who has capitulated. In the course of the evening, the Kapitulant is encouraged to tell the story of his former fiancée, Katharina von Baran. This starting point puts the civilized non-local narrator in the role of an anthropologist, thereby allowing sophisticated Viennese readers, secure in the comfort of their armchairs, to be educated and entertained about the exotic, wild East of the Habsburg multiethnic state. Balaban's fiancée is a devastatingly beautiful peasant girl who wants to elevate herself. True to the role of a "femme fatale," she tells our tragic hero directly that the Polish lord of the estate, to whom they are both subject, has eyes for her. She feels nothing for him, but his power and wealth have an irresistible charm for her. When Balaban obediently stammers to her: "Katharina . . . think of eternity!" Katharina answers him dryly: "That's just what I'm thinking of, . . . we're here for just a short time, but there forever."[54] Katharina lives like a lady, goes horseback riding, even smokes cigars and has the serfs whipped as suits her wish and mood. Thus, the transformation from a pretty farm maid to a power-addicted dominatrix is complete.

It is not without reason that von Sacher-Masoch positions Katharina's rapid inversion of sexual power relationships at the border of the Habsburg Empire. He projects this anxiety-provoking loss of manhood onto the margins of the empire to avoid unsettling his Viennese-educated bourgeois readers. The women's movement in the nineteenth century was viewed, together with the working class, as a perilous menace to Vienna's civic order. But while the sharpness of working-class demands was defused through social reforms, discrimination against women persisted. Women were seen as a gender-specific problem, which deeply affected attitudes toward sexuality, provoking anxieties among those in power. Hence, liberals did not believe the women's movement could be solved with social reform but was "more a matter of social control."[55]

Because sexual anxiety was so familiar, the familiar had to be alienated, kept remote, to maintain the comfort of distance. It had to be ghettoized, pushed to the outer reaches of empire where it melded with strangeness. As von Sacher-Masoch consciously breaks through the automatism of perception, he stylizes the periphery of the empire not only as a place of social progress but also as a repository for deeply held anxieties about female sexuality.

Moreover, when Katharina chases Balaban out of the village, he signs up for the Austrian imperial army in order to repair his broken sense of self and finds comfort in belonging to the emperor's military: as he says to himself, "Okay, you serve the emperor; you at least know to whom you belong."[56] During his long term of military service he regains his self-esteem and he gains telling and important insights from his military training: "I saw my prosperity there, more justice and humanity and more civilization than among us. I learned to respect the Germans and the Czechs who speak our language."[57] In other words, he comes to identify with the colonial power of Habsburg. This association with an empire more powerful than the Polish oppressors expresses Balaban's liminal position, as he identifies with the colonized Eastern Europeans and the colonial power of the Habsburg Empire at the same time.

Linking the private with the public sphere, von Sacher-Masoch sets the story of Balaban's traumatic separation in 1846 during the Polish landlords' revolution and the counterrevolution of the Galician peasantry. In response to these turbulent times, Balaban becomes increasingly politicized and projects his anger onto the Polish gentry. He actively seeks a trustworthy authority figure: "I looked up at the eagle, which hung over the gate, and I thought to myself: 'You are only a small bird and you have small wings, but they are strong enough to protect an entire people.'"[58] Claudio Magris comments precisely on this passage: "Folklore and supranational patriotism: that is the contribution of these rather modest tales from distant Galicia."[59] Yet Magris's cursory analysis is too abbreviated in its grasp of Balaban's supranational patriotism. Balaban's patriotism stems from a submissive personality, which—precisely through its affirmative character—throws the reverse side of patriotism into relief. This reverse side, this slavish following of military and national authority, allows him to publicly express his desire to become a "true" Austrian. In this respect, Balaban's ideology represents a desperate attempt to regain in the public sphere the structure and order that was taken from him in his private life by Katharina's cruel withdrawal of her love. During his sporadic visits home he has to concede that Katharina, who in the meantime has married the estate lord, has become his superior, his gracious lady. As this relationship with great social consequences emerged from lovers who were previously peasants, it immediately sexualizes the social contract. Contemporary readers could only conceive of such a breathtaking and awe-inspiring change of social circumstances on the paracolonial borders of the Habsburg Empire. Or, as Berman puts it, Galicia functions as "a site of destabilization where cultural hierarchies and truth values lose their credibility, leading to the possibility of new modes of cognition."[60] While von Sacher-Masoch projects the feared social upset outward to the periphery of the empire, this change costs Viennese society its "initial position of superiority and [subjects it to] a process of hybridization."[61] The periphery is no longer subordinated to the center, and its liminality offers a chance to recalibrate and reinvigorate the Viennese center.

As the conflict in Balaban's story reaches its apex, the Polish estate lords revolt against the Habsburg administration and try to bring the Galician peasants over to their side. They summon the peasants and appeal to them to join their lords' cause because, it was said, "the revolution had broken out, the peasants were free, the [Polish] estate lords had abolished forced labor, and they [the peasants] were allowed to attack [Habsburg] imperial treasuries and the Jews."[62] It would scarcely be possible to depict the social Darwinism of the Habsburg borderlands more drastically. In order to rid themselves of the German-Austrian administration, the estate lords offer their peasants self-determination, they call for the plundering of the state treasuries, and they are even callous enough to declare the Jews fair game. Balaban perceives his life as a series of such battles, and he explains his ongoing devotion to Katharina as determined by nature: "Everything is subordinate to necessity, every living being feels how tragic existence is and still fights with nature, struggles with man, and man with woman, and their love is just another battle for existence."[63] The Darwinian conflict between the sexes proves to be coterminous with the universal conflict for existence, which is itself masochistically justified, for "later, that which has hurt us, comes close to giving us pleasure."[64] With Balaban's unresolved situation and dire prospects in life, the novella closes with the inevitable appearance of Katharina in fully fetishized attire: "The sleigh stood now there, and out of the bearskins covering it arose a slender, beautiful lady in an expensive fur. As she pushed back the veil from her hood, she was still more beautiful but frightfully pale. Her blue eyes were feverish with anger."[65] Although the peasants would not allow her to pass the checkpoint, Balaban—true to his stance of personal renunciation—allows the lady to continue on her way undisturbed.

Two things stand out in this encounter. On the one hand, the dominating Katharina negates any connection to the friend of her youth. As a representative of condescending colonialism manifested on the periphery of the Habsburg Empire, she radiates a sadistic coldness that does not shrink from torment or violence. On the other hand, Balaban disavows the breakdown of his relationship with his young love and refuses to allow himself to be open to the possibility of falling in love with another woman. Even though he has recently won his freedom from the Polish estate lords, he sustains his masochism through the self-deception of a preordained inescapable love, which he can only bear in patience and silence. Thus, *Kapitulant* portrays Darwinian relationships in the private and public realms of Galicia. In particular, the novella can be read as a portrayal of gender power reversal. The projection onto the empire's periphery of contemporary misogynistic sentiments concerning gender conflicts illustrates the use of the paracolonial borderland as a less threatening discursive locus for innovative sociopolitical ideas. Galicia encompasses both restrictive boundaries and new possibilities for social progress and revitalization. Balaban's dire existential struggle reflects the utopian possibilities of the paracolonial space, even though the fulfillment of these possibilities—the conversion of a female peasant into an aristocratic lady—eventually turns against him.

Paradies am Dniester (1877)

If *Kapitulant* portrays an unresolved masochistic love relationship and power struggles within the multiethnic population in Galicia, the next novella, *Paradies am Dniester* (Paradise on the Dniester) provides the reader with resolution and reconciliation. Proposing pan-Slavism as the telos for Habsburg's multiethnic society, *Paradies* seeks to transcend the historical reality and spatial limitations of Eastern Europe. Following Mannheim's model of utopia, von Sacher-Masoch's vision of a new Eastern European order challenges the societal status quo. *Paradies*, in the novelistic cycle *Eigenthum* (Possession), is one of the two completed final novellas of *Vermächtnis Kains*. At the opening of *Paradies*, where the "wild Dniester [River] sends its green silver-foamed waves from the Galician plains into the forested Bucovina,"[66] the first-person narrator encounters a selfless soul named Zenon Miroslavski wandering among the people like a prophet. On his first trip away from the parental palace, the young nobleman Zenon comes across vagabond peasants. Their wretched existence affects him so much that he seeks counsel in the palace library. There he reads of Buddha, the Indian prince who was shaken by a glimpse of human misery, just as he was, and had "left his palace to wander into the wilderness to seek the solution to the agonizing mystery."[67] The account of Zenon's reading conveys another of von Sacher-Masoch's utopian ideas: the revitalization of the Habsburg realm through the spiritually redemptive mythology of the Far East. Zenon leaves his nurturing parents behind and sets forth to discover firsthand the impoverished life of the peasantry. Over time he evolves into a Galician Robin Hood who protects helpless young mothers from the oppressions of procreation and who frees young women from coerced sexual dependencies.

During a period of solitary contemplation, Zenon develops a social utopia of work, unity, and equality, while—drawn by his radiance—the exceedingly beautiful countess Maria Kasimira falls in love with him. With Zenon's support, the peasants refuse to perform their servile feudal duties and move, armed with their scythes and flails, to the palace. This peasant revolt, instigated and settled by a disguised nobleman, merely strengthens the prevailing authority, but it remains unclear if the narrator is conscious of its irony. With the social problems on the Dniester thus resolved, the narrative turns to bringing the two lovers from different social classes together. Although Zenon, with his strength and effectiveness, is in no way similar to von Sacher-Masoch's other heroes, he brings the usual masochistic disposition characteristic of von Sacher-Masoch's protagonists to the fore in a key romantic scene, in which Countess Kasimira playfully proclaims:

> "Don't you want be my slave?" Zenon knelt down before her. "I am that, . . . "Oh! Place your foot upon my neck," Zenon pleaded. "No, no," she countered full of majesty. "I swear to you it makes me happy," he cried, and threw himself face down on the ground at her feet. She blushed, breathed deeply, and finally placed her petite foot gently on his neck. "Are you really happy now?" she asked. "I am." "How wonderful it is to see a man who is strong, courageous, and noble before one in this way."[68]

Only through the enacted subjugation is Zenon's fantasy freed, thereby giving Maria sufficient courage to overcome her shame and to confess her desire and affection for the putative peasant. In von Sacher-Masoch's fictional reality, the protagonists can speak the truth liberated not only from confining class but also from traditional gender roles. Maria then flees with her revolutionary peasant, who, affirmed by her proof of love that transcends the apparent class differences between them, tells her of his noble birth.

If the novella ended here, one could criticize von Sacher-Masoch for glossing over the hard Galician social reality with a romantic love story. However, after Zenon and Maria are married and have moved to a grand estate, the narrator visits the couple. There, a conversation develops that sets von Sacher-Masoch's pan-Slavic utopia forth in detail. The German engineer Felbe, the French doctor Lenôtre, and the Russian aristocrat Popiel represent the competing contemporary social theories and thus juxtapose them. While the Frenchman is devoted to the unceasing progress of European civilization, the German questions the positive effects of civilization and dreams of a return to the natural state (*Naturzustand*). The Russian, in contrast, favors neither progress nor the natural state; instead he prefers the communities of Russian peasants. If it were up to him, everything would be destroyed in order to erect a new youthful world. Even if Popiel advocates a return to a premodern community, he still wants to demolish civilization in the service of modernization. With his emphasis on the destruction of the past, including history and art, in favor of a new youthful world, Popiel turns out to be a reactionary modernist par excellence.

As the host of the conversation, Zenon tries to mediate the different opinions by establishing a model for a work-based community for the Slavic peasant communities where inheritable property has been abolished. Consequently, his social philosophy enhances Popiel's reactionary modernism:

> [Possessions] will have to be returned to the community after the death of the owner, from which large return flows of money can fund major institutions and enterprises to benefit all mankind, similar to the Suez Canal or the transformation of the Sahara into an interior sea. Inheritance has never fulfilled its mission; it has not fulfilled it in the higher sense, because it seeks to assure the future of a few children at the expense of the majority.[69]

Shortly afterwards in the same conversation, Zenon states:

> [Possession] has also failed its mission as an attribute of parental love, because mere possessions are an insufficient assurance for the future of the children. Children are better cared for in common since the community and the state will prepare them for work and provide for their care until they have completed their education.[70]

Zenon's statement is a reflection of contemporary discussions about possession and inheritance. It is not without reason that von Sacher-Masoch entitles the entire second part of his Cain cycle *Das Eigenthum* (Possession). In Pierre Proudhon's book *Qu'est-ce que la propriété?* (What is property?) (1840), the French anarchist—and Popiel's alleged friend—condemns the kind of property gain by which one man exploits the labor of another, although he does not attack the widely valid ownership laws. Popiel, by contrast, in the cited conversation calls for a radical abolition of all rights of possession. But Zenon's principal criticism of such a radical position is that the categorical abolition of property would destroy personal freedom by taking away an individual's control over his means of production. To resolve this issue, Zenon proposes a compromise: individual wages and property should be retained but individual inheritance laws should be abolished. Perhaps most importantly, Zenon identifies von Sacher-Masoch's pan-Slavic idea as the motor for the Habsburg colonial utopia:

> Teutonicness is self-centeredness, inequality, aristocracy; Slavism is commonality, equality, democracy. For these reasons, I only expect a positive solution for all of the great questions that concern humankind from the Slavic race. Yes, from the Slavs I expect the regeneration of the world.[71]

While a key ideological tenet of the Habsburg myth portrays Austria as a harmonious place, too peaceable and unambitious to participate in vicious European colonialism, Zenon's expectations transcend even this wishful thinking.

In contrast to von Sacher-Masoch's usual portrayal of fierce ethnic conflicts as natural determinism within the paracolonial space of Eastern Europe, the conflict in *Paradies* is a prerequisite to his discussion of a utopian pan-Slavic community in Eastern Europe. With *Paradies*, von Sacher-Masoch propounds a colonial utopia, suspended in fantasy by being displaced onto the insurmountable spatial limitations of Europe. Although Zenon's utopia addresses the practical political problems of his time, and although von Sacher-Masoch locates his narratives in Eastern Europe, he is motivated by a utopian conception of a Europe-wide new order. He disassociates the characters in his novella from a limited and limiting reality to act out in an imagined space what is not possible in reality, so that the fictional conversation substitutes for the real. Or, as Deleuze writes: "He does not believe in negating or destroying the world nor in idealizing it: what he does is to disavow and thus to suspend it, in order to secure an ideal which is itself suspended in fantasy."[72] This suspension in fantasy also explains his depiction of a rapid inversion of sexual power relationships, set at the border of the Habsburg Empire, with its anxiety-provoking loss of manhood. Von Sacher-Masoch stylizes the periphery of the empire as a place of social reconstruction and reinvigoration, thereby elevating its status in relation to the center of the empire. Furthermore, by denying the spatial realities and political limitations of Europe, he creates utopian conversations that, through their suspension in fantasy, can take place within the Habsburg Empire itself. Using temporal and geographical borderlands, he is able to bring conflicts to light that were repressed or displaced by being set in exotic locations. He does not offer a way to remove all colonial, sexual, and psychological anxieties from the Habsburg sense of self but rather a way to project them onto the periphery of empire so that they become imaginable.

Notes

1. "Der Dichter fliegt kühn voran, und der Kritiker hinkt mühsam nach. Der Kritiker vertritt die Ideen und Prinzipien der Vergangenheit, der Dichter jene der Zukunft, folglich müssen sie auf dem Boden der Gegenwart jederzeit in Konflikt geraten." Leopold von Sacher-Masoch, *Über den Werth der Kritik: Erfahrungen und Bemerkungen* (Leipzig, 1873), 1.
2. "Wir werden das Oesterreicherthum vertreten als eine politische Nationalität, in der sich die natürlichen Nationalitäten, jede im vollen Genuße ihrer Rechte und Freiheiten, vereinen lassen." Leopold von Sacher-Masoch, *Materialien zu Leben und Werk*, ed. Michael Farin (Bonn, 1987), 337.
3. See Michael Gratzke, *Liebesschmerz und Textlust: Figuren der Liebe und Masochismus in der Literatur* (Würzburg, 2000); Barbara Mennel, "Leopold von Sacher-Masoch's *Ein weiblicher Sultan: Historischer Roman in drei Teilen* (1873): Public Sadism/Private Masochism," *Modern Austrian Literature* 34, nos. 1–2 (2001): 1–13; John K. Noyes, "Vernuft, Leidenschaft und der Liberalismus des 19. Jahrhunderts in Sacher-Masochs *Venus im Pelz*," in *Leopold von Sacher-Masoch*, ed. Ingrid Spörk and Alexandra Strohmaier, 146–66 (Graz, 2002).
4. See Friedrich Lindner's "Leopold von Sacher-Masoch: ein Vordenker der Einheit Europas"; and Marion Kobelt-Groch's "'Das Paradies am Dniester' und anderswo. Utopisches im Werk Leopolds von Sacher-Masoch," in *Leopold von Sacher-Masoch: Ein Wegbereiter des 20. Jahrhunderts*, ed. Marion Kobelt-Groch and Michael Salewski, 143–60 and 173–91 (Hildesheim, 2010).
5. Albrecht Koschorke, *Leopold von Sacher-Masoch: Die Inszenierung einer Perversion* (Munich, 1988), 55.
6. Koschorke, *Leopold von Sacher-Masoch*, 54.
7. See John K. Noyes, "The Importance of the Historical Perspective in the Works of Leopold von Sacher-Masoch," *Modern Austrian Literature* 27, no. 2 (1994): 1–20; Kai Kauffmann, "Slawische Exotik und Habsburger Mythos: Leopold von Sacher-Masochs Galizische Erzählungen," *Germanisch-Romanische Monatsschrift* 52, no. 1 (2002): 175–90; Torben Lohmüller, "Masochismus und Politik: Sacher-Masoch im Kontext seiner Zeit," *Seminar* 48, no. 2 (2012): 164–82; and Anne Dwyer, "The Multilingual Pleasure of Slavic Worlds: Sacher-Masoch, Franzos, Freud," *Comparative Literature* 65, no. 2 (Spring 2013): 137–61.
8. Noyes, "Historical Perspective," 16.
9. "Liest man also Sacher-Masochs Schilderungen lustvoller Unterwerfung in einem konkreteren gesellschaftspolitischen Zusammenhang, so zeigt sich, dass er seine Beschäftigung mit den Themen Furcht und Verführung als Mittel der Herrschaft in einem entweder geographisch oder historisch von der unmittelbaren Gegenwart entfernten Raum verlegt und dort einer spezifischen Umkehrung und Umarbeitung unterzieht. . . . Die Katharina-Novellen zeigen, dass ein Element der übereifrigen Unterwerfung des Individuums darin besteht, die von der Herrschaft ausgelöste Verführung und Furcht zu kontrollieren. Die Austreibung des eigenen erotischen *investissement* in diese Werkzeuge der Macht kann eine Voraussetzung für eine Überwindung realer Unterdrückung sein." Lohmüller, "Masochismus und Politik," 180.
10. John K. Noyes, *The Mastery of Submission: Inventions of Masochism* (Ithaca, NY and London, 1997), 53–54.

11. Noyes, *Mastery of Submission*, 109–10.
12. Ibid., 109.
13. Russell A. Berman, *Enlightenment or Empire: Colonial Discourse in German Culture* (Lincoln, NE and London, 1998), 222–23.
14. See John K. Noyes, "Sacher-Masoch's Africa," in *Deutsch als Herausforderung. Fremdsprachenunterricht und Literatur in Forschung und Lehre. Festschrift für Rainer Kussler*, ed. Rolf Annas, 215–24 (Stellenbosch, 2004).
15. See "Internal Colonialism," *Penguin Dictionary of Sociology*, 2006 edition. For an application of this concept to Austrian literature of the nineteenth century, see Joseph Metz, "Austrian Inner Colonialism and the Visibility of Difference in Stifter's *Die Narrenburg*," *PMLA* 121, no. 5 (October 2006): 1475–92.
16. "Dies könnte vielleicht sogar einen Paradigmenwechsel bedeuten, in jedem Fall aber einen Beitrag zu einer sinnvollen kulturwissenschaftlichen ›Globalisierung‹ der Philologien, die auf diese Weise ihre engen, d.h. willkürlich aufgezogenen nationalstaatlichen und -literarischen Grenzen überdenken könnten—und sich zugleich einen alten Traum erfüllen, nämlich einen ersten Schritt hin zu einer übernationalen Literaturgeschichte der k. (u.) k. Monarchie zu setzen." Clemens Ruthner, "K. (u.) k. postcolonial? Prolegomena zu einer neuen Sichtweise Österreich-Ungarns in den Kulturwissenschaften," in *Kakanien Revisited*, ed. Müller-Funk, Plener and Ruthner, 103.
17. See Lisbeth Exner, *Leopold von Sacher-Masoch* (Reinbeck, 2003), 16.
18. Leopold von Sacher-Masoch, *Souvenirs: Autobiographische Prosa*, trans. [from the French] Susanne Farin (Munich, 1985), 60.
19. Von Sacher-Masoch moves from Lemberg to Prague, Graz, Vienna, Budapest, Leipzig, Paris, and finally Lindheim in Hesse.
20. Von Sacher-Masoch, *Souvenirs*, 61.
21. Kauffmann, "Slawische Exotik und Habsburger Mythos," 178.
22. See Karl Mannheim, *Ideology and Utopia: An Introduction to the Sociology of Knowledge* (New York, 1954).
23. Leopold von Sacher-Masoch, "An unsere Leser," *Gartenlaube für Österreich* 1, no. 1 (1866): 1.
24. Oliver Bruck, "Die 'Gartenlaube für Österreich': Vom Scheitern des Projektes einer österreichischen Zeitschrift nach Königsgrätz," in *Literarisches Leben in Österreich: 1848–1890*, ed. Klaus Amann, Hubert Lengauer, and Karl Wagner (Vienna, 2000), 364.
25. Ibid., 384.
26. Ibid., 369.
27. Michael Hardt and Antonio Negri, *Multitude* (New York, 2004), xv.
28. Quoted in Bruck, "Die 'Gartenlaube,'" 386–87.
29. Ibid., 390.
30. Ferdinand Kürnberger, "Vorrede," in Leopold von Sacher-Masoch, *Don Juan von Kolomea: Galizische Geschichten*, ed. Michael Farin (Bonn, 1985), 192.
31. Ibid., 188.
32. Ibid., 193.
33. "Dort drüben das müde Europa, verwittert wie das Gestein, das unter unseren Füssen zur Tiefe bröckelt … Hier dagegen die jugendfrischen Nationen des Aufgangs, … ohne Furcht und Zweifel in die Zukunft blickend." Leopold von Sacher-Masoch, *Das Vermächtnis Kains: Zweiter Teil Das Eigenthum*, 2 vols. (Bern, 1877), vol. 2, bk. 1, 301.
34. Kürnberger, "Vorrede," 190.

35. Ibid., 191.
36. "Wie wäre es also, wenn wir statt des Grossrußen Turgenjew einen Kleinrußen, einen Ostgalizier, das heisst einen Oesterreicher, d. h. einen Deutschen hätten? Wie wär es, wenn in diesem Oesterreich, welches seinen Germanisirungsberuf bisher so schlecht erfüllt hat, wenn in dieser Zeit, welche die Nationalitäten Oesterreichs im hellen Aufstande gegen das Deutschthum sieht, ein slavisch geborener Dichter von den Ufern des Pruth eine vortreffliche deutsche Novelle an die Borde des Main und des Nekar zu senden hätte? . . . Aber die Tatsache könnte bedeuten, daß die deutsche Literatur ganz neue östliche Längengrade sich erobert, daß sie ganz frische Naturvölker sich annektirt hätte, welche bisher nicht deutsch geschrieben, welche aber im Laufe der Geschichte mehr und mehr es zu thun anfingen." Ferdinand Kürnberger, "Vorrede," 191–92.
37. Berman, *Enlightenment or Empire*, 224. To be sure, German cultural depictions did not always have positive connotations of the "Orient." As Ritchie Robertson shows, even Theodor Herzl's *Der Judenstaat* envisages the Zionist settlements in Palestine as a "bulwark against Asiatic barbarism." Ritchie Robertson, "'Urheimat Asien': The Re-Orientation of German and Austrian Jews, 1900–1925," *German Life and Letters* 49, no. 2, April (1996): 187.
38. Kauffmann, "Slawische Exotik und Habsburger Mythos," 164.
39. W. G. Sebald, *Unheimliche Heimat: Essays zur österreichischen Literatur* (Salzburg, 1991), 58.
40. Berman, *Enlightenment or Empire*, 224–25.
41. Leopold von Sacher-Masoch, *Don Juan von Kolomea: Galizische Geschichten*, ed. Michael Farin (Bonn, 1985), 179.
42. Koschorke, *Leopold von Sacher-Masoch*, 54.
43. "Der Wanderer der sich dem Mönchsstande zuzählt, die Ehe als Todsünde verwirft und bloß ein freies 'Zusammenleben der Geschlechter' gestattet, ist eine echt nationale Figur der großen slavischen Welt des Ostens." Von Sacher-Masoch, *Don Juan*, 9n.
44. "[Menschen sind] die vernünftigste, blutgierigste und grausamste der Bestien." Ibid., 11.
45. See Peter Sprengel, "Darwin oder Schopenhauer? Fortschrittspessimismus und Pessimismuskritik in der österreichischen Literatur," in *Literarisches Leben in Österreich 1848–1890*, ed. Klaus Amann, Hubert Lengauer, and Karl Wagner, 73.
46. "Die Völker, die Staaten sind große Menschen, und gleich den Kleinen beutelustig und blutgierig. Freilich—wer kein Leben schädigen will—kann ja nicht leben. Die Natur hat uns Alle angewiesen, vom Tode Anderer zu leben, sobald aber nur das Recht auf Ausnützung niederer Organismen durch die Nothwendigkeit, den Trieb der Selbsterhaltung gegeben ist, darf nicht allein der Mensch das Thier in den Pflug spannen oder tödten, sondern auch der Stärkere den Schwächeren, der Begabtere den Begabten, die stärkere weiße Race die Farbigen, das fähigere, gebildetere, oder durch günstige Fügungen mehr entwickelte Volk das weniger entwickelte." Von Sacher-Masoch, *Don Juan*, 11.
47. Koschorke, *Leopold von Sacher-Masoch*, 81.
48. The novella *Marzella oder das Märchen vom Glück* [Marzella or the Fairytale of Happiness] in the *Liebe* cycle portrays a plantation lord and a peasant daughter with a pure soul that the lord raises spiritually and morally, in a harmonious and equally entitled union.
49. Noyes, *The Mastery of Submission*, 55.
50. "Thus we know of two origins of the sense of guilt: one arising from fear of an authority, and the other, later on, arising from fear of the super-ego. The first insists upon a

renunciation of instinctual satisfactions; the second, as well as doing this, presses for punishment, since the continuance of the forbidden wishes cannot be concealed from the super-ego". Sigmund Freud, *Civilization and Its Discontents*, ed. and trans. James Strachey (New York, 1990), 88–89.
51. Michael O'Pecko, "Afterword," in *A Light for Others and Other Jewish Tales from Galicia* by Leopold von Sacher-Masoch, trans. Michael O'Pecko (Riverside, 1994), 335.
52. "Wie wir den kahlen Berg hinabflogen mit klingenden, hellen Glöckchen, lag die Ebene vor uns, unermeßlich, unfaßbar, unendlich. Der winterliche Hermelin gab ihr die höchste Majestät. Sie war ganz von ihm bedeckt, nur die kahlen Stämme der niederen Weiden, entfernter einzelne langarmige Heidebrunnen, in der Ferne ein paar verlorene russige Hütten, zeichneten sich schwarz auf dem weißen Schneepelz." Von Sacher-Masoch, *Don Juan*, 62.
53. Ibid., 192.
54. "Katharina . . . denke an die Ewigkeit! . . . Eben daran denke ich, . . . wir sind hier sehr kurz, dort aber ewig." Ibid., 83–84.
55. Karlheinz Rossbacher, *Literatur und Liberalismus: Zur Kultur der Ringstrassenzeit in Wien* (Vienna, 1992), 318.
56. "Gut, du dienst dem Kaiser; du weißt doch, zu wem du gehörst." Von Sacher-Masoch, *Don Juan*, 89.
57. "Ich sah dort mehr Wohlstand, mehr Gerechtigkeit und Menschlichkeit und mehr Civilisation als bei uns. Ich lernte den Deutschen achten und den Czechen, der eine Sprache spricht in der Weise wie wir." Ibid., 90.
58. "[D]a blickte ich zu dem Adler empor, der über dem Thore hing und dachte mir: 'Du bist nur ein kleiner Vogel und hast kleine Flügel, aber sie sind doch groß genug, um ein ganzes Volk zu schützen.'" Ibid., 89.
59. "Folklore und übernationaler Patriotismus: dies ist der Beitrag der eher bescheidenen Geschichten aus dem fernen Galizen." Claudio Magris, *Der habsburgische Mythos in der modernen österreichischen Literatur* (Vienna, 2000), 192.
60. Berman, *Enlightenment or Empire*, 225.
61. Ibid., 226.
62. "[D]ie Revolution sei ausgebrochen, das Landvolk in Freiheit, die Robot [the serfdom] geschenkt von den Edelleuten, auch durften wir über die kaiserlichen Kassen und die Juden herfallen." Von Sacher-Masoch, *Don Juan*, 93.
63. "Alles beugt sich der Nothwendigkeit, jedes Lebendige fühlt wie traurig das Dasein [ist] und doch kämpft Jedes verzweiflungsvoll darum und der Mensch kämpft mit der Natur, mit dem Menschen und der Mann mit dem Weibe und ihre Liebe ist auch nur ein Kampf um das Dasein." Ibid., 97.
64. "[S]päter macht uns das, was uns weh gethan hat, beinahe Freude." Ibid., 100.
65. "Da stand jetzt der Schlitten und aus den Bärenfellen, die denselben bedeckten, erhob sich eine schlanke schöne Dame in einem kostbaren Pelze. Wie sie den Schleier von ihrem Capuchon zurückschlug, war sie noch schöner, aber furchtbar bleich. Ihre blauen Augen fieberten vor Zorn." Ibid., 101.
66. "[D]er wilde Dniester [sendet] seine grünen silberschäumenden Wogen aus der galizischen Ebene in die waldreiche Bukovina." Von Sacher-Masoch, *Vermächtnis*, vol. 2, bk. 2, 461.
67. "[Der] seinen Palast verliess und in die Wüste ging, um die Lösung des qualvollen Räthsfels [sic] zu suchen." Ibid., 470.

68. "'Möchtest Du nicht gerne mein Sklave sein?'—Zenon kniete vor ihr nieder—'Ich bin es auch so,' rief er . . . 'O! setzen Sie den Fuss auf meinen Nacken,' flehte Zenon. 'Nein, nein,' entgegnete sie voll Hoheit. 'Ich beschwöre Sie, es macht mich glücklich,' rief er und warf sich mit dem Anlitz zur Erde vor ihr nieder. Sie errötete, holte Athem und stellte endlich den kleinen Fuss leicht auf seinen Nacken. 'Bist Du wirklich glücklich jetzt?' fragte sie. 'Ich bin es.' 'Wie schön das ist, einen Mann, der stark, muthig, edel ist, so vor sich zu sehen.'" Ibid., 528–29.
69. Ibid., 544.
70. Ibid., 546.
71. "Das Germanenthum ist der Selbstsinn, die Ungleichheit, die Aristokratie, das Slaventhum der Gemeinsinn, die Gleichheit, die Demokratie. Und deshalb erwarte ich eine glückliche Lösung aller grossen Fragen, welche die Menschheit bewegen, nur von der slavischen Race, ja von ihr erwarte ich die Regeneration der Welt." Ibid., 540.
72. Gilles Deleuze, *Masochism: Coldness and Cruelty*, trans. Jean McNeil (New York, 1991), 32–33.

Bibliography

Berman, Russell A. *Enlightenment and Empire: Colonial Discourse in German Culture*. Lincoln: University Press of Nebraska, 1998.
Bruck, Oliver. "Die 'Gartenlaube für Österreich': Vom Scheitern des Projektes einer österreichischen Zeitschrift nach Königsgrätz." In *Literarisches Leben in Österreich: 1848–1890*, edited by Klaus Amann, Hubert Lengauer, and Karl Wagner, 359–95. Vienna: Böhlau, 2000.
Deleuze, Gilles. *Masochism: Coldness and Cruelty*. Translated by Jean McNeil. New York: Zone Books, 1991.
Dwyer, Anne. "The Multilingual Pleasure of Slavic Worlds: Sacher-Masoch, Franzos, Freud." *Comparative Literature* 65, no. 2 (Spring 2013): 137–61.
Exner, Lisbeth. *Leopold von Sacher-Masoch*. Reinbeck: Rowohlt, 2003.
Freud, Sigmund. *Civilization and Its Discontents*. Edited and translated by James Strachey. New York: W. W. Norton, 1990.
Gratzke, Michael. *Liebesschmerz und Textlust: Figuren der Liebe und Masochismus in der Literatur*. Würzburg: Königshausen & Neumann, 2000.
Hardt, Michael, and Antonio Negri. *Multitude*. New York: Penguin, 2004.
Kauffmann, Kai. "Slawische Exotik und Habsburger Mythos: Leopold von Sacher-Masochs Galizische Erzählungen." *Germanisch-Romanische Monatsschrift* 52, no. 1 (2002): 175–90.
Kobelt-Groch, Marion. "'Das Paradies am Dniester' und anderswo. Utopisches im Werk Leopolds von Sacher-Masoch" and Friedrich Lindner "Leopold von Sacher-Masoch: ein Vordenker der Einheit Europas." In *Leopold von Sacher-Masoch: Ein Wegbereiter des 20. Jahrhunderts*, edited by Marion Kobelt-Groch and Michael Salewski, 143–60 and 173–91. Hildesheim: Olms, 2010.
Koschorke, Albrecht. *Leopold von Sacher-Masoch: Die Inszenierung einer Perversion*. Munich: Pieper, 1988.
Kürnberger, Ferdinand. "Vorrede." In Leopold von Sacher-Masoch, *Don Juan von Kolomea: Galizische Geschichten*, edited by Michael Farin, 188–94. Bonn: Bouvier, 1985.

Lohmüller, Torben. "Masochismus und Politik: Sacher-Masoch im Kontext seiner Zeit." *Seminar* 48, no. 2 (2012): 164–82.
Magris, Claudio. *Der habsburgerische Mythos in der modernen österreichischen Literatur.* 2nd edition. Vienna: Paul Zsolnay, 2000.
Mannheim, Karl. *Ideology and Utopia: An Introduction to the Sociology of Knowledge.* New York: Hartcourt, Brace & Co., 1954.
Mennel, Barbara. "Leopold von Sacher-Masoch's *Ein weiblicher Sultan: Historischer Roman in drei Teilen* (1873): Public Sadism/Private Masochism." *Modern Austrian Literature* 34, nos. 1–2 (2001): 1–13.
Metz, Joseph. "Austrian Inner Colonialism and the Visibility of Difference in Stifter's *Die Narrenburg.*" *PMLA* 121, no. 5 (October 2006): 1475–92.
Michler, Werner. *Darwinismus und Literatur: Naturwissenschaftliche und literarische Intelligenz in Österreich 1859–1914.* Vienna: Böhlau, 1999.
Noyes, John K. "The Importance of the Historical Perspective in the Works of Leopold von Sacher-Masoch." *Modern Austrian Literature* 27, no. 2 (1994): 1–20.
———. *The Mastery of Submission: Inventions of Masochism.* Ithaca, NY and London: Cornell University Press, 1997.
———. "Sacher-Masoch's Africa." In *Deutsch als Herausforderung. Fremdsprachenunterricht und Literatur in Forschung und Lehre. Festschrift für Rainer Kussler*, edited by Rolf Annas, 215–24. Stellenbosch: SUN Press, 2004.
———. "Vernuft, Leidenschaft und der Liberalismus des 19. Jahrhunderts in Sacher-Masochs *Venus im Pelz.*" In *Leopold von Sacher-Masoch*, edited by Ingrid Spörk and Alexandra Strohmaier, 146–66. Graz: Droschl, 2002.
O'Pecko, Michael. "Afterword." In *A Light for Others and Other Jewish Tales from Galicia*, by Leopold von Sacher-Masoch, trans. Michael O'Pecko, 329–37. Riverside, CA: Ariadne Press, 1994.
Robertson, Ritchie. "'Urheimat Asien': The Re-Orientation of German and Austrian Jews, 1900–1925." *German Life and Letters* 49, no. 2, April (1996): 182–92.
Rossbacher, Karlheinz. *Literatur und Liberalismus: Zur Kultur der Ringstrassenzeit in Wien.* Vienna: J. & V., 1992.
Ruthner, Clemens. "K. (u.) k. postcolonial? Für eine neue Lesart der österreichischen (und benachbarter) Literatur(en)." In *Kakanien revisted: Das Eigene und das Fremde (in) der österreichisch-ungarischen Monarchie*, edited by Wolfgang Müller-Funk, Peter Plener, and Clemens Ruthner, 90–103. Tübingen: A. Francke, 2002.
Sacher-Masoch, Leopold von. "An Unsere Leser." *Gartenlaube für Österreich* 1, no. 1 (1866): 1.
———. *Don Juan von Kolemea: Galizische Geschichten.* Edited by Michael Farin. Bonn: Bouvier, 1985.
———. *Materialien zu Leben und Werk.* Edited by Michael Farin. Bonn: Bouvier, 1987.
———. *Souvenirs: Autobiographische Prosa.* Translated from the French by Susanne Farin. Munich: Belleville, 1985.
———. *Über den Werth der Kritik: Erfahrungen und Bemerkungen.* Leipzig: E. J. Günther, 1873.
———. *Das Vermächtnis Kains: Zweiter Teil. Das Eigenthum.* 2 vols. Bern: Froben, 1877.
Sebald, W. G. *Unheimliche Heimat: Essay zur österreichischen Literatur.* Salzburg: Residenz, 1991.

Sprengel, Peter. "Darwin oder Schopenhauer? Fortschrittspessimismus und Pessimismuskritik in der österreichischen Literatur." In *Literarisches Leben in Österreich 1848–1890*, edited by Klaus Amann, Hubert Lengauer, and Karl Wagner, 60–94. Vienna: Böhlau, 2000.

Chapter 2

LAZAR VON HELLENBACH
Utopia or Theosophy

Hellenbach presents himself in this edition as one of those Janus-faced philosophers, who—just as they understand the present through the past—render an image of the future through their understanding of the present.
—Carl du Prel, "Vorrede des Herausgebers"[1]

Lazar von Hellenbach

According to Ernst Bloch, an abstract utopia is a bare conception for overhauling the existing society without regard to the readiness of the social conditions. That is to say, abstract utopias do not pay enough attention to the possibilities for their realization.[2] It is in this sense that Bloch views the post-Marxists' narrative utopias of the second half of the nineteenth century; he contends that abstract utopias devote nine-tenths of their pages to the portrait of the future state and the remaining one-tenth to the critical, often only negative, observation of the here and now. While at the same time utopian tendencies were at least kept afloat by these romantic devices, "the prophetic entertainment novel accomplished similar results among the non-proletarian classes like the curious petite bourgeoisie."[3] Hence, Bloch disapproves of these bourgeois utopias—such as Theodor Hertzka's *Freiland* (1890) or Edward Bellamy's *Looking Backward: 2000–1887* (1888)—which were intended as answers to Karl Marx's historical materialism. Although written some years earlier, Lazar Baron von Hellenbach's utopia *Die Insel Mellonta* (1883) would suit Bloch's simple categorization well if not for its intricate narrative structure. Using the case of *Insel Mellonta*, I will illustrate the extent to which von Hellenbach was not informed by "real" travel experience to the South Sea but rather by his keen observations of class- and race-related conflicts within the multiethnic Habsburg Empire. Even though the book thrives on inversions and transgressions of the dominant discourse on class and race, von Hellenbach's narrative style is steeped in contemporaneous European debates about colonialism. Furthermore, I will examine whether the author used the utopian genre merely as a vehicle to bring his theosophical philosophy before a broader audience of readers.

*

As a self-identified "hybrid product [*Kreuzungsprodukt*] of Magyar, Slavic and German blood,"[4] von Hellenbach was born in 1827 in Slovakia, went to school in Vienna, studied at Prague University, and traveled extensively in Europe and the Near East.[5] He spent the last twenty years of his life in Vienna working in the banking business, and after his retirement he focused on his scholastic publications. He died in 1887 in Nice, France.[6] Apart from his theosophical-philosophical writings and his colonial utopia *Insel Mellonta*, von Hellenbach published numerous works on current political issues of the Habsburg monarchy such as *Die Okkupation Bosniens und deren Folgen* (1878), *Der ungarisch-kroatische Konflikt* (1883), *Die öffentliche Meinung und die Nordbahnfrage* (1884), and the posthumous publication *Das neunzehnte und zwanzigste Jahrhundert* (1893). Aside from his career as a writer, von Hellenbach managed his estate in Paczolay, Croatia, and served as a representative in the Croatian state parliament from 1860 to 1867. He resigned from his public office due to his disappointment over the Austro-Hungarian Compromise of 1867, which he perceived as a proliferation of nationalism in Europe.

Today, von Hellenbach is primarily known within parapsychological circles. The field of parapsychology, which encompasses telepathy, hypnotism, and apparitions, examines the possibility of life after death. Von Hellenbach was friends with the philosopher Carl du Prel, as well as with the astrophysicist Friedrich Zöllner, who was known for his theory of four spatial dimensions. Von Hellenbach's pivotal parapsychological theory contends that humans are manifestations, which he calls "metaorganisms," residing in the physical body and the spiritual Self (i.e., soul). He deems this "metaorganism" capable of extrasensory perception and ascribes paranormal abilities to it: clairvoyance, telepathy, and thought transmission. Hence, he considers birth and death to be mere experiential transformations. An English language translation of his work refers to this phenomenon as a "change of perception."[7] In his view, humans have a double nature consisting of a phenomenological consciousness and a transcendental, reincarnating Self. The soul incorporates the unfolding story of life as it evolves toward the quest for fulfillment. As we will see, von Hellenbach's arguments are close to Helena Petrowna Blavatsky's modern Theosophy, which posits a general brotherhood of all men regardless of race, religion, or gender, recommends the study of Aryan literature, religion, and sciences of the East, and tries to explicate the unknown laws of nature as well as the latent power of the human soul.[8] Nevertheless, despite the close kinship of his views to those of the Theosophical Movement, von Hellenbach does not characterize himself as a spiritualist because he does not consider parapsychological phenomena an external revelation but sees them instead as indicators of an innate intelligent essence. As the visionary parapsychologist of the Habsburg Empire, von Hellenbach had a profound influence on fashionable philosophical circles in Vienna and Munich. Carl du Prel, who edited his literary estate, describes his social philosophy in the preface of von Hellenbach's *Das neunzehnte und zwanzigste Jahrhundert* :

> [It is as] if, before his death, from a high point of view, [von Hellenbach] had thrown a last objective glance at our condition. He criticizes the nineteenth century, uncovers the roots of our evil, presents the means of healing—yet with the gloomy presentiment that he is a voice crying in the wilderness—presents to us then a view of the twentieth century, convinced that this view of the future will be self-fulfilling, whether on the path to peace, or—if his proposals remain unnoticed—on the path to catastrophe.[9]

Perhaps not all contemporary social theorists espoused du Prel's enthusiastic appraisal of von Hellenbach's achievements. Even without Theodor W. Adorno's dire dictum that occultism depicts "a symptom of regression in consciousness" that replaces the "rationality of the real" with "hopping tables and rays from heaps of earth,"[10] one can imagine occultism as a bizarre breeding ground for chauvinistic ideas. For Jost Hermand, German occult utopias of the nineteenth century mirror the *völkisch* ideology, whose central idea is the *Volksgemeinschaft*, positing a mystical union of the Germanic people. This union encompasses the paramount ideal of German nationalists and chauvinists to make all class interest, as well as individual aspirations, insignificant. Closely allied to this desire for the mystical community is the notion of a leader whose charismatic personality directs his followers in what they should think and do.[11] The notion of a leader, according to Hermand, is ubiquitous in these right-wing writings.

Perhaps it is not by accident that the hero of *Insel Mellonta* is called Alexander and bears similarities to the charismatic Greek conqueror of the same name. In his historical study *Leben mit den Toten* (2002), Diethard Sawicki makes the point that many German-speaking proponents of spiritualism, who depicted a close association of occultism and theories of Germanic purity, enjoyed great popularity in the fin-de-siècle period. Sawicki concedes that, unlike many other spiritualists, von Hellenbach sympathized with "socialist ideas and saw himself as a philanthropist."[12] Still, the historian states that von Hellenbach's "philanthropic conviction did not hinder him from entertaining a discreet anti-Semitism and from delineating a Malthusian euthanasia program in which newborns should be killed with chloroform or zyankali in order to prevent overpopulation."[13] Yet Helmut Zander maintains that von Hellenbach also demonstrates how an impetuous embrace of occultism can be misconstrued as racist concepts of Germanic purity, whence Zander sees in von Hellenbach's writings foremost "a barrier to a hasty stigmatization of occultism with *völkisch* ideas,"[14] and locates the baron "politically on the side of socialism."[15]

Writing in Vienna at a time when the anti-Semitic discourse shifted from a cultural mode to a racial one, von Hellenbach addresses racial questions by stressing his sociopolitical inclination that shapes his explanation of ethnic phenomena:

> The physiognomy and speech of the Jews generally offers nothing inviting or attractive; . . . If one observes the narrow, dirty city quarters in which they have been everywhere confined, if one considers the contempt and persecution that they suffer, then one will no longer be surprised at their disadvantageous racial characteristics.[16]

The baron's racial discourse interprets the unattractive Jewish physiognomy as a result of their social situation for which they were not themselves responsible, but which was forced upon them, and he doubts that Jews have the ability to form their own nation-state because they are used to living as an "intercellular substance" of a state organism and "would perish in a proper cell complex."[17] But further along in the same essay, von Hellenbach states:

> This is one more reason why both parts should strive to set aside the limitations of a *specific nationality*, which is caricatured so easily by all nationalities. America, England, Hungary and other countries have sufficient examples of ridiculous, or even nasty, characterizations, which lead to stereotypes and disparaging names. It's high time that the concept of *nation* fades into darkness and that of *humanity* comes into the light.[18]

While von Hellenbach strives to abolish racial stereotypes, he cannot avoid using them when he describes Jews as parasites of their host economy. The baron disapproves of nationalism so vehemently that he cannot imagine a future Jewish state. This is noteworthy if we consider that Theodor Herzl, von Hellenbach's Viennese contemporary, published his Zionist manifesto *Der Judenstaat* as early as 1896.

Von Hellenbach's moderate political positions are exemplified in his essay *Die antisemitische Bewegung* (1883), a reprise of Eugen Dühring's *Die Judenfrage als Racen-, Sitten-, und Kulturfrage* (1881). Steven Beller describes Dühring's publication as the event that gave anti-Semitism "its theoretical backbone [by denying] the possibility of Jews ever becoming Germans" through conversion.[19] In his answer, von Hellenbach denounces Dühring's medieval demand that Jews be expelled from the German-speaking countries. Instead, von Hellenbach insists on their assimilation: "they have to become English, French, etc. in fact and not just nominally."[20] He points out that Voltaire, Schopenhauer, and even the utopian Fourier all speak disparagingly of the Jews, but he refuses to "condemn the bloodline."[21] Von Hellenbach limits his analysis of the etiology of the Jewish question to traditional Jewish childrearing, emphasizing ethnic solidarity. He asks why the Jewish emancipation has not unraveled, why it has yet to bear fruit. Then, he answers that Jewish assimilation into Viennese society will only succeed after the problem of Jewish solidarity is addressed. His argument is that false cosmopolitan solidarity needs to end because "the Jew is no cosmopolitan since he is not above the national squabble. He is much more a nomad moving about in the world; he shares this false cosmopolitanism with the Gypsies."[22] This statement, of course, shows how von Hellenbach was affected by the anti-Semitic discourse of the time, especially in defining Jews as nomadic outsiders, which resonates Georg Simmel's description of the stranger's position within a host society: "[A]s the man who comes today and stays tomorrow."[23] The outsider unites physical closeness and sociohistorical remoteness by allegedly lacking the ability to rise above the profane political squabble.

For von Hellenbach, the Jews' membership in the Viennese society is extraordinary despite their having been inorganically appended to the community. Seemingly, for the baron, true cosmopolitans are elite members of the Habsburg Empire (e.g., aristocrats) who have the liberty to wander around without endangering their connection to the community at home. Pushing von Hellenbach's line of argumentation, this would render the Jews a negative mirror image of the aristocracy. Later in the same essay, von Hellenbach makes a case against the accumulation of Jewish wealth as part of the existent inequality of wealth distribution in general. His sociopolitical plan involves a redistribution of the wealth of childless decedents to the social collective in order to rectify the disproportionality of individual and collective capital that arises from individual capital growing continuously (due to interest earnings) while collective capital steadily drops (state indebtedness). With his social welfare theory, which differs pointedly from the radical socialism of his day, he rejects the facile acceptance of mass poverty in Vienna as an economic, liberal necessity, and advocates an increase of collective wealth instead. He excoriates scientific positivism and its causally mechanistic explanatory models, which do not take the higher destiny of humankind into account. The central idea in von Hellenbach's essay *Die antisemitische Bewegung* is the struggle to improve the well-being not only of the Jews but of human society in general.

His utopia *Insel Mellonta* entails similar sociopolitical motives and was published in the same year as *Antisemitische Bewegung*. At that time, Germany was about to start its official colonial enterprise while Austria had taken a different course. Austrian nationalism and chauvinism was on the rise in reaction to the economic downturn of 1873, which had challenged the stable position of liberalism in the monarchy and the steady migration from the margins of the Habsburg Empire to Vienna. Undoubtedly, Austria's socioeconomic problems inform von Hellenbach's utopian image of "socialism without restriction of individual property."[24]

Insel Mellonta (1883)

In 1883, the respected Viennese publisher Carl Leopold Rosner brought *Insel Mellonta* onto the market, and over the years it went through three further editions.[25] Apart from publishing von Hellenbach's utopia, Rosner shared the credit with Heinrich Laube for having discovered the popular Austrian author Ludwig Anzengruber. Furthermore, he arranged for the Viennese flaneur Daniel Spitzer to collect his celebrated sketches in Austria's leading liberal newspaper *Neue Freie Presse*, and Rosner also published Ferdinand Kürnberger's essays.[26] The number of editions, and the renown of the publisher, indicate that von Hellenbach's novel was well received in its day by the intellectual public. In the third edition, the publisher's publicity release touted the book as a "corollary to Bellamy's *Looking Backward: 2000 to 1887*," which was one of the most influential American utopias of the late nineteenth century. The plot of *Insel Mellonta* unfolds as follows. Alexander, a cultivated German aristocrat, is shipwrecked and stranded in the Southern Pacific Ocean near a coral island, where he is rescued by natives. During his stay in the island paradise, Alexander learns about the history of Mellonta's inhabitants: the natives are descendants of noble French émigrés and their African wives who, since the French Revolution, have been living in a free-spirited commune far away from European civilization. In short order he is asked to report on the current state of European circumstances, in the course of which he becomes acquainted with the charming Aglaia, a "Bachantin" (a childless woman over twenty-two years old). The following morning he is taken on a hike by his guide Sophron to see Mellonta's tropical paradise in all its abundance. In the afternoon he participates in a business workshop led by Musarion, the attractive young leader of the "Vestals" (women under twenty-two years old), followed by an invitation to discuss possible technological improvements to the tropical island with the "Council of Grandfathers."

In the following weeks Alexander learns to appreciate the insular community, and at the same time he becomes quite popular among the inhabitants through his scientific presentations and his musical performances. After a sailing tour with Aglaia and Musarion, Alexander has a tête-à-tête with Aglaia. Although she prophesizes to him that Musarion will be his true soul mate, she makes love to him that night without apparent remorse. And indeed the romantic encounter does not hinder Alexander from pursuing Musarion, who initiates him into the island's Socratic–Platonic worldview, consisting of divine Providence and the immortality of the soul. Subsequently, Alexander and Musarion grow closer, and Musarion's passion for him is awakened when Alexander performs three captivating songs one evening during a communal event. Afterwards, she invites Alexander to her home where he tells her about his monotonous upbringing in rural isolation, his depression evoked by unhappy love affairs with egocentric European women, and the many journeys he undertook because he has loathed the politics of his homeland for a long time. But he promises that all his disheartening experiences will not affect their budding romantic relationship. Unfortunately, before the romance is consummated, a volcanic eruption submerges the entire island of Mellonta in the ocean.

The same glistening light that reveals the doom of their world to the lovers illuminates now a wise Brahman named Shakretes, who stands by Alexander as he awakens from what has been an intense dream. Shakretes makes it clear to him that, while Mellonta Island was only a dream, it must be seen as the manifestation of the inherent capabilities and experiential forms of the soul. As evidence for this, the Brahman master arranges a spiritual encounter for Alexander, in which important events of his stay on Mellonta are related to his acquaintances and friendships. Even his lover, Musarion, appears during the séance in the form of a light beam in "blue coloration."[27] This novel blue-toned ethereal light indicates that the lovers can only be reunited after Alexander's earthly demise. Through this moving experience, he finally says goodbye to all his social commitments and accepts his destiny. As the story ends, Alexander is solitarily striding over the spine of the majestic Himalayan mountain range and finds his solace in the conviction that the "future will justify . . . the vision of his dream."[28]

Up to the dramatic *peripeteia* resulting from the volcanic eruption, von Hellenbach's text structurally follows the scheme of an island utopia. In his book *Utopische Inseln* (1996), Horst A. Glaser differentiates between such island utopias and Robinson Crusoe sagas as follows:

> In the classic island utopia the arriving traveler is led around as a visitor, and a well-organized state system *in actu* is presented and explained. . . . In a Robinson saga in contrast, the character is not a visitor but a worker. While a visitor can calmly view the institutions of the utopia, a Robinson tale tells of the triumphs and setbacks in the organization of simple survival. The classic utopia is a completely institutionalized world, to which the Robinson saga in contrast offers a world in a raw state that can be developed into a community. To that extent it presents the genesis of a utopia.[29]

The utopian genre was based from the start on a spatial displacement (from the Greek *ou-topos*, or "not place," nowhere), and the location of the action is often set on an island. Thomas More's *Utopia* (1516), undisputedly the first utopia that launched an entire literary genre, Francis Bacon's *New Atlantis* (1624), as well as Tomasso Campanella's *City under the Sun* (1637), are only but a few of the best-known examples of these island utopias that follow this paradigm. Von Hellenbach's *Insel Mellonta*, following Glaser's description of island utopias, takes place almost in the present in order to emphasize the contrast between the historical reality (that is, the Habsburg Empire) and the island-based ideal state. In the conventions of the Robinson Crusoe saga, the main character is a first-person narrator with whom the reader can easily identify. However, von

Hellenbach instead unravels the educated aristocratic hero's experiences in the third person, which in turn helps to objectify the narrative. Mellonta's names of localities and persons follow the conventions of the genre in that they are all descriptive or allegorical names. With its epic structure and deep individual characters, *Insel Mellonta* is closer to a Robinson Crusoe saga than to a utopian narrative. But unlike a Crusoe tale, our shipwrecked hero is stranded on a remote island where he converses with the virtuous, yet simultaneously hedonistic, members of a humanistic community. It is possible that von Hellenbach was merely following an Austrian model to tell a Robinson Crusoe saga, as stated by Hermann F. Wagner: "A common trait of all Austrian Robinson Crusoe sagas is that instead of a 'Friday' character, the hero shares the loneliness with a female friend."[30] Accordingly, Alexander finds his soul mate Musarion, and due to his European education he is able to enlighten, like a "Habsburg Robinson," the graceful island people about the technological achievements of modernity.

Moreover, von Hellenbach inverts his utopian narrative through the dream. Perhaps due to the groundbreaking success of Louis-Sebastian Mercier's *L'An 2440* (1770), in which the dream of the narrator renders a temporal rather than a spatial displacement for the first time, dreams became a common feature in utopian novels of the nineteenth century. Jean Servier sees a reference to a dream figure in utopias:

> [Utopias] borrow from the dream state the sleeper's ability to transcend spatial boundaries and to set aside all barriers that are perceived by his waking consciousness. Heretofore, consciousness was constrained by the conflicted situation; now the dream appears and resolves them.[31]

However, in *Insel Mellonta* it is precisely Alexander's awakening from his dream that renders his utopian plan superfluous, unless the reader consents to von Hellenbach's spiritual program. In this respect, the author successfully weds the genre utopia to his belief in spiritualism, and carves out a space in between genre conventions for his novel.

Nonetheless, *Mellonta Island* also borrows from several utopian authors. First, the theme and structure of the book can be traced to Jules Verne, whose importance to the genesis of German science fiction literature was established by Roland Innerhofer.[32] One borrowing from Verne comes from *L'île mystérieuse* (1874). The island civilization in *Insel Mellonta* is demolished by a volcanic eruption in the end, just as in Verne's story; all traces of colonization are once more extinguished. Such natural narrative jolts instantly relocate the utopian societies to the imaginary realm.

Secondly, the story can be linked to Johann Gottfried Schnabel's enlightened novel *Insel Felsenburg* (4 vols, 1731–43). Schnabel's original adaptation of Daniel Defoe's *Robinson Crusoe* (1719) joins together the motif of the shipwrecked traveler stranded on a deserted island with the theme of an Ideal Commonwealth. The contrast between late feudal European society, with its intrigues, and the idyllic patriarchal social order on Felsenburg Island defines the structure of the novel and makes it appear to prefigure a bourgeois lifestyle. For members of the lower and middle bourgeoisie, who come there from Europe, an island is not a place of *exile*, as is the case for Robinson Crusoe, but an *asylum*—a place that replaces the land of their birth.[33] Aside from these striking content and structural agreements between the novels, there are also notable formal similarities. As Wilhelm Vosskamp points out, Schnabel's novel not only has "the form of a two-tiered narrative," but it achieves "a novelistic composition, which is characterized by an inherent duality. *Structurally*, there are two primary forms, the autobiographical narrative and the utopia-descriptive discourse."[34]

Thirdly, von Hellenbach adapts elements from Friedrich Leopold Graf zu Stolberg's *Insel* (1788) to advance his purpose. Stolberg tailors his outline for an ideal republic around the patriarchal structure of a society with little division of labor. By means of philosophical conversations between Sophron and his confidants (Glaukos, Kallias, Hilaros), which take place on a small island in the Danube, a utopian vision emerges: it consists of an isolated, self-contained, mountainous island with gentle climatic conditions that makes a "life of happy pious free naivety"[35] and a spiritual, Christian community possible. Complete equality of social status and wealth, and an informally regulated balance of work and leisure, create conditions for the education of a new breed of humans, subjected to as few laws and regulations as possible. The two novels are comparable not only because of the dream structure, the regressive form of the idylls, and the enthusiasm for Ancient Greek culture but also for the structural positioning between a Crusoe-like adventure tale and a utopian narrative. As Götz Müller demonstrates in *Gegenwelten: Die Utopie in der deutschen Literatur* (1989): "The basic model of the Crusoe tale is the forced dissociation from civilization; the formative thought of the classical utopia is the conscious break from tradition. With Stolberg a voluntary renunciation appears in place of the forced situation of a shipwreck."[36] The strongest indicator of an intertextual dependency between *Insel* and *Insel Mellonta* is the duplication of the central character Sophron: while Stolberg's Sophron is a rich heir and benefactor of the impoverished, who instructs his confidants through philosophical discourses, von Hellenbach's Sophron enlightens Alexander in the role of island leader and paternalistic friend. Sophron also symbolizes the connection to von Hellenbach's primary inspiration of his utopian community. Towards the end of the novel, in the séance, Alexander re-encounters his island guide Sophron, who rapidly morphs into the great French utopian philosopher Charles Fourier before he disappears entirely. Thus—at least figuratively—Fourier guides Alexander through the community on Mellonta Island. Just like the "Phalanstery" in Charles Fourier's utopian community, Mellonta offers communal life with constant meaningful encounters and carefree sexual relationships, only interrupted by abundant sessions at the dinner table.³⁷ Both writers consider bourgeois marriages and nuclear families as forms of enslavement or even prostitution, and von Hellenbach shares Fourier's disgust for civilization, which in their eyes seems to be the worst phase before humanity attains a higher plane of consciousness. The economic systems of the two utopian islands also bear striking similarities, consisting of cooperatives and limiting access to private property for their residents. Furthermore, von Hellenbach takes over Fourier's concepts of corporations for young women, "vestals" and "bacchants," and he does not even mind using the same terms for them.

Last but not least, the novel's title *Insel Mellonta* evokes Edgar Allan Poe's novella *Mellonta Tauta* (1849), which represents a fictitious message in a bottle from Pundit, an antiquarian scholar of the year 2848, who "has been allowed to examine the material exhumed by workers digging up the ground of the 'emperor's principal garden' of 'Paradies' for a new fountain."³⁸ The Greek title *Mellonta Tauta* is taken from the end of Sophocles' *Antigone* (441 BC) and means "these things are in the future." *Mellonta Tauta* approaches the borderline of science fiction, dealing plausibly with scenes that are fantastical, or beyond the bounds of everyday reality. Poe's science fiction stories often vacillate between romantic and occult discourse. Accordingly, *Mellonta Tauta* describes a complex future society radically different from his own and incorporates many scientific advances, and social and historical changes, from the society of his day; it is a warning against the totalitarianism of modern society, but at the same time it is not about a viable societal alternative. Considering the textual and ideological coincidences, and the availability of translations of Poe into German from 1853 onwards, it is plausible that von Hellenbach knew Poe's stories since they were celebrated on the continent for their sinister imagery and formal ingenuity.

*

According to Louis Marin, author of *Utopics: A Semiological Play of Textual Spaces* (1968), narrative utopias create a displaced vision in a fictitious non-temporality as well as non-spatiality, which neutralizes historical reality. For Marin a utopia is then: "[T]he neutral moment of a difference, the space outside of place; it is a gap impossible either to inscribe on a geographic map or to assign to history. Its reality thus belongs to the order of the text."³⁹ The narrative provides a neutral space, allowing the reader to reconstruct the underlying social conflicts and concealed ideological concepts of the present society, which the utopia inverts and neutralizes. Phillip E. Wegner states that the result is a critically productive reception for narrative utopias:

> [W]hen we attempt to translate the utopia back into the ideological enclosure of its immediate present, as would historicist or culturalist approaches, we discover blind spots, dislocations, erasures, and aporia marring the picture of the Utopian commonwealth. These absences and slippages are crucial, for they signal the

productive, critical neutralizations taking place in the narrative unfolding of the utopian figure.⁴⁰

Narrative utopias are neither literature presenting fictional experiences, nor depictions of social theory with systematized totalities, but rather, "an in-between form that mediates and binds together these other representational acts."⁴¹ Building on Marin's thesis Wegner asserts that these are forms of imaginary textual figuration or cognitive markers of cultural space, which merely permit a "pre-theoretical" view of historical development, a view that can only be completed later through social theory. Thus, Wegner contradicts the traditional view that literary utopias depict perfect societies. Utopias paradoxically achieve their greatest influence because of their incapacity to systematically represent potential alternatives. With this incomplete structure utopias leave possibilities open, inviting readers to play with alternatives and strive to avoid a definitive interpretation. Such an interpretative framework goes beyond historicizing *Insel Mellonta*'s intricate narrative structure, and carves out an in-between space for von Hellenbach's utopia that looks beyond the confrontation between the working class and the bourgeoisie in Europe at the end of the nineteenth century.

In 1883, at the time of *Insel Mellonta*'s publication, the erstwhile stable position of Viennese liberalism was challenged by the economic depression in the aftermath of the *Gründerkrise* of 1873. Until the mid-1870s, however, the liberalization of the economic system had immediate demographic consequences. There was tremendous mobility within the Habsburg monarchy because of improvements in the railway system and the liberalization of citizenship laws. As the Habsburg monarchy represented a multiethnic state, masses of people of different nationalities could change their residences. Vienna's population increased from around 600,000 in 1869 to almost two million in 1910.⁴² Unfortunately, Vienna's prosperity of the late 1860s came to a shrieking halt when the *Ringstrasse* investment bubble burst and the stock market crashed in 1873. Although the economy slightly rebounded after 1879, the widespread confidence in liberal economic principles had vanished, and nationalism and chauvinism were on the rise.⁴³ Once Viennese liberals became German patriots, the Slavic upper classes in Prague demanded autonomy. But when the liberals made concessions in the interest of the dual monarchy, they were considered traitors to the German cause by Vienna's petite bourgeoisie. Carl E. Schorske describes this moment of historical transition as follows: "*Laissez faire*, devised to free the economy from the fetters of the past, called forth the Marxist revolutionaries of the future."⁴⁴

These tremendous social and economic changes also influenced the aesthetic perception of intellectuals within the multiethnic Habsburg Empire. The Austrian situation at the time is reminiscent of the argument Wegner develops about the "turn inward" of Sir Thomas More and other English renaissance writers, "where that which could not yet be accomplished in the world was then achieved in the realm of imagination."⁴⁵ For von Hellenbach, this inward turn results in him articulating visionary political positions in a posthumously published essay collection:

> The task consisted ... in bringing about a regulation of the map of Europe and a federation of all or at least part of the preponderant states, a task which to many will seem to be insoluble. ... To believe that at a distant time the seven groups [English, French, Germans, Spanish, Italians, Benelux countries, and the Balkan states] could constitute themselves as federated states of Europe is not utopia, for they are compelled to a closer association through their financial situation, through the increasingly vocal demands of their worker population, and above all, however, through their large neighbors.⁴⁶

From today's perspective—with the European controversies concerning a common currency and market—von Hellenbach's federalist plan presents itself as a concrete utopia par excellence because he foresees accurately that without a political union, a union among the European powers is still on the horizon. Nevertheless, in case a European union should fail to materialize, he preventively puts the blame on the working class, warning that in the immediate future the workers may constitute a serious danger to the social peace and justice. In the previous chapter, we established that Leopold von Sacher-Masoch also develops pan-European fantasies. In a letter to his brother, von Sacher-Masoch describes the content of his planned volume, *Der Staat*, in the never-completed novella cycle, *Vermächtnis Kains* (1870–77): "the misery and business of the absolute monarchy; the mendacity of constitutionalism; rescue through democracy, United States of Europe; common legislation."⁴⁷ The Dual Monarchy of 1867, with its constitutional compromises, seemingly inspired intellectual aristocrats such as von Sacher-Masoch and von Hellenbach to develop various federalist European concepts at a time when nationalism in Europe was turning chauvinistic.

*

It may be that Vienna—as Alexander Honold puts it—was the European capital of "domestic strangers" in those days, and that alienated intellectuals viewed the political developments of the imperialist age all too casually. Thus, they found themselves "in the position of the other, the foreigner or even that of the uncanny."⁴⁸ One is willing to believe the description of the prevailing state of mind in Austria in those years conveyed by Robert Musil's narrator in his novel *Mann ohne Eigenschaften*: "[N]o man had an ambition for global economic or global political power; one was situated in the center of Europe, where the old world axes crossed; the terms 'colony' and 'overseas' sounded like something still completely untested and distant."⁴⁹ But whereas this description makes Austrians seem disinterested, they were far from it; Austrian literature of the last quarter of the nineteenth century was saturated with conscious and unconscious expressions of aspirations for alternative social and spatial organizations. Even if colonialism bypassed Austria, the empire also developed its own parallel discourse that led intellectuals to rethink Austria's position within Europe. In the same passage, Musil paraphrases Austria's utopian position:

> [W]ithout the world yet knowing it, [Austria was] the most advanced state; it was the state that somehow got along by itself, one was negatively free in it, continuously in the sense of the insufficient bases of one's own existence, and of the large fantasy of what hasn't happened, or not happened irrevocably, as if washed by the ocean breeze from which humanity sprang.[50]

Like this perception of Austria, Mellonta's utopian community, which had no contact with the outside world, embodies Musil's negative freedom—a freedom achieved only through Austria's imaginary disengagement in international affairs. Hence, this alleged freedom was found in the realm of the writer's fantasy. Even with Austria's disengagement, it is hard to imagine that the pervasive discourse on colonialism was absent from Viennese coffeehouses. Certainly, Austrian intellectuals valued the exotic and imaginary cultures just as other European powers did.

In *Enlightenment or Empire* (1998), Russell A. Berman insists on actual colonial experience (e.g., in travelogues) as a premise for colonial discourse. Yet without actual experiences in the tropics, von Hellenbach appropriates the rhetoric of the travelogue for his utopia.[51] But his experiences among the Habsburg Empire's heterogeneous population helped him craft an imaginary exotic community in the South Sea, in which the colonial perspective functions in a way that is similar to the exoticism in depictions of overseas colonies in contemporary travelogues. The imaginary utopia *Insel Mellonta* employs a similar colonial gaze and Eurocentric perception, since effective exoticist literature does not merely represent a foreign culture but also reflects self-perceptively on the home culture.[52] To paraphrase Hans Christoph Buch's *Nähe und Ferne* (1991), exotic relations are based on the dialectic of closeness and distance, on a mutual mixture where the distant seems near and the near distant. In poetological terms, exoticism is a special case of Bert Brecht's *alienation effect* meant to disturb the automatism of the spectator's usual reception; historically it reveals the results of five centuries of colonialism on the Western literary imagination.[53] Buch bases his argument concerning the closeness and distance of literary colonialism on Wolfgang Reif's exoticism theory, which Buch interprets in the following terms:

> The exoticist produces pictures, which as a projection of his inner being are intended to compensate for his alienated view of self and reality.... In the process of turning away from this proximity, the exoticist simultaneously ... projects a positive wish-concept at a distance, to which he can then turn with an equal passion.[54]

Illustrating Reif's exoticism, von Hellenbach's narrative utopia—through a process of inversions and transgressions—destabilizes the contemporary colonial discourse, as we shall see.

After *Insel Mellonta*'s beginning—describing a geographical natural history of the South Sea island world and its volcanic origins—the tale of a stranded victim of a shipwreck unfolds: "He awoke as from a dream and is unable to ascertain if he has dreamed or if, vice versa, he is now caught up in a dream."[55] This is the harsh awakening of our exhausted hero. As readers we are thus encouraged to understand his situation as a sobering reality, even though we learn—with the beginning of the frame story—that the paradise island has been merely the protagonist's dream. The narrator introduces his character with mysterious ambivalence: "[B]y the shape and color of his face one could only suppose a Mediterranean, but his deep-seated blue eyes lessened such an impression, so that it remained unclear to which European nationality he belonged. But his posture carried an aristocratic character."[56] And later, when asked for his name, the protagonist adapts to the island community's penchant for Greek names and "calls himself Alexander."[57] Caught on an island between dream and reality, the "Mediterranean" aristocrat chooses a name more suitable to his altered circumstances. Mellonta's liminality also recurs in a spatial dimension since the emigrants are not even sure where it is located. Having left their country in response to the nightmare of the French Revolution, the lonely island entices them, but they only know its latitude with certainty: 17 degrees 3 minutes south. The informant, a captain in the harbor at Rio de Janeiro, reveals: "[T]his island lies certainly not under 25, nor over 35, degrees easterly of Tahiti."[58] Consequently, Mellonta island is spatially, as well as temporally, *entre doux*, in Marin's terms, and its reality belongs to the order of the text. Yet even the island community itself is anything but a homogeneous descendant of the French aristocracy: back in Brazil, the colony founder Marquis de Chateau-Morand, who had been emancipated by the writings of Voltaire and Rousseau, had already bought a heterogeneous group of people to join the colony. It included:

> six young Negresses, who were just landed from an arriving ship, so as to have women workers who were accustomed to the high temperature and to be able to burden them with the care for the interior housekeeping. In addition the arrangement created a favorable relationship between female and male individuals. The purchase of Negros was not carried out because the creation of a wild race and the perpetuation of slavery was not in the interest of the colony.[59]

The reasoning by which the supposedly enlightened nobles take advantage of the slave trade is astonishing, at least from our present perspective. It not only undermines the Marquis's conduct and the ideal of individual freedom in a fundamental way, but strangely enough, with his "trade in women" and the allocation of the domestic duties to them, the aristocrat nonchalantly exports his Western chauvinism.⁶⁰ Georg Forster had already described this tradition in his Pacific travelogue *Entdeckungsreise nach Tahiti und in die Südsee 1772–1775* (1780): "The men didn't show the slightest respect towards the women while the women responded obediently to the slightest gesture and often had to take on the services of beasts of burden."⁶¹ Instead of taking the opportunity to imagine a just social order based on gender equality, von Hellenbach's misogynist Marquis generates a mixed race in Mellonta when he refrains from purchasing male slaves under the humanistic pretext of preventing the formation of a slave society. Thus, the narrator presents Mellonta as a successful multiethnic social order, and, needless to say, one finds flattering allusions to the island population along the lines of Louis-Antoine de Bougainville's Tahitians scattered throughout the text, although the narrative involves descendants of French aristocrats and African slave mothers. In keeping with the Marquis's gender preference, the men are portrayed first:

> [Alexander] found himself among honorable men who were unusually good-looking with very fine features, who had a markedly gentle manner; they were good-looking, but not with masculine good looks . . . It is conceivable that the continual scarcity, the exhausting work and the life struggles, always left traces in the faces [of the city dwellers], and it is conceivable that life on such islands, among the superfluity of natural gifts and the peaceful existence, is bound to result in a gentle character.⁶²

While metropolitan life leaves an ineradicable trace on men, the islanders' physiognomy has softened to the point of being an androgynous melding. In short, their beauty is so striking that the narrator feels obliged to explain this phenomenon in greater detail: the lack of heavy industrial work and the absence of the social-Darwinist structures of European metropolises allow even men to become gentle and beautiful on the island. While the men are conspicuous for their androgynous purity, the description of the women of Mellonta clearly emphasizes the mixing of the races:

> Three different racial qualities had successfully embodied themselves in Musarion, the fine gestures of a French lady from a good lineage and the dark tone of the Spanish race were not to be overlooked in her eyes and hair. This beautiful head was enthroned upon a figure such as is to be found among the daughters of the wilderness, which with Musarion appeared in a still ennobled form.⁶³

In Musarion, who later becomes Alexander's lover, Moorish-Spanish blood has encountered French noble blood. Undoubtedly, this multiethnic background contributes to a previously unknown refinement in the narrator's view. Her name might be an allusion to Christoph Martin Wieland's three-volume epic, *Musarion: oder die Philosophie der Grazien* (1768), which is tellingly set in a utopian Arcadian Greece.⁶⁴ Even Aglaia, Alexander's first love interest, has a similarly multiethnic ancestry, although the description of her assumes a sexually functional touch absent from Musarion:

> A young girl sat next to him. While she lacked beautiful gestures, she was large, wonderfully built, and had rich, reddish-brown hair, ivory white teeth, and bright facial coloring. What particularly distinguished her, however, was the glance from her dark blue eyes; her facial structure and nose were certainly such to mark her as a descendant of one of the Negresses brought along from Brazil, if the splendid whiteness of her arms and neck had not spoken against that impression. She was called, certainly not by chance, Aglaia.[65]

Her lack of beauty is offset by a "wonderfully built" body, and although in Greek mythology Aglaia represents one of the three goddesses of grace, the narrator is primarily cognizant of her sensual radiance by focusing on her African facial characteristics, thereby mixing a classical European beauty with the exoticized colonial subject.[66] The ethereal Musarion is virginally white, while Aglaia, like her African forebears, is dark skinned, sensual and sexually active.

The role of child-rearing in Mellonta is illustrated in a conversation about sexual practices that Alexander has with the patriarch: "Yes, yes, in that our women have the right instinct! They are afraid of contact with men with whom they have children, while the girls prefer precisely the proven, more mature men." Alexander answers, chuckling: "You approach it among humans as we do with breeding horses, which only rise in price when their progeny have proven themselves!"[67] Fourier's communal engineering takes precedence over the Christian ideal of lifelong married partners who grow old together. Instead, experienced women reproduce with young lovers, and young maidens do so with mature men.

In keeping with the theosophical literature, von Hellenbach sees the true future of humanity in the mixing of the races: the descendants of the refined French aristocracy with full-bodied African slave mothers. Neither European civilization nor the state of nature generate a public as cultured as the hybrid community of *Insel Mellonta*. This Viennese *melanche* à la von Hellenbach does not take place without a certain hierarchy. The Caucasian race is represented as the primus inter pares in the description of the leisure-time activities of the islanders:

> Amphibian-like graceful swimming is nearly universal among the wild tribes of Polynesia. It is therefore not surprising that the culture brought with the settlers from Europe brought about in this as well an advanced race, and the skill of the Mellontians in swimming surpasses that of the wild tribes.[68]

European superiority is palpable here, but it challenges the contemporary colonial discourse about European dominance, for only through the fruitful union of the advanced, but Europe-weary, French aristocrats with the exotic "Negresses" does a new, qualitatively better race emerge. Von Hellenbach underscores these natural preconditions for a better society by consciously distancing them from European marriage traditions:

Soon after the birth of the first few children, they came to the conclusion that all offspring—naturally without detriment to parental attention—would be viewed as communal children and that they would therefore be brought up in complete brotherliness. The aim was to form one large family, and thereby leave the young generation in ignorance of European marital customs, by substituting free love for the monopoly of marriage.[69]

While the revolutionary ideal of brotherhood is still put into practice in *Insel Mellonta*, France's erstwhile lauded civil society regulates almost all social relations. In Mellonta, the natives and European colonizers have merged to become one entity. The determinative moment of encounter is already a fait accompli and now, as the community is an emerging nation, the time has come to create a genesis myth. Perhaps the most important function of a national myth is to mold an integrated society, free of social conflicts and tensions. The meaning and purpose of this view of social harmony is to ameliorate societal anxieties while glossing over the actually existing injustices. Claude Levi-Strauss describes this as the "problem-solving" capacity in myth, whereby an imaginary synthesis between fundamental antinomies of a society (such as female vs. male, or life vs. death) is achieved and therefore provides legitimacy for its social organization.[70] Von Hellenbach's utopia envisions a spatial *and* temporal rapture from the European values of the nineteenth century. Mellonta's imagined community requires a radical break with tradition and with the past.[71] The author expresses this rupture from the rest of the world with the island's name, "Mellonta," which in classical Greek connotes "destined future." Thus, the baron deliberately creates a foundation myth:

> Since their relation to the rest of the world had broken down, and their future was to be decided on this island, they honored the Marquis's admiration of ancient Greek culture by giving the island the name *Mellonta* . . . The offspring were also left in complete ignorance of dogmatic religious teachings but instead were brought up in the belief in a divine Providence and an afterlife. In keeping with this purpose, all non-scholarly works that could infringe on this opinion were completely removed.[72]

The French philosopher of religion, Ernest Renan, seemed to support von Hellenbach's fictional character when he gave a lecture at the Sorbonne in Paris in 1882: "Forgetting is a crucial factor in the creation of a nation . . . The essence of a nation is that all individuals have many things in common, and also that they have forgotten many things."[73] In *Mellonta*'s case, however, it is control of memory that most troubles the protagonist—for example, when he has to inform the island community about recent historical developments in France:

> A chain of quite extraordinary circumstances and coincidences hurled me out of a world unknown to you that exists on the fringe of this paradise. I would almost like to believe that this happened merely so I could become a messenger of all the horrors from which you have been spared by what I believe to be a benevolent destiny.[74]

In the course of his lectures criticizing civilization within the context of political circumstances in France, it becomes clear why he feels like a latter-day Job who is in the process of destroying a happy idyll by teaching and enlightening his listeners about contemporary France, a state he called at one point a "European Work Colony":[75]

> Your fathers left the country when the monarchy was laid to rest and the First Republic was constituted. The bourgeois element seized the reins of power, and after that element had robbed the nobility, the owners of the major part of the estates, and where possible had slaughtered them, the bourgeoisie began to rage against itself. Mass executions followed, and as these let up, the sons of France were sacrificed by the hundreds of thousands in wars. A victorious field commander, named Napoleon, grabbed the reins, restored the monarchy, placed himself upon the throne, only then calling for blood and devastating Europe and, after 20 years, conceded the throne again to the descendants of the former ruling family. After 30 years of government by this dynasty, the previous drama repeated itself; once more a Napoleon assumed the throne, only to be toppled after various wars and horrendous devastations. Now a republican form of government is again in power, but the assorted pretenders to the crown are waiting for the opportune moment to again seize power for themselves.[76]

The aristocratic "Francophile" von Hellenbach shows a strong anti-bourgeois affect: the French bourgeoisie, who not only buried the monarchy but also devastated the rest of Europe afterwards, is blamed for the lamentable conditions in the nation. Alexander's depiction of the revolutionary developments creates an ideological bridge to the Marquis, who in light of the political circumstances in France then saw emigration and a break with the homeland as the only way to "sweep away with one swipe class differences and the conflict of situations."[77] Thus, the émigré aristocrats try with their utopian community to realize the idealistic goals of the revolution, which were the cause of their forced emigration in the first place.

In his address, Alexander portrays a French population that is "subjugated to war service"[78] and, in particular, he points to the misery of the working classes: "[T]he situation of the workers has become something wretched because work developed through strength and intelligence is shifted to costly machines, so that the worker is becoming more and more dependent on those who have these tools."[79] If a "disarmament of the mass armies" and a "guarantee of work and existence" does not emerge soon, Europe will inevitably devolve to catastrophes, "in contrast [with which] the Reign of Terror of the French Revolution will seem like an idyll!"[80] In connection with the fate of the working classes, von Hellenbach's blind spot becomes clear. If Alexander attributes the excellent productivity of Mellonta to the "magnificent climate" and, above all, to its inhabitants' "fine morals," then he thereby recognizes in the "coarseness of the masses" the greatest obstacle to introducing the superb conditions on Mellonta into Europe, with its disease of civilization: "A turn to the better could only be achieved by the building of labor facilities, which aside from other advantages would allow the bearing and upbringing of the children to be carried out communally and systematically."[81] Further along in the text, Alexander offers the disturbing insight "that human society is comparable to a fermenting and boiling mass that is suited to nothing more than the development and crystallization of human character, which, as it were, gains refinement through the pressure of his purity and through the experiences of life."[82] In the same context, Shakretes darkly prophesizes: "Most people are not at all aware that they are standing on a volcano, and the few who sense the approaching eruption hope to be able to escape it."[83] The recurring image of a volcanic eruption thus serves not only formally as a dramatic turning point but displays von Hellenbach's anxiety about the revolutionary masses. These masses could instigate a bloody proletarian revolution in future that could surpass the bourgeois French Revolution in its destructiveness. Jost Hermand describes the confrontation between the bourgeoisie and the proletarian masses in the nineteenth century as a process that led to a "global *Endkampf* after 1885, as the opposition of both classes rapidly worsened."[84] It was this situation that made von Hellenbach anxious about the proletarian movement.

To escape this pessimistic prognosis for the future, Alexander recognizes the true alternative in the island commune of his dream: "The ideal inhabitants of Mellonta owe their happy existence to the circumstance that—completely in contrast to the condition of European civilization—a large communal wealth lay at their disposal by which concerns for raw existence and for the upbringing of children ceased to apply and, therefore, distress and misery—these sources of all suffering and vice—were unknown."[85] The fragmentation of this communal harmony is the essential ill of civilization, yet Alexander was "intelligent enough to recognize that the splintering of the European commonwealth brought with it an enormous squandering of the productive workforce. The societal splintering alone makes it impossible to come close to attaining the good life of the islanders."[86] The island commune is bound together by a "solicitous paternalism" and marked by "sympathetic relationships among relatives and old acquaintances." Still, the merits of communal living are not only advantageous in the social context but have a solid economic significance:

> On Mellonta there were no tradesmen who, as in Europe, would cut off a poor girl's ponytail for 5 fl., only to sell it for 50 fl. More to the point, there was an absence of the whole chain of middlemen who grow rich without contributing their own work effort while the producers and consumers groan under their pressure.[87]

While von Hellenbach's utopia is more than merely a reflection of the contemporary social situation, his unconscious aversion toward migrating tradesmen from Eastern Europe is apparent. As von Hellenbach explains in *Antisemitische Bewegung*:

Now, however, "trading" is in actuality a line of lies, in which the overcharging of one's neighbor is the guiding principal. He who sows a wind will reap a storm. Moreover, the almost comical trading in Genesis, in which Abraham bargains Jehovah or Yahweh down from 50 righteous men to 45, then to 40, 30, 20, and finally 10, shows that traders were very early at home among the Jewish people.[88]

Like the exoticist described in Buch's *Nähe und Ferne*, von Hellenbach is not fully aware of his biases, even if he comprehends the plight of workers and Jews alike. In order to compensate for his anxieties about modern society, he portrays his utopian island as a primordial community. By turning away from what is around him, von Hellenbach projects a positive wishful ideal into the distance to which he is passionately fleeing.

The putative danger of the masses in the European metropolises manifests itself in the text through lengthy discussion about the contrast between modern society and traditional communal culture. Community is maintained by traditional rules and a universal sense of solidarity, which fits the organic theory of social union. In the life of the community, man participates with all his sentiments. The real controlling agent is the people (*Volk*). Likewise, the community as a whole embodies rural village life folkways and mores, with the people entering into this form of existence with full minds and hearts. While the Mellonta community is characterized as a large family group, the portrayal of the European metropolis emphasizes the increasing moral depravity and egoism inherent in them. Marriages, it suggests, are entered into on the basis of "predicaments and support concerns," though this is nothing other than "lifelong prostitution."[89] Alexander describes the false morality of Europe:

> In Africa, and to an extent also in Asia, women are sold in the market like animals. By one very numerous sect, they are penned in for their entire life like cows in a stall, and in civilized Europe one can very easily purchase a wife for the cost of her maintenance, and often much less expensively; yes, it even occurs that women buy men.[90]

The criticism of European customs is not so much directed at chastity and prudery, but more toward the commodification of erotic love. While, Alexander points out, the founding father of Mellonta bought female slaves in Brazil, women also buy men in the civilized Moloch of Europe. The trope of European love slaves threads through the entire text. After the sensuous Aglaia gives herself to Alexander without regret or ulterior motive, she tells her lover as he declares his fidelity: "It's clear that you come from the land of slaves!"[91] When Alexander afterwards begins his great romance with Musarion, he tells her of his earlier unhappy relationship: "This conniving woman understood the demonic power that she had over me, and although not at all a demon but good-hearted, it gave her pleasure to test her power and to content herself with that."[92] In other words, European civilization turns men into slaves. Only escape fantasies free Alexander from his masochistic position. The sexual economy of Mellonta brings von Hellenbach's critique of European civilization close to von Sacher-Masoch's representation of gender relationships with his apparently weak male characters who are nevertheless in control of the situation. If sadism follows the logic of institutional dominance and the oppressor's pleasure in the victim's feeble resistance, then in contractual masochism the victim is the one who authorizes his own humiliation and who is paradoxically in charge of the scenario. Accordingly, von Hellenbach's main protagonist needs a colonial setting to get rid of the burden of European civilization.

Alexander's sailing excursion reveals how strongly von Hellenbach's cultural pessimism remains evident in his eroticized image of the beautiful savage:

> The nasty north wind blew on Aglaia, who sat opposite him, drawing back from moment to moment her coat, now at the top, then at the bottom, allowing indiscreet glimpses. Aglaia was not at all as hasty in the restitution of the *status quo ante* as her European sisters would have been; also she had no reason to be, it was all so marvelous that one would have had to be a native Mellontan not to be influenced by such a sight in his views and speeches.[93]

Unlike in Europe, erotic passions are neither vicious nor perverted in Mellonta, since it is civilization that distorts and represses them. Von Hellenbach's sensuous creature, free of societal shame, is reminiscent of Rousseau's glorification of the natural condition.

But von Hellenbach ends this romanticized depiction of the beautiful savage with the volcanic eruption. The social utopia of Mellonta is transformed by the protagonist's awakening into a dreamlike fantasy world. When Alexander inquires about the possible concrete realization of his dream world, he receives an evocative answer from his fatherly friend, Shakretes:

> Futile effort, my son! Earth does not yet shine forth in blue love's light! The problems of work and the recognition of the natural still weigh heavily on the shoulders of humanity. You are among a small group of others to those citizens of this world who have a heart for humanity and understanding for its suffering, but there have always been such, and the teachings, deeds, and sacrifices of these friends of humanity have nearly always caused more harm than good because one ought not to take unripe fruit from the tree.[94]

On the one hand, this rejection of the transcendental orientation of the utopia represents a further inversion of the text. It perceives the elimination of suffering from society as an unworthy pursuit since misery results from the incongruity between the constitution and the conditions of the commonwealth. On the other hand, the frame story confirms the validity of Alexander's dream, not only through the improvised séance in which we again encounter Musarion, leaving behind as evidence of her existence a fetishistic "thin, bluish fabric," but also through the enunciation of Alexander's exceptional position, for he is one of the few humans whom "the veil of Maja has not entirely entwined."[95] In other words, these are the visions of a solitary seer whose only misfortune is to live before his time. Hence, his Indian Brahmin advises him:

> The dream was given you far more as a comfort than as doctrine, for you have to struggle and suffer in the interest of your own development. Therefore, return to your life enriched through the comforting knowledge that humanity, however slowly, is progressing toward better conditions, and that love will compensate you when you have suffered much, for only suffering can lead to love's magic palace.[96]

The demand that Alexander return to his private life comes closer to the ideology of the bourgeois *Bildungsroman* than to a social utopia. Shakrates' sobering insight that humanity is slowly progressing is not only indicative of von Hellenbach's anxieties about the revolutionary proletarian masses but opposes Bloch's concept of a concrete utopia. For although the fatalistic Brahmin puts the hope of rapid change to rest and dismisses Alexander's Mellonta as an idealistic social utopia, his dream analysis and séance can be interpreted as promoting the philosophy of theosophy, which holds that all humans will come to perceive birth and death as experimental changes, untouched by the universal cosmic kernel of the human soul. In his essay *Das neunzehnte und zwanzigste Jahrhundert*, von Hellenbach summarizes his vision for humanity in the twentieth century:

> (1) Human birth and death is nothing more than a change of experiential form. (2) The motif for this metamorphosis lies in the interest in the development of our character and our abilities. (3) This development requires a corresponding quantity of suffering, work, and experience, which can be completed more quickly or more slowly. (4) There is consequently no injustice in the world because suffering and work translate into a transcendental capital, and everyone becomes what he [has] made of himself. (5) Human life is in a certain sense fatalistic because humans enter the world with a determined intention regarding their own education or that of another, and therefore conduct themselves instinctively in accordance with this intention. (6) Humans have a vital interest to spare no effort in the pursuit of their own or another's ethical, intellectual and physical development. (7) No action, no thought is for naught. The action and inaction of each individual is decisive for his own ethical and intellectual value and is transparent through all time.[97]

Thus, in von Hellenbach's view, our life is predetermined and all earthly injustice will be abolished. Therefore, there is no need for social utopias; the Mellonta dream is rather a preview of the happy condition that will come into being when humans have reached the enlightened stage. Moreover, humans first have "to lift the mystical veil" and to learn "that we have interests in solidarity with humanity, because death neither separates us permanently from humanity's destiny nor from other people."[98]

The dreamlike community in *Insel Mellonta* sets forth a model of society by which "the excesses of capital and the limitations of ownership can be removed without disturbing the freedom of acquisition."[99] That is to say, von Hellenbach advocates a redistribution of the inheritance of wealthy childless couples to increase Vienna's collective wealth. Von Hellenbach's social welfare plans aim to eliminate unemployment and poverty in Vienna, which the liberal bourgeoisie saw as an immutable evil necessary for securing a profitable economy. Von Hellenbach's vision of the island community, therefore, does not constitute a concrete utopia for the oppressed working masses of the European metropolises to rediscover themselves, but offers a showcase for societal circumstances that solves social problems "through the initiative from above."[100] Written in Vienna at a time of economic depression and social disparity, the author's conservative approach with his hope of a return to a preindustrial community of brotherly love serves as a vanishing mediator between two different ways of organizing social life whose particular effectiveness disappears once the transition has been accomplished.[101] The growing social tension, expressed through the author's anxiety about the "boiling mass,"[102] and the resentments towards the East European Jews who had recently immigrated to Vienna, renders *Insel Mellonta* an in-between space.

For Wegner, one function of a narrative utopia is "to mediate between two different cultural and social realities, between the world that is and that which is coming into being."[103] The social tension between the bourgeoisie and proletarian masses that troubled von Hellenbach and his contemporaries was partially eased in the twentieth century through an increase in the power of social democracy and the extension of the welfare state. However, the pervasive authoritarian structures in the text seem to undermine the liberation of the working class. Only through the frame story does *Insel Mellonta* become a utopia, albeit a conservative one, in which the human potential to explicate previously unknown laws of nature as well as the latent power of the human soul is demonstrated. Von Hellenbach seeks to discredit the notion that humans live but once since only the knowledge of the immortal life of the soul justifies Mellonta's dream. The innovative narrative structure distances von Hellenbach's dream temporally from the present. Its "play within a play" form achieves a different sense of reality. That the author's creative narrative structure did not always achieve the sought-after effect on readers or critics can be discerned from his foreword to the second edition, where he explains: "What surprised me very much . . . was the perception that only very few readers were able to draw conclusions and render it into a prose of the common sense, which was clear and distinctly expressed in the book although in dramatic form."[104] Von Hellenbach therefore feels compelled to add an explanatory chapter, even if the creative structure of the text suffers from this editorial measure.

*

In *Orte, Irgendwo: Formen utopischen Denkens* (1981), Jost Hermand appraises *Insel Mellonta*, along with William Alexander Taylor's *Intermere* (1901), merely as "utopian island" adventures that "take up the conventional shipwreck motif and allow their travelers to become stranded" there.[105] This cursory assessment of von Hellenbach's versatile novel neglects the imaginative frame story, with which the author uses the utopian discourse to convey his theosophical philosophy. As this chapter has demonstrated, *Insel Mellonta* is steeped in the contemporary debates about colonialism and nationalism, while it also thrives on inversions and transgressions of the dominant discourse. Finally, von Hellenbach appropriates the colonial rhetoric for his narrative without having had actual travel experience in the South Sea. Rather, his experience as an intellectually minded aristocrat living in Vienna, who found himself in the position of "the other," enabled him to project his utopia to a faraway and indeterminate space in the Pacific Ocean.

Notes

1. "Hellenbach zeigt sich in der vorliegenden Schrift als einer jener janusköpfigen Philosophen, die, wie sie die Gegenwart aus der Vergangenheit verstehen, so aus der Gegenwart ein Bild der Zukunft gewinnen." Carl du Prel, "Vorrede des Herausgebers," in Lazar Baron von Hellenbach, *Das neunzehnte und zwanzigste Jahrhundert: Kritik der Gegenwart und Ausblicke in die Zukunft*, ed. Carl du Prel (Leipzig: O. Mutze, 1893), viii.
2. See Ernst Bloch, *Abschied von der Utopie? Vorträge*, ed. Hanna Gekle (Frankfurt, 1980), 110.
3. Ernst Bloch, *Das Prinzip Hoffnung* (Frankfurt, 1959), 2:714.
4. Lazar von Hellenbach, *Die antisemitische Bewegung* (Leipzig, 1883), 41.
5. "In 1846 he traveled by sea from Hamburg to Malta, where he remained for a year in the Mediterranean Sea and the Orient (as far as Baghdad)." Wilhelm Hübbe-Schleiden, *Hellenbach: Der Vorkämpfer für Wahrheit und Menschlichkeit* (Leipzig, 1891), 6.
6. See Anton Neuhäusler, "Lazar von Hellenbach," *Neue Deutsche Biographie* (Berlin, 1969), 8: 467–68.
7. Lazar von Hellenbach, *Birth and Death, as a Change of Form of Perception: Or, The Dual Nature of Man*, trans. "V." (London, 1886), 3.
8. Cf. Lazar von Hellenbach, *Geburt und Tod als Wechsel der Anschauungsform oder die Doppelnatur des Menschen* (Vienna, 1885), 217–22.
9. Prel, "Vorrede," in von Hellenbach, *Das neunzehnte und zwanzigste Jahrhundert*, viii.
10. Theodor W. Adorno, *Minima Moralia: Reflections from a Damaged Life*, trans. E. F. N. Jephcott (New York, 1999), 238 and 240.
11. See Jost Hermand, *Old Dreams of a New Reich: Volkish Utopias and National Socialism* (Bloomington, 1992), 26–74.
12. Diethard Sawicki, *Leben mit den Toten: Geisterglauben und die Entstehung des Spiritualismus in Deutschland* (Paderborn, 2002), 334.
13. Ibid., 334.

14. Helmut Zander, "Sozialdarwinistische Rassentheorien aus dem okkulten Untergrund des Kaiserreichs," in *Handbuch der 'Völkischen Bewegung' 1871–1918*, ed. Uwe Puschner, Walter Schmitz, and Justus H. Ulbricht (Munich, 1996), 226.
15. Ibid., 236.
16. Lazar von Hellenbach, Volkswirtschaftliche Vorurtheile. Politische Vorurtheile. Gesellschaftliche Vorurtheile, *Die Vorurteile der Menschheit*, 3 vols. (Leipzig, 1893), 1:265.
17. Ibid., 268.
18. Ibid.
19. Steven Beller, *Vienna and the Jews 1867–1938: A Cultural History* (Cambridge, 1989), 191.
20. Von Hellenbach, *Die antisemitische Bewegung*, 45.
21. Ibid., 10.
22. Ibid., 51–52.
23. Georg Simmel, "The Stranger," in *On Individuality and Socials Forms: Selected Writings*, ed. Donald N. Levine (Chicago, 1971), 143.
24. Von Hellenbach, *Das neunzehnte und zwanzigste Jahrhundert*, 21.
25. After the first edition (Vienna: C. Rosner, 1883), the book was reprinted by W. Braumüller (Vienna, 1885), followed by a third edition by O. Mutze (Leipzig, 1896) and a fourth printing by R. Besser (Leipzig, 1926). More recently, Dieter Reeken (Lüneburg, 2012) reprinted von Hellenbach's utopia.
26. See Murray G. Hall, *Österreichische Verlagsgeschichte 1918–1938* (Vienna, 1985).
27. Lazar Baron von Hellenbach, *Die Insel Mellonta* (Leipzig, 1896), 228.
28. Ibid., 248.
29. Horst A. Glaser, *Utopische Inseln: Beiträge zu ihrer Geschichte und Theorie* (Frankfurt, 1996), 31.
30. Hermann F. Wagner, "Robinson und die Robinsonaden in unserer Jugendliteratur," in *28. Jahresbericht der k.k. Franz Joseph Realschule in Wien* (Vienna, 1903), 16.
31. Antoon Berentsen, *Vom Urnebel zum Zukunftsstaat: Zum Problem der Popularisierung der Naturwissenschaften in der deutschen Literatur (1880–1910)* (Berlin, 1986), 35.
32. See Roland Innerhofer, *Deutsche Science Fiction 1870–1914: Rekonstruktion und Analyse der Anfänge einer Gattung* (Vienna, 1996), 29–85.
33. See Fritz Brüggemann, *Utopie und Robinsonade: Studien zu Schnabels 'Insel Felsenburg' 1731–1743* (Weimar, 1914), 85.
34. Wilhelm Vosskamp, "'Ein Irdisches Paradies': Johann Gottfried Schnabels *Insel Felsenburg* (1731–43)," in *Literarische Utopien von Morus bis zur Gegenwart*, ed. Klaus L. Berghahn and Hans Ulrich Seeber (Königstein, 1983), 95–96. (Italics in the original.)
35. Friedrich Leopold Graf zu Stolberg, *Die Insel* (Heidelberg, 1966), 28. Stolberg's vision of a "Leben in froher frommer freier Einfalt" anticipates the motto of *Turnvater* Jahn's volkish sport youth movement during the Napoleonic era.
36. Götz Müller, *Gegenwelten: Die Utopie in der deutschen Literatur* (Stuttgart, 1989), 132.
37. See M. C. Spencer, *Charles Fourier* (Boston, 1981), 13.
38. Burton R. Pollin, "Politics and History in Poe's *Mellonta Tauta*: Two Allusions Explained," *Studies in Short Fiction* 8, no. 4 (Fall 1971): 627.
39. Louis Marin, *Utopics: Spatial Play*, trans. Robert A. Vollrath (Atlantic Highlands, 1984), 57.

40. Phillip E. Wegner, *Imaginary Communities: Utopia, the Nation, and the Spatial Histories of Modernity* (Berkeley, 2002), 36.
41. Ibid., xviii.
42. "In the meantime, the monarchy's railway network expanded seven-fold to 42,000 kilometres and its coal production five-fold to 55 million tons. Four million people left the empire, of whom about a third returned." Robin Okey, *The Habsburg Monarchy: From Enlightenment to Eclipse* (New York, 2001), 228.
43. The end of liberal era brought about the rise of labor unions, which helped to improve the social situation for workers. At the time, laissez-faire market policies were replaced with national protectionism curtailing the international free trade agreements. See Karl Gaulhofer, "Finanzkrise: Genau wie damals beim Gründerkrach," *Die Presse*, 11 July 2009 <http://diepresse.com/home/wirtschaft/finanzkrise/494325/Finanzkrise_Genau-wie-damals-beim-Gruenderkrach>.
44. Carl E. Schorske, *Fin-de-Siècle Vienna: Politics and Culture* (New York, 1981), 117.
45. Wegner, *Imaginary Communities*, 56.
46. Von Hellenbach, *Das neunzehnte und zwanzigste Jahrhundert* (Leipzig, 1893), 6.
47. Leopold von Sacher-Masoch, *Don Juan von Kolemea: Galizische Geschichten*, ed. Michael Farin (Bonn, 1985), 178.
48. Alexander Honold, "Peter Altenbergs *Ashantee*: Eine impressionistische cross-over Phantasie im Kontext der exotischen Völkerschauen," in *Grenzüberschreitungen um 1900: Österreichische Literatur im Übergang*, ed. Thomas Eicher and Peter Sowa (Oberhausen, 2001), 137.
49. Robert Musil, *Der Mann ohne Eigenschaften*, 2 vols. (Reinbek, 2005), 1:32–33.
50. "[O]hne dass die Welt es schon wusste, der fortgeschrittenste Staat; es war der Staat, der sich selbst irgendwie nur noch mitmachte, man war negativ frei darin, ständig im Gefühl der unzureichenden Gründe der eigenen Existenz und von der großen Phantasie des Nichtgeschehenen oder doch nicht unwiderruflich Geschehenen wie von dem Hauch der Ozeane umspült, denen die Menschheit entstieg." Musil, *Mann ohne Eigenschaften*, 1:35.
51. See Russell A. Berman, *Enlightenment or Empire: Colonial Discourse in German Culture* (Lincoln, 1998), 8.
52. See Michael Mayer, *'Tropen gibt es nicht': Dekonstruktion des Exotismus* (Bielefeld, 2010), 10.
53. Hans Christoph Buch, *Die Nähe und die Ferne: Bausteine zu einer Poetik des kolonialen Blicks* (Frankfurt, 1991), 12.
54. Ibid., 30–31.
55. Von Hellenbach, *Insel Mellonta*, 5.
56. Ibid., 9.
57. Ibid., 49.
58. Ibid., 29.
59. Ibid., 29–30.
60. See Buch, *Nähe und Ferne*, 29.
61. Ibid.
62. Von Hellenbach, *Insel Mellonta*, 14.
63. Ibid., 167.
64. Wieland's text also evoked a poetic "resonance" in Goethe: "*Musarion* had the deepest effect on me . . . Here was where I was able to experience the ancients alive and new."

Johann Wolfgang von Goethe, "Aus meinem Leben: Dichtung und Wahrheit", in *Werke: Hamburger Ausgabe*, ed. Erich Trunz, vol. 9 (Munich, 1998), 271.
65. Von Hellenbach, *Insel Mellonta*, 50–51.
66. John Ruskin's art-historical essay, "Cestus of Aglaia" (1866), may also have inspired the name of von Hellenbach's Aglaia.
67. Von Hellenbach, *Insel Mellonta*, 146.
68. Ibid., 84–85.
69. Ibid., 32.
70. Claude Levi-Strauss, *Structural Anthropology*, trans. Claire Jacobson and Brooke Grundfest Schoepf (New York, 1963), 237.
71. Von Hellenbach's imagined utopia has the characteristics of imagined communities as described by Benedict Anderson in his *Imagined Communities: Reflections on the Origin and Spread of Nationalism* (New York, 2006), where he states, "The striking nineteenth-century imaginings of fraternity, emerging 'naturally' in a society fractured by the most violent racial, class and regional antagonisms, show as clearly as anything else that nationalism in the age of Michelet and Renan represented a new form of consciousness" (203).
72. Von Hellenbach, *Insel Mellonta*, 32.
73. Ernest Renan, "What Is a Nation" (1882), in *Nation and Narration*, ed. Homi K. Bhabha, (New York, 1990), 11.
74. Von Hellenbach, *Insel Mellonta*, 43.
75. Ibid., 35.
76. Ibid., 44.
77. Ibid., 24.
78. Ibid., 45.
79. Ibid., 45–46.
80. Ibid., 47–48.
81. Ibid., 116–17.
82. Ibid., 247.
83. Ibid., 245.
84. Jost Hermand, *Orte, Irgendwo: Formen utopischen Denkens* (Königstein, 1981), 21.
85. Von Hellenbach, *Insel Mellonta*, 242.
86. Ibid., 85.
87. Ibid., 96.
88. Von Hellenbach, *Die antisemitische Bewegung*, 13.
89. Von Hellenbach, *Insel Mellonta*, 241.
90. Ibid., 114.
91. Ibid., 133.
92. Ibid., 199.
93. Ibid., 120–21.
94. Ibid., 236.
95. Ibid., 237.
96. Ibid., 236.
97. Von Hellenbach, *Das neunzehnte und zwanzigste Jahrhundert*, 122–23.
98. Ibid., 122 and 126.
99. Ibid., 127.
100. Ibid., 137.

101. Frederic Jameson, *The Ideologies of Theory: Essays 1971–1986*, 2 vols. (Minneapolis, 1988), 1:3.
102. Von Hellenbach, *Insel Mellonta*, 247.
103. Wegner, *Imaginary Communities*, 37.
104. Von Hellenbach, *Insel Mellonta*, vii–viii.
105. Hermand, *Orte, Irgendwo*, 23.

Bibliography

Adorno, Theodor W. *Minima Moralia: Reflections from a Damaged Life*. Translated by E. F. N. Jephcott. New York: Verso, 1999.

Anderson, Benedict. *Imagined Communities: Reflections on the Origin and Spread of Nationalism*. New York: Routledge, 2006.

Beller, Steven. *Vienna and the Jews 1867–1938: A Cultural History*. Cambridge: Cambridge University Press, 1989.

Berentsen, Antoon. *Vom Urnebel zum Zukunftsstaat: Zum Problem der Popularisierung der Naturwissenschaften in der deutschen Literatur (1880–1910)*. Berlin: Peter Oberhofer, 1986.

Berman, Russell A. *Enlightenment or Empire: Colonial Discourse in German Culture*. Lincoln: University of Nebraska Press, 1998.

Bhabha, Homi K., ed. *Nation and Narration*. New York: Routledge, 1990.

Bloch, Ernst. *Abschied von der Utopie? Vorträge*. Edited by Hanna Gekle. Frankfurt: Suhrkamp, 1980.

Bloch, Ernst. *Prinzip Hoffnung*. 3 vols. Frankfurt: Suhrkamp, 1959.

Brüggemann, Fritz. *Utopie und Robinsonade: Studien zu Schnabels 'Insel Felsenburg' 1731–1743*. Weimar: Duncker, 1914.

Buch, Hans Christoph. *Die Nähe und die Ferne: Bausteine zu einer Poetik des kolonialen Blicks*. Frankfurt: Suhrkamp, 1991.

Glaser, Horst A. *Utopische Inseln: Beiträge zu ihrer Geschichte und Theorie*. Frankfurt: Peter Lang, 1996.

Goethe, Johann Wolfgang von. *Werke: Hamburger Ausgabe*. Edited by Erich Trunz. Vol. 9. Munich: dtv, 1998.

Hall, Murray G. *Österreichische Verlagsgeschichte 1918–1938*. Vienna: Böhlau, 1985.

Hellenbach, Lazar Baron von. *Birth and Death, as a Change of Form of Perception: Or, The Dual Nature of Man*. Translated by "V." London: Psychological Press, 1886.

———. *Das neunzehnte und zwanzigste Jahrhundert: Kritik der Gegenwart und Ausblicke in die Zukunft*. Edited by Carl du Prel. Leipzig: O. Mutze, 1893.

———. *Die antisemitische Bewegung*. Leipzig: O. Mutze, 1883.

———. *Die Insel Mellonta*. 3rd edition. Leipzig: O. Mutze, 1896.

———. *Geburt und Tod als Wechsel der Anschauungsform oder die Doppelnatur des Menschen*. Vienna: Wilhelm Braunmüller, 1885.

———. Volkswirtschaftliche Vorurtheile. Politische Vorurtheile. Gesellschaftliche Vorurtheile, vol. 1: *Die Vorurtheile der Menschheit*. 3 vols. Leipzig: O. Mutze, 1893.

Hermand, Jost. *Old Dreams of a New Reich: Volkish Utopias and National Socialism*. Bloomington: Indiana University Press, 1992.

Hermand, Jost. *Orte, Irgendwo: Formen utopischen Denkens*. Königstein: Athenäum, 1981.

Honold, Alexander. "Peter Altenbergs *Ashantee*: Eine impressionistische cross-over Phantasie im Kontext der exotischen Völkerschauen." In *Grenzüberschreitungen um 1900: Österreichische Literatur im Übergang*, edited by Thomas Eicher and Peter Sowa, 135–57. Oberhausen: Athena, 2001.

Hübbe-Schleiden, Wilhelm. *Hellenbach: Der Vorkämpfer für Wahrheit und Menschlichkeit*. Leipzig: Max Spohr, 1891.

Innerhofer, Roland. *Deutsche Science Fiction 1870–1914: Rekonstruktion und Analyse der Anfänge einer Gattung*. Vienna: Böhlau, 1996.

Jameson, Frederic. *The Ideologies of Theory: Essays 1971–1986*. 2 vols. Minneapolis: University of Minnesota Press, 1988.

Levis-Strauss, Claude. *Structural Anthropology*. Translated by Claire Jacobson and Brooke Grundfest Schoepf. New York: Basic Books, 1963.

Marin, Louis. *Utopics: Spatial Play*. Translated by Robert A. Vollrath. Atlantic Highlands, NJ: Humanity Press, 1984.

Mayer, Michael. *'Tropen gibt es nicht': Dekonstruktion des Exotismus*. Bielefeld: Aisthesis, 2010.

Müller, Götz. *Gegenwelten: Die Utopie in der deutschen Literatur*. Stuttgart: Metzler, 1989.

Musil, Robert. *Der Mann ohne Eigenschaften*. Edited by Adolf Frisé. 2 vols. 20th edition. Reinbek: Rowohlt, 2005.

Neuhäusler, Anton. "Lazar von Hellenbach," *Neue Deutsche Biographie*. Berlin: Duncker & Humblot, 1969.

Okey, Robin. *The Habsburg Monarchy: From Enlightenment to Eclipse*. New York: St Martin's Press, 2001.

Pollin, Burton R. "Politics and History in Poe's *Mellonta Tauta*: Two Allusions Explained." *Studies in Short Fiction* 8, no. 4 (Fall 1971): 627–31.

Prel, Carl du. "Vorrede des Herausgebers," in Lazar Baron von Hellenbach, *Das neunzehnte und zwanzigste Jahrhundert: Kritik der Gegenwart und Ausblicke in die Zukunft*. Edited by Carl du Prel. Leipzig: O. Mutze, 1893.

Sacher-Masoch, Leopold von. *Don Juan von Kolomea: Galizische Geschichten*. Edited by Michael Farin. Bonn: Bouvier, 1985.

Sawicki, Diethard. *Leben mit den Toten: Geisterglauben und die Entstehung des Spiritismus in Deutschland 1770–1900*. Paderborn: F. Schöningh, 2002.

Schorske, Carl E. *Fin-de-Siècle Vienna: Politics and Culture*. New York: Vintage, 1981.

Simmel, Georg. "The Stranger," in *On Individuality and Socials Forms: Selected Writings*, edited by Donald N. Levine, 143–49. Chicago: University of Chicago Press, 1971.

Spencer, M. C. *Charles Fourier*. Boston: Twayne Publishers, 1981.

Stolberg, Friedrich Leopold Graf zu. *Die Insel*. Heidelberg: L. Schneider, 1966.

Vosskamp, Wilhelm. "'Ein Irdisches Paradies': Johann Gottfried Schnabels *Insel Felsenburg* (1731–43)." In *Literarische Utopien von Morus bis zur Gegenwart*, edited by Klaus L. Berghahn and Hans Ulrich Seeber, 95–105. Königstein: Athenäum, 1983.

Wagner, Hermann F. "Robinson und die Robinsonaden in unserer Jugendliteratur." In *28. Jahresbericht der k.k. Franz Joseph Realschule in Wien*, 3–20. Vienna: Franz Joseph Realschule, 1903.

Wegner, Phillip E. *Imaginary Communities: Utopia, the Nation, and the Spatial Histories of Modernity*. Berkeley: University Press of California, 2002.

Zander, Helmut. "Sozialdarwinistische Rassentheorien aus dem okkulten Untergrund des Kaiserreichs." In *Handbuch der 'Völkischen Bewegung' 1871–1918*, edited by Uwe Puschner, Walter Schmitz, and Justus H. Ulbricht, 224–51. Munich: KG Saur, 1996.

Chapter 3

THEODOR HERTZKA
Seeking Emptiness

Hertzka's *Freiland* is a complicated machine with lots of teeth and wheels that even engage each other, but nothing proves to me that they could be put into operation. And even seeing Freeland clubs arise, I shall regard the whole thing as a joke.
—Theodor Herzl, "Der Judenstaat"[1]

Theodor Hertzka

Theodor Herzl's contemptuous remark on Theodor's Hertzka's *Freiland* (1890) is rather surprising when one compares his own novel *Altneuland* to it, as the two utopias share many themes and narrative structures, to say the least, and both utopias critique Vienna's fin-de-siècle decadence. While Herzl's *Altneuland* went on to become the world-renowned manifesto of Zionism, Hertzka's *Freiland* enjoyed popularity only at the time of its publication. Herzl's utopia is set in Palestine; Hertzka's narrative takes place in the empty space of East Africa. If *Altneuland* oscillates between a vision of a sparsely populated Near East and a geopolitical action plan, *Freiland* seeks to inhabit previously unpopulated territory. Hertzka's vision to found a new civilization on vacant land in Africa coincided with European colonialism and the surge of anti-Semitism in Vienna. In what follows, I investigate if Hertzka merely posits *Freiland* as a critique of Vienna's fin-de-siècle culture or if he produces a viable alternative.

Utopian fiction as a literary genre dramatizes the need for social change; these visions of a better society are meant to shatter and overcome society's ideological status quo. Yet narrative utopias are neither literature presenting fictional experiences nor social theory presenting totalities. Paradoxically, utopias achieve their greatest influence because of their inability to represent future societies systematically, and their use value for the readers resides in positing imperfect alternatives to the status quo of a given society. Hence, what renders Hertzka's utopia productive is not its literal representation of a perfect society but, rather, its contradictions, dislocations, and blind spots.

*

In the context of European colonial expansion and the intensification of anti-Semitism in Vienna, a journalist had a sudden vision of founding a new civilization in eastern Africa:

> My intense delight at making this discovery robbed me of the calm necessary to continue the abstract investigations with which I was engaged. Before my mind's eye arose scenes that the reader will find in the following pages—tangible, living pictures of a commonwealth based upon perfect freedom and equality, which has no other precondition to become reality beyond the will of a number of resolute men.[2]

Needless to say, the author who was thus diverted from his scholarly pursuits was Dr. Theodor Hertzka, a well-known commentator on current affairs in Vienna at the turn of the last century. He was born in 1845 in Budapest and studied macroeconomics in Vienna and Budapest. From 1872 to 1879 he was responsible for the economic section of the liberal Viennese daily *Neue Freie Presse*, and for the ensuing six years he was in charge of the *Wiener Allgemeine Zeitung*. At the time, Hertzka published several academic studies regarding financial and currency issues of the day, in which he stated his liberal convictions, advocating individual freedom in all economic aspects of life and approving of individual self-interest as a driving force for economic growth, for example. Until the late 1870s, Hertzka adhered to the tenets of the Manchester school of economic liberalism, but with the publication *Die Gesetze der sozialen Gerechtigkeit* (1886) and his utopia, *Freiland*, he started to mediate between economic individualism and the principle of absolute justice.

Like von Hellenbach before him, Hertzka was affected by the surge of chauvinism and anti-Semitism spurred by the economic crisis from 1873 to 1896, and the mass immigration in Vienna in the 1880s, which challenged the stable position of liberalism in Viennese society. Austria's socioeconomic problems inspired Hertzka's utopianism as they had von Hellenbach's, but their propositions for economic improvement were different. For Hertzka, the problems of existing society were generated by capital and rental income, because the earnings of the owning class limited the demand and consumption of the working class, preventing the modern production facilities from being fully utilized. Gustav von Schmoller, a contemporary economist, agreed with Hertzka: "An improvement of the situation of the lower classes must be easier to facilitate now than before, in an era of such unprecedented technological progress, as we experience it, with the millions of iron-machine slaves."³ To achieve the desired situation, Hertzka proposed abolishing land ownership, with associations managing the "free land" and the state providing these cooperatives with the necessary operating capital. However, this capital, he believed, should be repaid in annual installments, and the state should also levy 15 percent taxes. In short, Hertzka believed that societal affluence comes about "through planned growth, but, above all, [through] a synthesis of communal ownership, individual effort, and free trade."⁴

In the 1890s, with the publication of the novel *Freiland* and the accompanying journal *Zeitschrift für Staats- und Volkswirtschaft*, Hertzka's professional life came under the spell of his utopian vision. With the growing public interest, Hertzka published a sequel, *Eine Reise nach Freiland*, in 1893. Soon "Freeland committees" were founded throughout Austria and Germany. In 1894, a mere four years after *Freiland*'s initial publication, a small group of dedicated activists organized a poorly supported expedition to the Freeland region in East Africa, but they soon encountered insurmountable problems and had to cancel the project after only six weeks. As Franz Oppenheimer notes in his memoirs:

> Like all utopians, Hertzka clearly saw the goal but not the way toward its attainment. If it had been possible to transport even just a few thousand people to Kenya, together with the minimally necessary simple tools and weapons, it might have been possible to bring about the development, albeit much more slowly than Hertzka had hoped . . . The English prevented the expedition from proceeding into the interior, and that was lucky for them; the Masai would most likely have slaughtered them.⁵

With the complete failure of the expedition, public interest rapidly ceased, and Hertzka adopted instead, in his little-known third novel, *Entrückt in die Zukunft* (1895), a temporal displacement scheme for a utopian colony.

By the beginning of the twentieth century, he had left Vienna and moved to Budapest, taking over an editorial position with the newspaper *Friss Újság* and later with the daily *Magyar Hírlap*. At the end of his professional career, Hertzka published *Das sociale Problem* (1912). In this study, he tries to elaborate and prove the real reasons for mankind's oppressive living situation. Hertzka ardently argues for the intertwined relationship between economics and religion. In the book's preface, he states that "religion, and only religion, has the spiritual potential to succeed in domesticating the naturally free human species to alienated purposes."⁶ He spent the last years of his life quietly at his daughter's residence in Wiesbaden, Hesse, where he died in 1924.

According to Carl E. Schorske, Austrian bourgeois liberals during Hertzka's formative years perceived "themselves to be combating the socially superior, and the historically anterior."⁷ Liberalism represented rational progress and enlightenment. As mentioned in the previous chapter, this optimism of action shifted by the 1880s, when economic and political developments made it impossible for Austrian liberals to respond to perceived failures in the political arena in a positive way. Following Schorske's paradigm, the cultural elite of alienated bourgeois liberals withdrew into the aesthetic and artist realm, thereby shaping modernist fin-de-siècle Vienna. Suffice it to say that numerous scholars have revised Schorske's theory. For instance, Steven Beller objects to the suggestion that Vienna's modernism was the product of the cultural elite of an alienated liberal bourgeoisie. In his reading, Viennese culture around 1900 appears to be "something more particular: the response of a culture elite of an alienated *Jewish* liberal bourgeoisie."[8]

As we will see, Hertzka never abandoned his enlightened liberal convictions. Even in the face of an ever-growing tidal wave of anti-Semitism in Vienna, he continued to publish and lecture on contemporary politics. With the rise of nationalistic politicians like Georg von Schönerer and Karl Lueger, vicious anti-Semitism became more pervasive, and Jews found it ever more difficult to assimilate into Austrian society. In fact, anti-Semitists attacked Hertzka's novel and movement early on. One criticism leveled against it was its Jewish financing: since Jews financed the Freeland movement, the whole enterprise could only be dirty business. Furthermore, racist remarks like these deceitfully convinced Christian workers that Dr. Hertzka only sought to lure them to Freeland in order to sell them through "his capitalistic middlemen as slaves down there."[9] In reality, Hertzka sought to develop communities that were regulated by custom and tradition. Interestingly enough, such communal longing is close to Ferdinand Tönnies's conservative concept, which "rests on harmony and is developed and ennobled by folkways, mores and religion."[10] However, Hertzka also emphasized enlightened universal values and proposed to supersede the opposition of town and country through radical land reforms and revised zoning laws.

The decline of liberalism and the surge of anti-Semitism in Vienna inspired Hertzka—beyond writing *Freiland*—to become a civic activist and give many political speeches. To better understand Hertzka's motivations, it is revealing to read his speech "Arischer und semitischer Geist," which he presented at the "Society of Austrian-Israeli Union" and published in Joseph Samuel Bloch's *Österreichische Wochenschrift* on 20 January 1893. In it, explaining religious and technological progress, Hertzka expounds a dichotomy between Jews and Christians: "We Semites are suited to ethical inquiries, to philosophy, while the Aryan races have a great talent for natural scientific inquiries." But as an enlightened liberal, he is equally interested in the synthesis of the two strands that should follow: "It seems, therefore, that fate has preordained for these two races the achievement of a great purpose through their united powers."[11] Judaism and Christianity share the biblical dictates of "love thy neighbor" and equal justice under God for all the faithful, while the Romans, like the ancient Germanic tribes, believed in a plurality of deities, which runs contrary to an equality of justice: "The Aryan nobles were descended directly from the various gods, and the common people were the herd rising from the dust."[12] Nevertheless, Christ explicitly calls for the brotherly equality advanced by the Jews. Hertzka dryly alludes to this insight by commenting that "Christ was, in a word, a *Jewish Socialist* and was executed as such in Jerusalem. If he had lived in Vienna, his destiny would not have been different."[13] In other words, both Jews and Christians emerged from the same Old Testament tradition, and the contemporary anti-Semitism was not in any way attributable to the murder of Christ by the Jews.

Mindful of his bourgeois audience, Hertzka considers the uprooting of the Jews from Viennese society as a harsh critique of their assimilated self-identity, and characterizes anti-Semitism in Viennese society as a rapidly spreading disease: "At least a third, perhaps half (voice from the hall: 75 percent!) of our fellow Viennese citizens who are otherwise noted for their good-naturedness and harmlessness have been infested with this plague."[14] In light of this alarming premise, Hertzka might have been able to conclude without further discussion that Zionism provided the only realistic reaction to the prevailing anti-Semitism. Yet Hertzka sees instead in this distressing situation a chance for a fresh start rooted in brotherhood:

> Hand in hand, and only hand in hand, with our Christian fellow citizens, we are called to manage a revolutionary transformation such as has never been seen before. We are poised on the *threshold of a new era*, which will be so different from that which preceded it that, in the entire course of the history of mankind, only one such transformation can be compared with it, and that is the advance from cannibalistic barbarism to civilized culture.[15]

Although the utopian Hertzka seems unaware of the dialectic of enlightenment in this, he realizes all the possibilities of the pivotal moment of modernity in which he lives. Walter Benjamin calls those moments "messianic holes in time . . . that mark the uneven, lurching and deeply contested movement of modernity."[16] In these liminal moments, Benjamin believes that utopias could bridge the differences between different social structures. But Hertzka's confidence in mutual Judeo-Christian resolution stems from the nineteenth-century liberal ideal of the good society situating the free individual at the center of the social world: "On that day in which liberalism proclaims that political freedom is only the beginning of freedom, that economic freedom must first be brought into existence."[17]

Emphasizing the economic aspect of this ontological crisis, Hertzka's analysis is grounded in the liberal concept of free market forces seemingly able to overcome even anti-Semitism and finally making the assimilation of the Jews possible. Hertzka posits the synthesis of the active, though xenophobic, research mentality of the Aryans with the contemplative ethics of the Jews. In this future heaven on earth, arts ("the incarnation of the beautiful" = Jewish) and science ("the incarnation of the sublime" = Christian) will reciprocally fulfill each other. Although Hertzka is fully aware of anti-Semitism in Vienna, he portrays xenophobia as a catalyst of a beautiful liberal world to his assimilated audience. In this light, the freedom of the African plains that Hertzka describes in *Freiland* appears to be a reflection of a partially unperceived, but real, lack of freedom for Jews in Vienna.

Freiland (1890)

Freiland recounts the utopian story of a settlement of enlightened European colonists in Kenya, near the nomadic Masai. The first part of the novel describes the proclamation of an international society for the project of a colony in the East African lake highlands. The main character, Dr. Karl Strahl ("beam of light"), a thinly disguised alter ego of the author, is part of the Viennese establishment and, like Hertzka himself, a well-respected publicist in macroeconomics. His announcement, published in all the leading European and American newspapers, petitions for support of his endeavor to settle down on an "ownerless, but fertile" area.[18] The news of the proposed undertaking evokes an overwhelming and immediate response, and at the beginning of the following year a first expedition of two hundred Freeland followers is sent to the region between Mt. Kilimanjaro and Mt. Kenya. Another significant character is Henry Ney, a young engineer, who leads the expedition and narrates the story in the form of a diary.

Because of organizational commitments, Dr. Strahl remains in Europe while preparations for the expedition move forward without interruption. A beautiful, young American, Ellen Fox, stirs up some controversy when she insists on joining the otherwise exclusively male expedition corps. In Henry Ney's sister, Klara, she finds a well-intended companion who ultimately manages to broker a marital union between her brother and Ellen. The bulk of the first part of the novel is dedicated to a detailed description of the expedition to Kenya. The assembly point is Alexandria; from there the route takes the Europeans to Zanzibar and finally to Mombasa in Kenya. On the fourth day of the journey, the expeditionary corps has a peaceful encounter with a regional warrior tribe, the Masai. At the beginning of the summer, merely one year after Dr. Strahl's announcement, Freeland, with its capital of Edenthal, is founded.

The second part of the book reports on the development of Freeland in the following five years from the perspective of a European visitor to Edenthal. Already within a year of its founding, 95,000 people live in the city and work in 218 different associations incorporating 87 diverse trades. Only three years later, the number of inhabitants has grown to 780,000, and merely twenty-five years after the inception of the colony, 26 million whites and 15 million natives peacefully share Freeland territory. The narrator's diary meticulously describes the technological progress in the newly founded colony. Three thousand freight ships distribute the products of Edenthal throughout the world; an interlaced network of artificial canals (17,800 ships) and rail lines (combined length 575,000 kilometers) provide the transportation infrastructure for this economic wonderland set in the heart of Africa.

Shortly after the twenty-fifth anniversary of the colony, Freeland is attacked by Ethiopia, but its youthful militia heroically defeats the aggressor. The victory also marks the final triumph of the colony's economic ideas and is an attempt to show the global proliferation of Edenthal's flourishing model. Committees from all over the world send delegates to an international congress. Leftist followers from Russia debate the historical and philosophical implications of Freeland with right-wing skeptics. The congress participants conclude: "We have seen that all the foundations of justice, such as reason, speak in favor of the transition from exploitative to free economic activity, with the transition accomplished peacefully through the acknowledgement of collectively acquired rights, and that the means are readily obtainable."[19] That is to say, utopian Freeland was intended to become global reality.

*

In his work, Hertzka describes empty space as a possibility for another order of meaning containing the potential for cultural alterability. He defines progress quantitatively in numbers, with scientifically measured space, plans for economic growth, and urban development. The new technological paradise embraces the trajectory of enlightenment in the malleable African environment. Tellingly, Frank and Fritzie Manuel see in Hertzka's colonial project that "[t]echnology and rational organization of labor took the place of ancient magic and gave the imaginary society verisimilitude and, alas, a deadly earnestness."[20] Freeland rapidly develops new technologies and methods of production, which yield national prosperity. This technological superiority comes in handy once the peace-loving Freelanders encounter the belligerent Masai. Within ten minutes of meeting them, they have already set up heavy and light artillery, and these otherwise nonviolent colonists transform themselves into a straight line of cavalry ready to fight.

After the Masai demand a levy as tribute, the seasoned Africa traveler Thomas Johnston, who happens to speak the Masai dialect, asks the warriors if the land belongs to them and explains what the Masai's options are: "We won't pay levy to anyone; we offer gifts to our friends, and horrible weapons to our enemies!"[21] In a courtly gesture, Johnston demands instead that the Masai free their African hostages, who are from a tribe that is already allied with the Freelanders. Disregarding this threat, the Masai warriors start the fight. The Masai, however, only endure one cannon salvo: "When the guns thundered, the rockets, hissing and crackling, swept over their heads, and, above all, the uncanny creatures with four feet and two heads rushed upon them, they turned in an instant and fled away howling."[22]

Hertzka portrays this first encounter as a confrontation between civilization and nature. In his description, the African warriors merely perceive this encounter with civilization as the earthly manifestation of an uncanny mythological figure. The reference here is, of course, to the horse-mounted cavalry. In the following paragraph, the narrator depicts the African "other" in detail for the first time:

> The captured Masai were fine daring-looking fellows, and maintained a considerable degree of composure in spite of their intense alarm and of their expectation of immediate execution. Fortunately, there was among them their leitunu, or chief and absolute leader of the party—a bronze Apollo standing 6 ft. 6 inches high. He looked as if he would like to thrust his sime [short sword] into his own breast when the Wa-Duruma, who had begun to gather about us, ventured to mock him and his people, and to loudly demand their death.[23]

Rather than suffer the loss of his honor and pride, this brave fighter would prefer to take his own life with his short sword. Hertzka's narrator, Henry Ney, represents the Masai as "noble savages" with a graceful bearing, despite their looming defeat. Their leitunu is a "bronze Apollo" of imposing stature. With this description, the savage warrior turns into the Greek god of light and muses, which figuratively transfers him from the African highlands to the cradle of Western civilization. It is remarkable how the European narrator instantly idealizes the exotic African warrior, projecting noble traits of ancient Greek mythology to the "native" other but without wanting to share his fate. What follows sounds like one of Karl May's "exotic" Native American stories. The Europeans invite the hostile Masai to become their blood brothers, thus swiftly resolving the first serious conflict of the expedition. After the blood brotherhood is sealed, however, Henry Ney insists that the Europeans and Africans remain separated because he imagines that sexual transgressions might occur between the European colonizers and African women:

> It was almost sunset before the last of the Masai men left our camp whilst the prettiest of the girls and women showed no inclination to return to their household gods. The men realized this but obviously did not mind that their women and daughters accompanied the generous strangers even after sunset. Masai custom demands this, and we had difficulty saving ourselves from the consequences without insulting the brown ladies who, though they smelled of rancid oil, were well-figured.[24]

The European travelers resist the feminine lure of the "dark continent," and they repress their desires seemingly because of the awful oily smell of the otherwise "well-figured" women. Interestingly enough, in the English translation of *Freiland* and in the last German edition (tenth), which is commonly used in the research literature, the last sentence of the text passage is omitted.[25] On another occasion, Hertzka concedes that the high number of male immigrants to Freeland, and especially the resulting involuntary celibacy, at first caused intrigues involving native girls and women in Masai country. Only after the foundation of Edenthal, he asserts, did the young European settlers resist temptation without exception:

> In Taveta and Masailand, a few isolated affairs with native girls and wives had occurred. In Kenya, our young people had, without exception, resisted the enticements of the very ugly Wa-Kikuyu women; but they could not perpetually be required to exercise self-denial, which, particularly in this luxurious country, would be contrary to nature.[26]

Moreover, only the first edition of *Freiland* admits the existence of "natural" desires and especially the initial sexual contact between Freeland "conquerors" and native women. The savage beauties are brazen about their sexual desires, which calls for a reserved and cultured response. The prudery of the two white ladies on the expedition is indicative of the civilizing that first must be done to these "naïve" people:

> Prudery is unknown in Equatorial Africa; and the Taveta beauties would have been as little able to understand why anyone should think it wrong to open one's heart to a guest as their white sisters would have been able to conceive of the possibility of talking freely and in all innocence of such matters without giving the least offense to friends and relatives.[27]

Suffice it to say, as the journalist Hertzka must have been aware of the fledgling women's liberation movement, the two "white sisters," the beautiful American Ellen Fox, and Henry Ney's smart sister find their fulfillment in traditional roles—marriage and the social sphere. Apparently, women's freedom in Freeland is limited to natural reproduction and the aesthetic realm. Consequently, it is Ellen Fox who first describes the natural splendor of East Africa. When the expedition arrives in the lush Mt. Kenya region, the breathtaking beauty of the pristine mountain peaks affect both Europeans and the Swahili, although each quite differently: "Even the Swahili, who are generally indifferent to the beauties of nature, break out into deafening shouts of delight; but we whites stand in speechless rapture, silently pressing our hands together, and not a few furtively brushing tears from their eyes."[28] While the cultured Europeans honor the natural beauty with a respectful and restrained silence, the Africans cannot help but childishly voice their emotions. To paraphrase Hertzka's inspiration, Johann J. Winckelmann, the simple-minded cannot quietly appreciate majestic grandeur. Speechlessness occurs again as a trope when our explorers come across a natural valley surrounded by hills and a crystal-clear lake. The only creatures residing in this stunning arena are elephants, zebras, and antelope. The European reaction to this paradise is silent delight. But Ellen Fox regains her speech first, and ecstatically stammers: "Let us call this place Eden."[29] Like the Jews in Hertzka's speech

"Aryan and Semitic Spirit," his female characters are relegated to contemplation, while industrious white males guarantee Freeland's technological progress.

The enchantment of this unspoiled natural setting, together with the absence of any sign of civilization, exemplifies a uniquely Germanic colonial gaze within the larger context of European colonialism. As Russell A. Berman notes, the "difference vis-à-vis France and England is this: in place of threatening multiplicity, [and] the confrontation with barbarian hordes, its primal scene involves a self-assertion in a vacuum, emptied of any potential threat, an enforced singularity and a return to an origin."[30] Accordingly, rather than dwelling on the confrontation with hostile warrior tribes, Hertzka presents an idyllic empty space waiting to be civilized. That is to say, it is not the encounter with Africans that brings about an altered self but, rather, the imagined spatial transfer, with its revelation of natural beauty, that is to resolve Vienna's social and xenophobic problems. Berman observes in the German colonial literature contemporary with Hertzka a "capacity to recognize and appreciate—appreciate even at the moment of colonial appropriation—the other culture" and further hypothesizes "that there is a strain in German culture that allows for the appreciation of difference."[31] But even if Hertzka's utopian armchair colonialism stresses peaceful European intentions and assures the Africans that they will not be forced to give up their land, he overlooked the potential for the appreciation of African culture and the alteration of European attitudes as a direct result of the colonial experience in *Freiland*. Not having traveled to Africa himself, Hertzka apparently felt the need to justify his fictional image of Africa: "The highlands in Equatorial Africa exactly correspond to the picture drawn in this book. Whoever doubts this, check my narrative against Speekes, Grant, Livingstone, Baker, Stanley, Emin Pascha, Thomson, Johnston, Fischer; in short, all who have visited the paradisiacal area."[32] Quite literally, Hertzka's utopia is informed by contemporary European travel writing, and involuntarily reproduces the Occidental image of Africa in the late nineteenth century. Furthermore, Hertzka is caught up in the codes and models of his metropolitan lifestyle, so his narrative lacks the meaningful colonial cross-cultural encounter he might otherwise have written about.

Toward the end of the book, Karl Strahl, Hertzka's fictional alter ego, presents his universal, historical conception of human evolution. In the gray mist of prehistory, mankind lived in the tropics in paradisiacal tranquility alone and with nature. Through the process of civilization people learned to exploit nature and its riches for human purposes, and the peaceful coexistence of mankind with nature lost its binding force. At the same time, a large part of the populace migrated to the temperate northern zones of the earth. Now situated in this inhospitable environment, people were compelled to subjugate nature. If mankind could reverse this process and learn to master the elements with the help of technology, then people could return to their place of origin in the tropics and inhabit a utopian dream.[33] Heinz Eberdorfer calls Hertzka's vision a gnostic scheme involving "alienation from the essential origin—reversal—return to origin and with it, redemption, [that] is able to explain the nearly hymn-like description of the Central African highlands. Paradise is regained; humankind is redeemed."[34] The reversion and return to tropical origins elucidate Hertzka's rhapsodic description of the African highlands and his allusion to a regained paradise. Put differently, Hertzka opts for an enlightened evolutionary approach whereby humans ought to move out of their present dire situations to search for a more suitable place.

*

Edward Said's understanding of French and British Orientalism focuses on the nexus of nation-state, colonial expansion, and cultural production. Yet he saw German Orientalism differently. As he states: "The German Orient was almost exclusively a scholarly, or at least a classical, Orient: it was made the subject of lyrics, fantasies, even novels, but it was never actual, the way Egypt and Syria were actual for Chateaubriand, Lane, Lamartine, Burton, Disraeli, or Naval."[35] In the case of Hertzka's fiction, Said's statement rings true—at least partially. Instead of creating a nation-state, Hertzka envisions a pan-European empire, guided, however, by leadership grounded in the tenets of Germanic culture. The "International Association of Freelanders" claims a common European identity that extends beyond the narrow confines of the nation-state. Still the Europeans are so superior, technologically and scientifically, that they see it as their task to educate the Africans while treating them like children. Thus, Hertzka portrays colonization not as a hostile act toward the natives but, rather, as a pedagogical necessity to achieve advancement for all. Hence, the "reverse migration" of the Europeans does not cause Hertzka to have any qualms of conscience, and accordingly he mentions the cross-cultural encounter merely in passing.

Hertzka's ideal is closer to an elitist multicultural state than to a nation-state. Although he proposes an ideal of equality and ponders the employment of Africans free from the usual colonial exploitation, a real Freeland would be a caste system with little social contact between Africans as menial workers and whites as rulers. Effectively, Freeland would not be too different structurally from actual nineteenth-century European colonies in Africa. Like Mary Louise Pratt's imperial travelers, Freelanders mention animals, humans, and cultural artifacts, but they "are most often disembodied, erased and robbed of their subjectivity."[36] Thus the distant African people and landscape provide Hertzka, unlike Berman's appreciative German explorers at the end of the nineteenth century, with a screen onto which reflections of the self are projected.

As a narrative, Hertzka's novel may lose some of its appeal through its detailed depiction of the future society, or as Theodor W. Adorno dryly puts it: "As [utopias] have been realized, the dreams themselves have assumed a peculiar character of sobriety, of the spirit of positivism, and beyond that, of boredom."[37]

Still, Edenthal is not merely an image of Vienna in reverse order but, rather, an attempt to mediate between two different ways of organizing a society. *Freiland* endeavors to resuscitate the positive aspect of technological progress by repressing the negative social implications of Viennese modernism.

In his recent article, "Utopia, Science, and the Nature of Civilization in Theodor Hertzka's *Freiland*," Elun Gabriel addresses the effects of Hertzka's uncritical use of scientific knowledge. He contends that the success of *Freiland* was related to Hertzka's claim that the application of scientific reason to social problems could peacefully transform emerging societies into affluent economies. But Gabriel cautions that Hertzka thereby advances "a vision of potential universal human equality that denie[s] the significance of class and race to the ability and right of individuals to prosperity and happiness."[38] Even though Hertzka's utopia addresses the economic uncertainties of this liminal modernist moment, his prescription to overcome these uncertainties fails to fully realize his liberal concept of mutualism. For contrast, one could consider French philosopher Pierre-Joseph Proudhon's vision of a mutualist society, in which everyone possesses the same means of production. For Proudhon mutualism balances individual and collective needs in order to avoid class struggles. By this standard, Hertzka's narrative overlooks the plight of native Africans. Even if he sympathized with the Viennese proletariat because of his liberal consciousness and empathetic conscience, Hertzka was seemingly blind to the similarities between the plight of the Viennese working poor and that of the Masai whose land he sought to colonize. While this limited perspective is characteristic of his time, it shows an inconsistency between his willingness to dispossess the indigenous inhabitants and his progressive utopia, which strives to achieve "a social synthesis between economic individualism and the principle of absolute justice."[39] Hertzka, true to the conceits of his time, never questioned his belief in the moral superiority of European culture.

*

In the introduction to *Freiland*, Hertzka compares himself to Francis Bacon. Like the British philosopher, the Viennese economist suspends his academic pursuits to compose a political novel based on sober reality. As he puts it: "First of all, I hoped to make an understanding of these difficult questions—which are the topic of the book—through vibrant and descriptive presentations, accessible to a much broader audience than a dryly systematic report would have found."[40] While Bacon's explorers encounter a superior society in New Atlantis from which they learn, bringing home new scientific methods, Hertzka's Freelanders assert themselves by cutting through the umbilical cord joining them to the motherland while trying to export enlightened European values to Africa. Hertzka's Freeland in the heart of Africa and Herzl's Zionist state in the Near East were located in these empty or sparsely populated regions in order to avoid collision with existing societies. The fanciful travel narratives and social utopias fulfilled the popular yearning for openness, untrammeled by economic or political oppression. Undoubtedly, Hertzka had a profound influence on Herzl's Zionist utopia *Altneuland*. In addition to all sorts of technical inventions that Herzl adopted from Hertzka, Altneuland also has a cooperative economic order that mediates between individualism and collectivism, revealing the affinities between the two authors. As put by Israel Zwangwill, president of the Jewish Territorial Organization for the Settlement of the Jews within the British Empire: "Herzl would not be without a Jewish State, . . . but there would not have been a Jewish State without *Freiland*."[41] In fact, it was Zwangwill who opted to accept British colonial secretary Joseph Chamberlain's offer to allow his group to take possession of 6,000 square miles in the Ugandan highlands. If the Zionists had settled in Uganda, they would have been in the immediate vicinity of the Freeland territory. However, history played out differently, since the majority of Russian Zionists voted against Chamberlain's proposal at the Sixth Zionist Congress in Basel in August 1903.

But Hertzka's utopia is of more than mere historical interest to a present-day reader. Some of its central issues are still relevant: alternative communities, free markets, property regulations, a welfare state, and the impacts of technological progress. Yet it is not the novel's innovations that set *Freiland* apart from comparable utopias of its time; rather, it was that Hertzka's colonial utopia managed to influence contemporary Viennese debates. Moreover, Hertzka reconceptualized the social fabric of the Habsburg Empire at a time when most of his contemporaries were mired in the concept of the nation as something permanent and transhistorical. He developed instead the idea of a transnational European empire and envisioned a common European identity beyond the imperial nation-state. This vision alone, I contend, qualifies Hertzka as a true utopian thinker.

Notes

1. "[Hertzka's] *Freiland* ist eine komplizierte Maschinerie mit vielen Zähnen und Rädern, die sogar ineinander greifen; aber nichts beweist mir, dass sie in Betrieb gesetzt werden könne. Und selbst, wenn ich Freiland-Vereine entstehen sehe, werde ich es für einen Scherz halten." Theodor Herzl, "Der Judenstaat. Der Versuch einer modernen Lösung der Judenfrage," in *Theodor Herzl oder Der Moses des Fin de siècle* ed. Klaus Detthloff (Wien: Böhlau, 1986), 187.
2. "Das Entzücken über diese Entdeckung raubte mir die Ruhe, die im Zuge befindlichen abstrakten Untersuchungen fortzusetzen. Vor meinem geistigen Auge bauten sich jene Gestaltungen auf, die der Leser in den nachfolgenden Blättern finden wird, greifbare, lebendige Bilder eines auf vollkommenste Freiheit und Gleichberechtigung begründeten Gemeinwesens, das, um sofort reale Wirklichkeit zu werden, keiner anderen Vorbedingung bedarf, als des Willens einiger tatkräftiger Menschen." Theodor Hertzka,

Freiland: Ein soziales Zukunftsbild, 10th ed. (Dresden, 1896), xvi. This edition will be quoted, unless otherwise noted.
3. Gustav von Schmoller, *Zur Litteraturgeschichte der Staats- und Sozialwissenschaften* (Leipzig, 1888), 270.
4. Paul Jackson, "Freiland. Theodor Hertzka's Liberal-Socialist Utopia," *German Life and Letters* 33, no. 4 (July 1980): 270.
5. Franz Oppenheimer, *Erlebtes, Erstrebtes, Erreichtes: Lebenserinnerungen* (Düsseldorf, 1964), 139–40.
6. Theodor Hertzka, *Das sociale Problem* (Berlin, 1912), ix.
7. Carl E. Schorske, *Fin-de-Siècle Vienna: Politics and Culture* (New York, 1981), 117.
8. Steven Beller, ed., *Rethinking Vienna 1900* (New York, 2001), 9.
9. [Anonymous], "Journalstimmen," *Zeitschrift für Staats- und Volkswirtschaft* 5, no. 13 (1894): 14.
10. Ferdinand Tönnies, *Community and Society*, ed. Charles P. Loomis (New York, 1957), 223.
11. Theodor Hertzka, "Arischer und semitischer Geist," *Österreichische Wochenschrift* 1, no. 20 (1893): 37.
12. Ibid., 39.
13. Ibid., 38.
14. Ibid., 40.
15. Ibid., 41 (my emphasis).
16. Walter Benjamin, paraphrased in Phillip E. Wegner, *Imaginary Communities: Utopia, the Nation, and the Spatial Histories of Modernity* (Berkeley, 2002), 10.
17. Hertzka, "Arischer und semitischer Geist," 43.
18. Hertzka, *Freiland*, 3.
19. Hertzka, *Freiland*, 352.
20. Frank Manuel and Fritzie Manuel, *Utopian Thought in the Western World* (Cambridge, MA, 1979), 767.
21. Hertzka, *Freiland*, 24.
22. Ibid., 24.
23. Ibid., 25.
24. Theodor Hertzka, *Freiland: Ein soziales Zukunftsbild* (Leipzig, 1890), 57–58.
25. "So will es die Sitte in Massailand, und wir hatten Mühe, uns vor deren Konsequenzen zu bewahren, ohne die zwar nach ranzigen Fett duftenden, sonst aber selbst nach europäischen Begriffen wohlgebildet zu nennenden braunen Damen zu beleidigen." Ibid.
26. "In Taweta und im Massai-lande hatte es einige, wenn auch sehr vereinzelte Intrigen mit eingeborenen Mädchen und Weibern gegeben; am Kenia hatten unsere jungen Leute ausnahmslos den Verlockungen der grundhässlichen Wakikuja-Damen widerstanden; auf die Dauer aber durfte von ihnen keine Entsagung gefordert werden, die in diesem üppigen Lande vollends gegen die Natur gewesen wäre." Ibid., 176–77.
27. "Prüderie ist im äquartorialen Afrika eine gänzlich unbekannte Sache und die Taweta-Schönen würden ebensowenig begriffen haben, dass irgend jemand Übles darin finden könne, wenn man einem Gaste ohne sein Herz entgegenträgt, als ihre weissen Schwestern begriffen hätten, dass man derlei Dinge in aller Unschuld ausplaudern könne, ohne dass Freunde und Verwandte daran den geringsten Anstoss nähmen." Hertzka, *Freiland*, 33.
28. "Selbst die Suahelis, die sonst Naturschönheiten gegenüber stumpf sind, brechen bei diesem Anblicke in betäubendes Jubelgeschrei aus; wir Weissen aber stehen in Entzücken

versunken, drücken uns stumm die Hände und gar Mancher wischt sich verstohlen eine Thräne aus dem Auge." Ibid., 45.
29. Ibid., 51.
30. Russell A. Berman, *Enlightenment or Empire: Colonial Discourse in German Culture* (Lincoln, NE, 1998), 102.
31. Ibid., 235.
32. Hertzka, *Freiland*, 354.
33. Although Robert Müller's anti-exotic *Tropen: Der Mythos der Reise* (1915) clearly opposes Hertzka's colonialism, Müller's theory of miscegenation has certain parallels to Hertzka's idea of a "return to the tropics."
34. "Dieses in seinem Wesenskern gnostische Schema: Entfremdung vom Urgrund, von der eigentlichen Wesenheit—Umkehr—Rückkehr zum Ursprung und somit Erlösung, vermag die geradezu hymnische Beschreibung des zentralafrikanischen Berglandes zu erklären." Heinz Eberdorfer, "Africa Utopica: Das Bild Afrikas und der Afrikaner in literarischen Utopien und utopischen Projekten," *Geschichte und Gegenwart* 6, no. 2 (1984): 125.
35. Edward Said, *Orientalism* (New York, 1979), 19.
36. Mary Louise Pratt, *Imperial Eyes: Travel, Writing, and Transculturation* (London, 1992), 125.
37. Theodor W. Adorno, "Something's Missing: A Discussion between Ernst Bloch and Theodor W. Adorno on the Contradiction of Utopian Longing," in Ernst Bloch, *The Utopian Function of Art and Literature: Selected Essays*, trans. Jack Zipes and Frank Mecklenburg (Cambridge, MA, 1988), 18.
38. Elun Gabriel, "Utopia, Science, and the Nature of Civilization in Theodor Hertzka's *Freiland*," *Seminar* 48, no. 1 (February 2012): 26.
39. Birgit Affeldt-Schmidt, *Fortschrittsutopien: Vom Wandel der utopischen Literatur im 19. Jahrhundert* (Stuttgart, 1991), 110.
40. "Erstlich hoffte ich durch möglichst lebensvolle und anschauliche Gestaltungen das Verständnis jener zum Teil höchst schwierigen Fragen, deren Lösung das eigentliche Thema des Buches ist, einem weitaus grösseren Leserkreis zugänglich zu machen, als es bei trocken systematisierender Behandlungsweise zu erwarten gewesen wäre." Hertzka, *Freiland*, xvi.
41. Quoted in Franz Neubacher, *Freiland: Eine liberalsozialistische Utopie* (Munich, 1987), 55.

Works Cited

Affeldt-Schmidt, Birgit. *Fortschrittsutopien: Vom Wandel der utopischen Literatur im 19. Jahrhundert*. Stuttgart: Metzler, 1991.
[Anonymous]. "Journalstimmen" in: *Zeitschrift für Staats- und Volkswirtschaft* 5, no. 13 (1894).
Beller, Steven, ed. *Rethinking Vienna 1900*. New York: Berghahn Books, 2001.
Berman, Russell A. *Enlightenment or Empire: Colonial Discourse in German Culture*. Lincoln: University of Nebraska Press, 1998.
Bloch, Ernst. *The Utopian Function of Art and Literature: Selected Essays*. Transl. Jack Zipes and Frank Mecklenburg. Cambridge, MA: MIT Press, 1988.
Dethloff, Klaus, ed. *Theodor Herzl: oder der Moses des Fin de siècle*. Vienna: Böhlau, 1986.

Eberdorfer, Heinz. "Africa Utopica: Das Bild Afrikas und der Afrikaner in literarischen Utopien und utopischen Projekten." *Geschichte und Gegenwart* 6, no. 2 (1984): 117–43.
Gabriel, Elun. "Utopia, Science, and the Nature of Civilization in Theodor Hertzka's *Freiland*." *Seminar* 48, no. 1 (February 2012): 10–27.
Glass, Hildegard F. *Future Cities in Wilhelminian Utopian Literature*. New York: Peter Lang, 1997.
Hertzka, Theodor. "Arischer und Semitischer Geist." *Österreichische Wochenschrift* 1, no. 20 (1893): 37–41.
———. *Das soziale Problem*. Berlin: Georg Reimer, 1912.
———. *Freiland: Ein sociales Zukunftsbild*. 10th edition. Dresden: E. Pierson, 1896.
———. *Freiland: Ein sociales Zukunftsbild*. Leipzig: Dunker & Humblot, 1890.
Jackson, Paul. "*Freiland*. Theodor Hertzka's Liberal-Socialist Utopia." *German Life and Letters* 33, no. 4 (July 1980): 269–75.
Manuel, Frank, and Fritzie Manuel. *Utopian Thought in Western World*. Cambridge, MA: Harvard University Press, 1979.
Müller, Robert. *Tropen: Der Mythos der Reise. Urkunden eines deutschen Ingenieurs*. Munich: Hugo Schmidt, 1915.
Neubacher, Franz. *Freiland: Eine liberalsozialistische Utopie*. Munich: R. Oldenbourg, 1987.
Oppenheimer, Franz. *Erlebtes, Erstrebtes, Erreichtes: Lebenserinnerungen*. Düsseldorf: Johannes Melzer, 1964.
Pratt, Mary Louise. *Imperial Eyes: Travel, Writing, and Transculturation*. London: Routledge, 1992.
Reifowitz, Ian. *Imagining an Austrian Nation: Joseph Samuel Bloch and the Search for a Multiethnic Austrian Identity, 1846–1919*. New York: Columbia University Press, 2003.
Said, Edward. *Orientalism*. New York: Vintage Books, 1979.
Schmoller, Gustav von. *Zur Litteraturgeschichte der Staats- und Sozialwissenschaften*. Leipzig: Dunker & Humblot, 1888.
Schorske, Carl E. *Fin-de-Siècle Vienna: Politics and Culture*. New York: Vintage, 1981.
Servier, Jean. *Der Traum der großen Harmonie: Eine Geschichte der Utopie*. Munich: List, 1971.
Tönnies, Ferdinand. *Community and Society*. Edited by Charles P. Loomis. New York: Harper & Row, 1957.
Wegner, Phillip E. *Imaginary Communities: Utopia, the Nation, and the Spatial Histories of Modernity*. Berkeley: University Press of California, 2002.

Chapter 4

THEODOR HERZL
Vienna in Palestine

The mere will to action was something so startlingly new, so utterly revolutionary in Jewish life that it spread with the speed of wildfire. Herzl's lasting greatness lay in his very desire to do something about the Jewish question.

—Hannah Arendt, *The Jew as Pariah*[1]

Theodor Herzl

"The most priceless and indispensable part of a philologist's heritage," writes Erich Auerbach, "is still his own nation's culture and heritage. Only when he first separates from this heritage, however, and then transcends it, does it become truly effective."[2] For Auerbach, a philologist's heroic return is based on his experience abroad. One could also apply his dictum to Theodor Herzl, whose visionary Zionism was informed by his cosmopolitan upbringing in the Habsburg monarchy and refined by his *éducation politique* in Paris. This chapter interprets Herzl's utopia *Altneuland* (1902) and his Zionist imagination as a refracted image of Vienna. The metaphor of refraction is used since Herzl's view of Vienna was significantly shaped by his journalistic engagement in Paris. Herzl's Zionism attempts to overcome contemporary Viennese racism by envisioning a Jewish nation in Palestine. His colonial vision thereby connects Vienna with Palestine through a "literary-historical process, in the course of which the homeland (*die Heimat*) is subjected to the same colonial gaze as are the foreign country (*die Fremde*)."[3] Whereas von Sacher-Masoch's novels portray fierce ethnic conflicts in the paracolonial space of Eastern Europe as the trigger for his utopian concept of pan-Slavism, Herzl's colonial vision, written almost twenty-five years later, struggles to surmount the endemic anti-Semitism in Europe at the time. Thus, this chapter shows how Herzl's *Altneuland* not only renders a colonial utopia in the Near East but also, by transcending the sociohistorical realities, produces a space in which his European experiences and Oriental imaginations collapse into each other.

In his essay "Politics in a New Key: An Austrian Trio," Carl E. Schorske claims that Herzl's thought is rooted both in Austrian liberalism and in German nationalism alike. Schorske links Herzl to Georg von Schönerer and Karl Lueger, two of Vienna's most notorious anti-Semitic politicians, in their mutual reliance on fantasy and dreams in order to transcend purely political policies.[4] Without precipitously discarding Schorske's psychological observation, one can also see Herzl as an enlightened thinker who seeks "to fulfill the promise of Jewish emancipation."[5] Aware of the utopian dimensions of his work, and the chance that they might therefore be dismissed as unrealistic fantasy, Herzl insisted throughout his career on the realism and practicality of his Zionist project. Peter Loewenberg claims that this led some Herzl scholars to interpretations that make a dichotomy of aesthetic creativity and empirical rationality.[6] This dualism, I argue, is an epistemological fallacy that fails to consider Herzl's imaginative playing with possibilities so that they can assume a rational character when the utopia comes into being. This alleged opposition is part of the indivisible character of Herzl's creativity, within which he is simultaneously capable of entertaining utopian possibilities as well as making rational plans.

Tivadar Herzl was born in 1860 in Pest, Hungary, to parents indebted to the German language and culture of the Habsburg Empire. After the death of his sister Pauline in 1878, the family moved to Vienna. Theodor—as he called himself from then on—studied law at the university and received his doctorate of law in 1884. The cultural atmosphere of fin-de-siècle Vienna deeply impressed the young man. The spirit of the time "emerge[d] from confronting the possibility of ending," unleashing a vital and creative energy.[7] Along these lines, some of his biographers see Herzl as a prototypical Viennese dandy caught between appearing to be nonchalant, enjoying a life of leisure, and longing for an aristocratic lifestyle.[8] But unlike most contemporary dandies and dilettantes, Herzl used writing to work through his existential problems; the literary form generated the distance necessary for him to express himself freely. In this respect, Herzl's longings could also indicate a sense of alienation in his adopted city. After all, Herzl traveled extensively as a young man, and the dandy phenomenon is intrinsically connected to the cosmopolitan capitals of Paris and London.

Accordingly, in an autobiographical sketch from 1898, Herzl hardly mentions his experiences in Vienna but stresses the freedom of Salzburg, where he had moved after completing his studies in Vienna: "In Salzburg the work seemed to be much more attractive [than in Vienna], the scenery in and around the town being most beautiful. . . . Of course I wrote much more for the theater than for the law-courts. In Salzburg I spent some of the happiest hours of my life."[9] Salzburg gave him enough free time and space to pursue his greatest ambition: to become a writer. Upon returning to Vienna, he yearned to conquer the Burgtheater and the *Neue Freie Presse*, that is, the chief local bastions of cultural production. His output as a playwright was substantial, though his success proved to be short lived.[10] While lasting fame as a dramatist eluded him, his travel reports from Italy and Spain eventually earned him a position as foreign correspondent in Paris for the *Neue Freie Presse*.[11] In the same autobiographical sketch Herzl describes the circumstances as follows: "I accepted the position, though until then I had detested and despised politics. In Paris I had occasion to learn what the word politics means."[12] During his four-year stay in Paris, Herzl wrote regular commentaries about the parliamentary government of the French Republic, later published as *Das Palais Bourbon: Bilder aus dem französischen Parlamentsleben* (1895).

The four years in which Herzl resided in the French capital (1891–95) were fraught with scandals, crises, and increasing hostilities against Jews. The Panama scandal of 1892, in which two Jewish financial counselors had bribed various members of parliament, gave the radical daily *Libre Parole* an opportunity to popularize its anti-Semitic propaganda. These events deeply affected Herzl as they politicized him for the Jewish cause. In Paris, Herzl was transformed from an itinerant literary dandy to a Zionist political lawyer and leader. Nonetheless, Klaus Dethloff is right to question Herzl's transition from writer to statesman: "Herzl never gives up the role of the German writer. But he redefines it and mobilizes it not only when he arrives at new insights into relevant constitutional law, but especially once he starts with political action, which would not have been possible without his role as a writer."[13]

There have been many attempts to explain Herzl's turn to Zionism. At times, Herzl himself casts it as a quasi-mythological experience, "a work of infinite grandeur" or "a mighty dream,"[14] and he attributes it to "the realm of the unconscious."[15] Literary critics of a psychoanalytic bent assess Herzl's ceaseless efforts for the Zionist cause as an unconscious flight from an unfulfilled marriage. His wife Julie apparently showed little interest in his intellectual pursuits.[16] Following this line of argument, one can interpret Herzl's political engagement as a libidinal cathexis in which he sought (and found) fulfillment. But his flight into the world of grandiose ideas also generated a "withdrawal of interest in the external world of people and things."[17] Elsewhere, Herzl states that he became a Zionist during his deployment as a correspondent of *Neue Freie Presse* in Paris. Stefan Zweig, a young Viennese writer at the time, was reminded of Herzl's telling assertion in his final encounter with him: "Everything I know I have learned abroad. Only abroad does one get used to thinking in distances. I am convinced that here [in Vienna] I would never have had the courage to utter the first concept [of *The Jewish State*]. Someone would have torn it to pieces before it had a chance to grow."[18] Naturally, this claim by an already ailing Herzl recalls his frustration as a Jewish outsider within Viennese society. This existential position might explain why Herzl directed his attention to several bloody assassination attempts, and related financial relief efforts for the poor of Paris, whose unrest helped the anarchist Ravachol disturb the bourgeois order. In brief anecdotes, Herzl depicts the festering mood in Paris: one account describes a proud hotel owner who is humbled when the mere announcement of the name Ravachol leads his guests to hastily depart. Another tells of the sudden generosity of the bourgeois passersby toward panhandlers. And in a fictitious dialogue between an attractive young lady and her admirer, Herzl's psychological investment in the destiny of the anarchist Ravachol becomes evident:

He: Don't you feel anything for me?
She: No, not for you!
He: Ah, so there is someone else? Is he here (at the ball)?
She: (Sighing) No.
He: (Jealous) What does he look like? What is so special about him?
She: He has what women love. He makes me shiver and dream.
He: I suppose you won't tell me his name?
She: (With half-open eyes) Oh yes, I will. (Breathes rapturously) Ravachol![19]

In this characterization of a sexually demanding woman forgetting all social graces, and the self-tormenting admirer eagerly seeking to know more about the object of her desire, we see the familiar trope of inverted gender relations in fin-de-siècle Vienna. As John K. Noyes puts it in *Mastery of Submission* (1997), the stylization of deeply held fears of emasculation allowed the author and his readers "to take on a position of relative powerlessness and at the same time retain power over this position."[20] In this respect, Herzl's characters demonstrate similarities to the dynamics described in Leopold von Sacher-Masoch's novellas. Yet, in contrast to von Sacher-Masoch's proposed solution of sexual renunciation, Herzl incites readers to identify with the erotic explosiveness of the "selfless" anarchist Ravachol, who promises to fulfill Herzl's desire for recognition. Or, in the words of his biographer Ernest Pawel, Herzl, at that moment, defines "the subtle nexus between libido and politics."[21] After Ravachol's arrest, Herzl ventures to describe the "Robin Hood" personality of the Parisian anarchist:

And this is the man who committed murder, who dug up corpses to rob their graves, who forged money and blew up houses in which innocent victims died—victims even by his own lights. What, then, is he—dreamer or villain? . . . Probably the closest we can come to the truth is to assume that he started as a bad man and ended as a good one. Today he believes in himself and in his mission. In committing his crimes, he became an honest man. The ordinary killer rushes off to the brothel with his booty. Ravachol has discovered lust of a different kind: the voluptuous pleasure of a great idea, and martyrdom.[22]

Herzl's depiction of Ravachol's motives reads like a preview of his own life's work: the voluptuous pleasure of a grand idea, and martyrdom in the service of Zionism. In this respect, it should not be surprising if we wonder whether Herzl's sympathies for Ravachol are also reflected in his penchant for a mutualist economy, a system that envisions a society where everyone possesses the means of production.[23]

*

Herzl's concept of mutualism can be traced back to Pierre-Joseph Proudhon, Charles Fourier, and Peter Kropotkin. Fourier had previously proposed what Herzl formulates in *Der Judenstaat*, namely, a joint-stock communal partnership, in which "each person who joined the community would, if possible, purchase some stock." Fourier also relied on finding some wealthy people who might not want to join the community at the outset, but who would be willing "to provide the risk capital to start the phalanx on the assumption that they would make profit."[24] Herzl's fascination with Parisian anarchism could explain his willingness to take on mutualist economic policies. Of course, Herzl corresponded later with Franz Oppenheimer, the German sociologist most renowned for his mutualist economic system.[25] But there is little reason to believe that Oppenheimer shaped Herzl's affinities for mutualism.[26]

"The best way of explaining Herzl's gradual obsession with the Jewish question," writes Steven Beller, "is to see it as a result of a dialectic between his Viennese experience of anti-Semitism and his perception of Parisian politics and French anti-Semitism."[27] In late summer 1892, Herzl began—albeit hesitantly— to deal openly with the problem of anti-Semitism. In the article "French Anti-Semites," he seeks to depict the situation in a playfully ironic tone reminiscent of his literary model, Heinrich Heine:

> French anti-Semites are more kindhearted than those of other countries; they are even willing to admit that Jews, too, are human beings . . . What the French hold most against the Jews is that they come from Frankfurt—an obvious injustice, since some of them come from Mainz or even Speyer. Their money is resented only if they have any . . . And if a Jew carries native cunning to the point of sacrificing his life in a noble and knightly manner, he will earn widespread murmurs of approval . . . The [anti-Semitic] movement here will pass, though probably not without excesses and isolated disasters.[28]

As it turns out, Heine and Herzl shared more than a flair for irony: they also loved living in Paris. As early as 1826, Heine described his motivation for living and working in Paris in the following terms: "There is no question that it is difficult for me to bid farewell to the German fatherland. It is less wanderlust than the anguish of my personal circumstances, i.e., the ineradicable Jew (*nie abzuwaschende Jude*) that drives me away from there."[29] For Heine, the move to Paris signified a deep, transformative biographical event, just as it later would for Herzl. As soon as Heine touched ground in Paris, he felt as though he had been born anew and freed. For Heine, as for Herzl, a second great creative period began in Paris, one in which he defined a new life aim for himself after years of malaise in Germany: "[I] dream every night that I am packing my bag and traveling to Paris to scoop up a breath of fresh air."[30]

With his observations of the Paris scene, Herzl came to the insight that anti-Semitism is social in nature, and he became increasingly indignant that the "Jewish debate" or "Jewish question" was still always treated as a religious problem in the Viennese Reichsrat: "If the Jewish question were really on the agenda, then none of those named parliamentarians would have spoken on the topic, for it has been for a while no more than a matter of theological stories or of religion and conscience."[31] Relating French political circumstances to those in Vienna, Herzl believed that the same processes were underway but at different points in history; that which was occurring in France would also occur in Austria, only later.[32] In 1893, he writes: "France is a 'fast' country and Austria a slow one, but it will perhaps turn out that the difference in the political outcome between fast and slow countries is not great."[33] Thus, Herzl projects his Parisian experiences of politics and anti-Semitism onto the Viennese situation.

Merely a year later, in mid-October 1894, France became embroiled in the Dreyfus affair, in which a Jewish officer of Alsatian origin was scapegoated, tried, and convicted of treason. The affair of Alfred Dreyfus, the purported German spy, polarized liberals and conservatives and greatly enflamed debate across Europe regarding the Jewish question. Having witnessed a mob shouting "à mort les juifs" (murder the Jews) while in Paris, Herzl resolved that the Jews had only one way out: mass migration to a land that they could call their own. Concluding that anti-Semitism was an enduring and immutable factor in human society, which assimilation could not resolve, he mulled over the idea of Jewish sovereignty, and, despite ridicule from various Jewish leaders, he published *Der Judenstaat* (1896). As the subtitle of the first edition indicates, it is Herzl's attempt to find a "Modern Solution to the Jewish Question." For him, the answer resides in modern nation building. He postulates that Jews could only gain acceptance from the rest of the world if they became a nation themselves. That is to say, despite its religious connotation, Zionism was a secular nationalist movement like those of the Czechs, Rumanians, and the southern Slavs. Herzl understands the Jewish question as an issue for the arena of international politics. Whether his political vision was generated during the Dreyfus affair, or from earlier experiences, as Loewenberg and Beller have suggested, is not crucial to my argument.[34] What is crucial, however, as we can see in his Parisian writings, is that the shift in location enabled him to address the Viennese Jewish question.

Herzl's liminal stance in Paris in regard to the Jewish question becomes clear in his drama *Das neue Ghetto* (1897). Although the plot unfolds in Vienna, Herzl had written it in Paris in 1894. The play's main character is Dr. Jacob Samuel, a Jewish lawyer. His brother-in-law, Rheinberg, is a business partner of the gentile Rittmeister von Schramm. They trade together in shares of an unprofitable coal mine. We are told that, years before, von Schramm had challenged Jacob to a duel, but due to his father's illness, Jacob had to bow out instead of taking up the challenge. Needless to say, Jacob has felt ashamed ever since. His lingering shame compels him to defend the coal miners, and when there is a deadly accident in the mine, Jacob accuses von Schramm of exploiting the miners. When their argument escalates, another duel becomes inevitable. This time, Jacob does not bow out and gets gravely injured. At the end of the drama, Jacob is brought in, in his death throes. His last prophetic words are: "I want to get—out—out of the ghetto."[35]

As mentioned earlier, although *Das neue Ghetto* was written in Paris, it is set entirely in Vienna, and thus the title pointedly describes the situation of the Jews in Vienna. They endured a pseudo-emancipated existence but lacked genuine assimilation. For all the legal freedom they had obtained during Austrian liberalism, they enjoyed little integration in certain circles of society. In the play, Herzl articulates a perceived otherness of Jews, a negative identity formation, which is to be overcome through ethical sublimation and aristocratic ideals. As Gisela Brune-Firnau points out: "The absurdity of this ultimately anti-Semitic command is demonstrated by the protagonist, in that he looks to fulfill the command through indirect self-obliteration."[36] The significance of this desolate portrait of Viennese Jewry lies in Herzl's refusal to offer simple solutions to the situation, ultimately emphasizing unresolved social tensions. Karl Kraus, who made no secret of his contempt for Herzl,[37] depicts *Das neue Ghetto* as a "tendentious piece that combats anti-Semitism from a sincere Jewish-nationalistic perspective, while partially confirming it by portraying an exceptionally corrupt Jewish milieu."[38] The writer Arthur Schnitzler, one of Herzl's Viennese acquaintances, also reacted critically to the play: "Even the 'Jew with the wounded honor' doesn't appeal to me—give your Jacob somewhat more inner freedom. The basic concept of the drama won't suffer by that and the figure will then appear more sympathetic to us."[39] Yet with his consciously unsympathetic portrait, Herzl wanted to reveal the viciousness of the political and social circumstances that "emasculated" the Jews and thus forced them to compensate internally by inflating their own self-importance. Predictably, the play was only performed a few times in Vienna in 1898 and was not very favorably received.[40] Hence, Herzl's quest to modify the liminal position of Jews in Vienna, caught between self-annihilation and escape from the ghetto, remained unresolved.

Towards the end of his appointment in Paris, Herzl wrote the first version of *Der Judenstaat*, a 22-page set of notes prepared for the meeting with Baron von Hirsch in Baden-Baden, before he left Paris for good to assume the position of feuilleton editor at the *Neue Freie Presse* in Vienna.[41] The primary objective of

Der Judenstaat is to form a new autonomous state for the Jews. Herzl, who had still been advocating Jewish assimilation in *Das neue Ghetto*, now began emphatically to oppose the possibility of Jewish integration in the Habsburg Empire. To support his proposition, which his contemporaries rejected for the most part, he invoked the two thousand years of suffering in the Jewish diaspora. Herzl was able to compose a practical political-colonial plan, as evinced by the precise ethnic, natural, and civil law manner in which he formulated his theses. This textual strategy enabled Herzl to avoid the issue of the existing non-Jewish residents in Palestine. Rather, he attempted to legitimate the "seizure" of Palestine under international law: "The emigration also makes sense when its foundation is the assurance of our sovereignty. The 'Society of Jews' will negotiate with the current sovereign authorities in the country, and namely under the protectorate of the European Powers, as soon as the matter becomes clear to them."[42] Herzl knew that the concept of Jewish emigration to resolve the Jewish Question was anything but new and therefore looked to the law for support for the particular emigration process: "I don't assert at all that the idea must be new. It is two thousand years old. What is new is only the process as I am launching it and how later I organize the society and eventually the state."[43] With the concept of *Der Judenstaat* in hand at the end of his time in Paris, Herzl took a radical, qualitatively new position on the Jewish Question, finally attaining through this grand political idea the recognition that had previously eluded him.

The short story "Das lenkbare Luftschiff" (The Steerable Zeppelin, 1896), which Herzl wrote at the time, demonstrates just how important this recognition was to him.[44] The frame story consists of a small group of socialites who gather to "fantasize out loud and to tell each other modern tales."[45] This beginning—unlike that in *Der Judenstaat*—leans on sources such as Johann Wolfgang Goethe's novella cycle *Unterhaltungen deutscher Ausgewanderten* (1795), and literary utopias like Friedrich Leopold Graf zu Stolberg's *Insel* (1788) to advance Herzl's Zionist agenda.[46] In the story, a doctor who had recently returned from Paris tells the group about the rapid technological advances in the French capital, and explains that "living circumstances are now changing more rapidly than in any other time in history."[47] The painter Robert tells a story within the story about the Viennese engineer Joseph Müller, who, unappreciated and laughed at by those around him, invents an airship and is interned in an insane asylum for a time. After his release he accumulates sufficient resources from several smaller inventions to be able to realize his dream without the help of others. After completing the construction of his airship, he invites a select group of friends to join him on a maiden flight over the Mediterranean Sea. Tellingly, Müller has given his invention the peaceful name of Halcyone.[48] The narrator describes the airship as being like a "dragonfly, with its structural parts of aluminum, while the softer elements were of hundred-leaved white silk."[49] A dragonfly, with its horizontal wingspan and stable, well-balanced flight, seems to be a particularly fitting metaphor for a stern but malleable Zionist project. Yet, the dragonfly is just as colorful as it is predatory, seeking to dominate its surroundings with its acute, faceted eyes. The engineer destroys the airship because he cannot forgive his doubters, and he believes humanity is not yet ready for progress. The airship dances about on the waves like a "dead seagull."[50] In the end, the Parisian in the frame story criticizes Müller's actions:

> Joseph Müller was wrong, and above all he did not grasp the scope of his invention. He ought not to have thought only of the people of his own era, and should at least have considered the poor unfortunates in his immediate vicinity. He who prepares the future must be able to look beyond the present. Better people will come.[51]

Herzl's Parisian experiences, thus, demanded that he not let his Zionistic project be smothered while it was just germinating. The frame story consequently takes the misanthrope of the story within the story, Joseph Müller, to task, and illustrates a way that the steerable airship (that is, Zionism) can achieve success. In other words, Müller's difficult life situation accords in many particulars with Herzl's own life issues. Both Müller and Herzl suffer from an ambivalent relationship with women and a shame-filled sense of the lack of their own importance in comparison with their Viennese fellow citizens. But Müller's story differs from Herzl's biography in at least two points: despite recurrent anxiety attacks Herzl was never interned in an insane asylum, nor—to stay within the imagery of the narrative—did he fully sever his attachment to the "dead seagull" of Zionism. By means of his Parisian interlude, Herzl was able to outgrow "the poor unfortunates of his immediate vicinity" and to bring the steerable Zeppelin of Zionism into existence and ultimately to forgive his Viennese antagonists. In his diary entry one day after the publication of the story, Herzl recorded that his story "Das lenkbare Luftschiff" was generally interpreted as he had intended it, namely, "as an allegory for the Jewish state."[52]

Altneuland (1902)

On 2 July 1899, on a train trip from Paris to Frankfurt, Herzl wrote the first lines of his Zionist novel *Altneuland*, which takes place predominantly in Palestine, where he had met with the German emperor Wilhelm II the previous autumn to discuss the forthcoming Jewish colonization. The novel attempts the aesthetically difficult task of imagining precisely the picturesque details that he had left out of *Der Judenstaat*. The hero of *Altneuland* is Dr. Friedrich Löwenberg, a young Jewish lawyer, whose chances of finding his moorings in fin-de-siècle Vienna are limited. In addition, Löwenberg is unhappily in love with a simple-minded but seductive daughter of affluent socialites. In order to set himself free he enters a contract with a wealthy Prussian-American aristocrat, Adalbert von Kingscourt, to accompany him to an uninhabited Pacific island. Both men cherish hunting, drinking, and playing chess, and share a dislike of women. Fed up with civilization and its discontents, they travel south across the Mediterranean Sea, briefly stopping over in Palestine before they retire to Kingscourt's island in the South Sea. Palestine in 1902—the year in which the narrative starts—offers little apart from arid lands and desolate living conditions. In contrast, Kingscourt's island is a paradise regained, equipped with all the modern conveniences, though deliberately cut off from communications with the outside world.

After twenty years of companionable bliss they decide to return briefly to Europe in 1922. Along the way, Kingscourt's yacht stops off again in Palestine, where a veritable miracle awaits them. Already at the port in Haifa, they meet David Littwak—whom Löwenberg had met as a struggling boy in Vienna—now a grown man who plays an important role in the "New Society for the Colonization of Palestine," an association that, in the meantime, has provided the country with a modern infrastructure. Littwak invites them to his mansion and, in the tradition of classical utopias, leads them through the blossoming country. They learn about equal rights for women there, and the society's universal welfare system.

What had been plain desert on their previous visit twenty years earlier is now a flourishing landscape with thriving cities, vast smokeless industries, and prosperous cooperative farms. The Arab population has welcomed the prosperity brought by the Jewish society, and only Jewish orthodox nationalists present a problem to the country's freedom and equality. Once they arrive at the Sea of Galilee, they visit the research institute of Professor Steineck, a biologist searching for a cure for malaria to make the colonization of Africa possible. Book IV, entitled "Passover," shows how the exiled Jews have become a new people while managing to retain their traditional roots. The visitors learn about the exodus from Europe and the first trying years of settlement in Palestine via a speech transmitted by a modern phonograph. The last chapter culminates in Löwenberg's visit to Jerusalem, a city in which the old structures are preserved and the modern additions provide spacious comfort for its residents. The citizens of the Holy City enjoy the re-creation of Vienna's charm without the cloud of anti-Semitic Jew baiters. Löwenberg's journey to Jerusalem becomes a spiritual homecoming, and he finally comprehends and overcomes the reasons for his self-contempt in Vienna.

The structure of *Altneuland* is symmetrical (five books, each with six chapters of nearly the same length), yet the temporal framework of the plot is not so straightforward. After Löwenberg and his new "master" Kingscourt depart, the following twenty years of fictional time are skipped, and the story resumes in Palestine only after their return. Jeremy Stolow proposes that this leads to a "transubstantiation of Palestine from desert to garden . . . [which] occurs without conflict, resolution, or mediation: a chiasmus that is simply posited without any accompanying frame. This temporal juxtaposition of Palestine 'before' and 'after' functions strategically in the text to reinforce the 'miraculous' character of what the Jews were able to achieve."[53] However, the historical developments in Palestine are not entirely overlooked, since the director of the Zionist Industrial Office, Joe Levy, explains the "transubstantiation" in great detail in Book IV. Left out of the narration are Löwenberg's and Kingscourt's twenty years on the lonely Pacific island. Following the motto of "don't ask, don't tell," Herzl integrates both protagonists into the new society. In Kingcourt's case, a curious transfer of homosocial love takes place, when he develops a close bond with Littwak's toddler Friedrich, named after his former companion Dr. Löwenberg.

By March 1901, the political success of the Zionist movement had lost some of its momentum, and Herzl resumed working on *Altneuland*, although, as he wrote in his diary, "[m]y hopes for practical success have been dashed. My life now is no novel, and so the novel has become my life."[54] Contradicting the well-known epigraph, "If you like, then this is not a legend," which prefaces *Altneuland*, Herzl's statements raise the question of whether he really intended it as a utopia because it involves a rhetorical inversion, which Na'ama Rokem elucidates: "If the reader lacks will, it is nothing but a legend; if, on the other hand, the reader is inspired into action, it will turn into descriptive prose."[55] Although Herzl's descriptive prose is set in a cartographically specific place, chosen for its historical significance, *Altneuland* still seeks to fulfill an important function of the utopian genre: to bridge different ways of organizing a society. Nevertheless, the novel undermines its utopian aspiration with its problematic premises for a peaceful Jewish settlement in Palestine. To further a dystopian reading, *Altneuland* was written at a time when utopias had lost their credibility as a result of Western global explorations and colonization. With the onslaught of modernity and technology, the difference between the perceptions of closeness and distance was replaced by "an experience of simultaneity of the non-simultaneous, the simultaneous coexistence of what used to be worlds apart."[56] In this sense, if Vienna can be transferred imaginatively to Palestine, *Altneuland*'s time and space coordinates become increasingly relative.

Despite Herzl's emphasis on his Zionist dream being realizable in historical reality, *Altneuland* borrows substantially from popular nineteenth-century utopian literature such as Etienne Cabet's *Voyage en Icarie* (1840),[57] Edward Bellamy's *Looking Backward* (1888),[58] and Theodor Hertzka's *Freiland* (1890)[59] discussed in the previous chapter. In *Altneuland*, the economic concept of mutualism[60] can be traced back to the Irish Ralahine community, whose goal was to acquire enough common capital to take care of its members when they became too old or sick to provide for themselves.[61] Even though Herzl rejected any notion of socialism and favored the opportunities of a liberal market economy, in *Altneuland* he seizes the idea of the distribution of the means of production. Thus, it becomes apparent how nineteenth-century socialist utopian writers "modified his legalistic liberalism and gave an anti-democratic tinge to some of his writings."[62] Suffice it to say, *Altneuland* also contributed to the contemporary Zionist discourse. At the end of the nineteenth century, there were numerous Zionist utopias that were indicative of the social reformist enthusiasm and the unbroken belief in progress through technology among the Jewish bourgeoisie. Neither Herzl's *Judenstaat* nor *Altneuland* was the first, much less the only, literary Zionist manifesto.[63] But even more important than the Zionist discourse in the conception of *Altneuland* is Vienna's fin-de-siècle culture, which shaped Herzl's aesthetic ability to mold a utopia from the "fragments of modernity, glimpses of futurity, and resurrected remnants of a half-forgotten past."[64]

At the turn of the nineteenth century, rapid industrialization and urbanization were breaking down many of traditional structures of society. Modernism and technology provoked anxiety and awe at the same time. Hence, Herzl's fellow Zionist, Max Nordau, accused intellectuals and artists of giving in to decadent mysticism, leading to nihilism, narcissism, and sexual aberration. Although Nordau's popular book *Entartung* (1892) reflects the reactionary strain of European thought, the writer condemns, like Herzl, the rising anti-Semitism of the time as a product of what he calls "degeneration." Likewise, *Altneuland* represents Vienna as a degenerate Moloch. Herzl apparently subscribes to Nordau's dire outlook on modernity while he presents the visionary New Jewish Society in Palestine as vibrant and spotless.

As for literary models, Herzl was seemingly inspired by Victorian literature and culture,[65] such as *Tancred* (1847), by British prime minister Benjamin Disraeli. Born Jewish and converted to Christianity, Disraeli not only expresses a romantic visionary Toryism but also makes a case to reinstitute Jewish national independence in this novel: "The vineyards of Israel have ceased to exist but the eternal law enjoins the children of Israel still to celebrate the vintage. A race that persists in celebrating their vintage, although they have no fruits to gather, will regain their vineyards." Disraeli's influence on young Herzl seems evident in the fact that Tancred is Herzl's *nom de combat* for his student fraternity, Albia. If Disraeli's *Tancred* appealed to Herzl for its political romanticism, George Eliot's novel *Daniel Deronda* (1876) seems to have influenced the structure of *Altneuland*. Like Löwenberg, Deronda is a high-minded young man searching for his path in life who finds himself drawn by a series of dramatic encounters into two contrasting worlds: that of English country-house life complete with a high-spirited beauty trapped in an oppressive marriage, and the very different lives of a poor Jewish girl and her family. As Deronda uncovers the long-hidden secret of his own parentage, the suspenseful narrative opens up a world of Jewish experiences previously unknown to the Victorian novel.[66] According to Edward Said, for George Eliot Zionism represented a "genuinely hopeful socio-religious project in which individual energies can be merged and identified with a collective national vision, the whole emanating out of Judaism."[67] Furthermore,

Said points out that existential homelessness, which is shared by both Jews and Englishmen, is an unavoidable part of the human condition. Undoubtedly, this is an observation Herzl could have readily related to.

*

At the beginning of *Altneuland*, Herzl's alter ego Löwenberg perceives himself as an outsider in Vienna, and it is through him that the text creates an external view of the ailing fin-de-siècle society.

> Several young men stood about the billiard table, making bold strokes with their long poles. They were in the same boat as himself, but for all that not too unhappy—these budding physicians, newly minted jurists, freshly graduated engineers. They had completed their professional studies, and now they had nothing to do. Most of them were Jews.[68]

The hopeless atmosphere of the Viennese coffee houses, in which unemployed Jewish academics spend their days reading newspapers, is contrasted with the fashionable but meaningless world of assimilated Jewish businesspeople. The Jewish bourgeoisie are all too comfortable with their standing within Viennese society, and laugh openly about the idea of Zionism. Only a rabbi from Moravia seems interested in the movement and tries to explain the future goals of Zionism to the dinner party guests: "Its aim is to solve the Jewish problem through colonization on a large scale."[69] But instead of generating understanding, the rabbi is surprised by the effect of the simple word "Palestine": "The laughter ran every gamut. The ladies giggled; the gentlemen roared and whinnied. Friedrich alone was indignant at this brutal and unseemly merriment at the old man's expense."[70] Nauseated by such an insensitive materialistic worldview, Löwenberg feels superfluous in "this room, in this city, in this world altogether."[71] Nevertheless, before he finally turns his back on his birth city, he experiences still another facet of Jewish life in Vienna. He encounters Littwak's bare, one-window room, devoid of even basic furniture, such as a cupboard or a chair: "A whimpering baby lay on the woman's flabby chest. The mother stared at him anxiously out of her hollow eyes."[72] At this moment, Löwenberg realizes the extent of the poverty Eastern Jews in Vienna have to endure. This naturalistic depiction of the milieu not only completes the fatalistic picture of the Viennese Jews but also consciously addresses the hopeless masses of families immigrating from the Pale of Settlement. The dire scene is put in stark relief when later in the novel David Littwak, the son of the poor family described above, is chosen to be president of the new company, and when his attractive sister, Miriam, comes to marry our hero Löwenberg. That Herzl did not entirely sympathize with Jews from Eastern Europe becomes evident in an earlier outline for the novel: "The hero has blond characteristics, blue eyes, a hard look. His lover is a Spanish Jewess, slender black-haired, fine race. She sees him for the first time as the commander of a ship of conquest. He dreams about her in his tent."⁷³ Tellingly, in Book III, "The Prosperous Land," Herzl's reservations towards the mumbling [*mauscheln*] of the Eastern European masses becomes apparent (in the portrayal of the populist supporter Dr. Geyer) when orthodox nationalists with their populist appeal threaten to undermine the New Society's freedom and equality. David Littwak and the star architect Steineck undertake a lecture tour through the province to propagate the immigration policy and the humanitarian values of the Zionist movement. After Steineck's moving speech at the cooperative farm in Neudorf, the spokesman for the Eastern European peasants speaks up impudently:

> 'Architect Steineck has just delivered an address to us. You might say that it was good, and again you might say that it was uncouth. I say it was uncouth.' Friedman interrupted him: 'You Mendel! I won't allow you to be insulting.' 'Who is insulting?' Mendel retorted. 'I say he is! He said we were not worthy to have the sun shine upon us. Why aren't we worthy of it? Because we don't want to let everyone in.'⁷⁴

Mumbling in Yiddish, Mendel stands in for East European Jews who had little in common with Herzl's universal aims and allegedly sought to claim the new state exclusively for Jews. Herzl wanted to liberate the Zionist movement not only from the oppressive situation of decadent Vienna but also from what he perceived as the backwardness of the East European shtetl. In this respect, the text undermines Herzl's overtly stated agenda to integrate East European Jews. For Muhammad Ali Khalidi, the portrayal of East European Jews in *Altneuland* provides further evidence that due to the "general applicability of [Herzl's] ideas and their universal aspects . . . this novel seems mainly aimed at non-Jews."⁷⁵ Similarly, Herzl's contemporary adversary, Ahad Ha'am, the leader of Cultural Zionism and an advocate of Hebrew, criticizes the complete lack of Jewish identity in *Altneuland*. For Ha'am, instead of looking for solutions for the Jews, the novel tries to answer the big questions for humanity at large. In this vein, he continues to polemicize against Herzl's utopia by saying: "Without distinction of nationality or religion—that is the spirit that animates the entire story, stressed in almost every chapter with such emphasis that it seems as though the author were chiefly concerned with assuring the 'outside world' that Zionism was a completely harmless enterprise."⁷⁶

To explore the world outside, Löwenberg sees the solution to his existential crisis in Vienna in a journey to a Pacific island with his new acquaintance Kingscourt. On their outbound way, they come to know—more by chance than design—the "old land of the Jews":

> Jaffa made a very unpleasant impression upon them. Though nobly situated on the blue Mediterranean, the town was in a state of extreme decay. Landing was difficult in the forsaken harbor. The alleys were dirty, neglected, full of vile odors; everywhere lurid Oriental misery. Poor Turks, dirty Arabs, timid Jews lounged about—indolent, beggary, hopeless. A peculiar, tomblike odor of mold caught one's breath.⁷⁷

This first description of Palestine is reflected in Herzl's diary entry on his own trip to Jerusalem to meet the German emperor Wilhelm II. Coming from Alexandria, on 26 October 1898 Herzl's ship dropped anchor in Jaffa's shallow harbor, which made the landing difficult. Herzl writes about his first impressions: "Again poverty and misery and heat in lurid colors. Confusion in the streets, at the hotel, not a carriage to be had."[78] But Herzl's disappointment does not disappear after Jaffa. According to his diary entry, even the ancient city of Jerusalem needs a heavy makeover, and he reflects on the urban cleaning and clearing he would do first thing upon returning to the city:

> I would clear out everything that is not something sacred, set up workers' homes outside the city, empty the nests of filth and tear them down, burn the secular ruins, and transfer the bazaars elsewhere. Then, retaining the old architectural style as much as possible, I would build around the Holy Places a comfortable airy new city with proper sanitation.[79]

Herzl's ceaseless desire for hygiene also enables him to arrange his dream in a new and meaningful order. Like a collector, Herzl prefigures imaginary spaces in his mind. For Walter Benjamin, the collector comprehends not only the historical fate of objects but also knows about their hidden structure and their relationship to each other. In this sense, cleaning and clearing necessarily precede a desired new order. As Benjamin explains, "the true, but often overlooked, accomplishment of the collector is always anarchic and destructive. Because this is its dialectic: his faithfulness to the unique, well preserved object is combined with an obstinate, subversive protest against the typical and classifiable."[80]

Palestine's destiny seems to unfold in Herzl's hands, and *Altneuland* makes the Jewish state's entire passage visible from its humble beginnings to prosperity. It is as if Herzl's deep-rooted disappointment triggered his fictional new order for Palestine. In Herzl's peculiar way of plotting events, Palestine is turned upside down into the new and improved state of Israel. Upon their return from twenty quiet years on a lonely Pacific island, Kingscourt and Löwenberg stop over in Palestine again, this time in the northern harbor city of Haifa:

> Brilliant Oriental robes mingled with the sober costumes of the Occident, but the latter predominated. There were many Chinese, Persians and Arabs in the streets, but the city itself seemed thoroughly European. One might easily imagine himself in some Italian port. The brilliant blue of sky and sea was reminiscent of the Riviera, but the buildings were much cleaner and more modern.[81]

The projection of a modern, clean metropolis bathed in a blue Italian sheen, at the same time, turns away from the oppressive nearness of social realities in Palestine and Vienna. Herzl overcomes the traumatic loss of his illusion through a vision of *Altneuland* projected into the distance. Herzl's evasive aesthetic rendition of the host culture bespeaks the contemporary colonial gaze of many

European travel narratives of the late nineteenth century. Accordingly, rather than dwelling on the possibility of conflict with a hostile Arabic populace, Herzl presents instead an idyllic Oriental scene. The imagined spatial transfer, with its revelation of uplifting architecture, is intended to resolve the social and xenophobic problems of contemporary Vienna. Central to this colonial vision is the absence of Arabic protagonists in the novel. The sole exception is Raschid Bey, educated in Germany, who metonymically represents the Arabs:

> A handsome man of thirty-five was standing beside a wrought-iron gate as they drove by. He wore dark European clothing and a red fez. His salute to them was the Oriental gesture, which signifies lifting and kissing the dust. David called to him in Turkish, and Raschid replied in German—with a slight northern accent. 'Wish you much joy of your guests!' Kingscourt stared. 'Who's this little Muslim?' he asked. 'He studied in Berlin,' replied David laughingly. 'His father was among the first to understand the beneficial character of the Jewish immigration, and enriched himself, because he kept pace with our economic progress. Raschid himself is a member of our New Society.'[82]

The acceptance of the "little Muslim fellow" (*Muselmännchen*) in the New Society is not only rooted in the universal tolerance Herzl touts but also in Bey's ability to assimilate. Paradoxically, Herzl demands of the Arab minority in Palestine what he thought it impossible for Viennese Jews to achieve. Sophie Perriaux and Daniel Steuer have described Herzl's strategy as a negative utopia:

> Zionism, moreover, and this is what Herzl's text must hide by all means, marks the point where the arithmetic of nationalism breaks down. In the equation of state, people and territory into a nation, someone somewhere tends to get short-changed. "The land without people for a people without a land" (in Zwangwill's famous phrase)[83] would solve this equation. But there is no land without people.[84]

That Herzl was in touch with the demographic realities of Palestine is demonstrated in the following passage from *Der Judenstaat*, which develops his "progressive" settlement plan, and thereby reiterates his fantasies of clearing the space and creating a *tabula rasa*:

> If nowadays one wishes to found a nation, one cannot do it in the way that was the only way possible a thousand years ago. It is foolish to hark back to the old cultural levels as many Zionists advocate. For instance, if we had to clear a country of wild animals, we would not do it in the same way as Europeans of the fifth century did it. We would not go forth individually with spears and lances to slay bears, but we would put together a big, enjoyable hunt to drive the beasts together and then we would throw a melinite bomb among them.[85]

The wish to clean and clear the colonial space of its historicity reflects a desire for a new social order. The thinly disguised animal metaphor depicts explicitly how Herzl sought to legitimate the production of open space in Palestine through technological advances. "When nations wandered in historic times," Herzl remarks in the same text, "they let chance carry them, fling them hither and thither, and like swarms of locusts they settled down indifferently anywhere . . . But this modern Jewish migration must proceed in accordance with scientific principles."[86] Apparently, Herzl's *Der Judenstaat* functions as a pragmatic blueprint for a tolerable colonization understood as an inevitable evil. Along these lines, *Altneuland*'s American director of the Zionist industrial office promotes the following geopolitical cartography:

> I divided a map of Palestine into squares, which I numbered. It was kept in my office, and an exact copy given to Alladino [a real estate agent]. He was simply to wire me the numbers of the parcels he had bought, and so I knew from hour to hour just how much land we already owned, and what kind of land it was.[87]

Altneuland oscillates between a utopian view of a sparsely populated Near East and a concrete geopolitical plan. Even though Herzl's colonial utopia depicts a possibility of rescue for his fellow believers from the threats of homelessness, anti-Semitism and persecution in Central Europe, his strategy rests on the assumption of the indigenous Arab population being absent.[88] This hypothesis makes this concrete colonial plan of action for the establishment of a Jewish nation-state possible, and it is not necessarily confined to the Near East. In Book III, Kingscourt and Löwenberg get to visit a medical research institute on their journey through the country. In the ensuing conversation, bacteriologist Dr. Steineck (the brother of the architect) announces that he is looking for a cure for the tropical disease of malaria to "open up" the African continent:

> We have overcome it here in Palestine, thanks to the drainage of the swamps, canalization, and the eucalyptus forests. But conditions are different in Africa. The same measures cannot be taken there because the prerequisite—mass immigration—is not present. The white colonialist is lost in Africa. That country can be opened up to civilization only after malaria has been subdued. Only then will enormous areas become available for the surplus populations of Europe. And only then will the proletarian masses find a healthy outlet. Understand?[89]

Kingscourt makes sure that he understands the implications of Steineck's agenda, and ironically responds: "You want to cart off the whites to the black continent, you wonder worker!"[90] But Steineck insists that he has even bigger plans in mind:

> Not only the whites! . . . The blacks as well. There is still one unresolved problem of racial misfortune. The depths of that problem, in all its horror, only a Jew can fathom. I mean the Negro problem. Don't laugh, Mr. Kingscourt. Think of the hair-raising horrors of the slave trade. Human beings, because their skins are black, are stolen, carried off, and sold.[91] Their descendants grow up in alien surroundings, despised and hated, because their skin is differently pigmented. I am not ashamed to say, though I

be thought ridiculous, now that I have lived to see the restoration of the Jews, that I should like to pave the way for the restoration of the Negroes.[92]

The Jewish colonization of Africa is proposed, like the one already planned for Palestine, as a project of enlightenment and global improvement. The planned immigration, made possible by modern science, would not only result in resolving latent anxieties about the proletarian masses of Vienna, but would also allow the Jews, afflicted by persecution, poverty, and existential homelessness, to claim for themselves an empathetic and humane colonial policy toward other marginalized groups.

Tellingly, the cultural Zionist group around Ahad Ha'am does not criticize Herzl's biased colonial discourse but his universal, cosmopolitan posture, which seeks to keep the Zionist state open to all religious orientations. Apart from his cosmopolitanism, Professor Steineck, with his colonial plans, not only mirrors humanism but also identifies with the victims of imperialism. Steineck's condemnation of the slave trade shows Herzl's consistent compassion towards socially inferior groups. Taking the fin-de-siècle imperialist discourse into account, Derek J. Penslar posits a clear link between Zionism and colonialism, but he also sees in the Zionist rhetoric the response of an oppressed people to "racist discrimination," which "has often been expressed in orientalist terms."[93] It is the experience of endemic anti-Semitism that shapes Herzl's paramount goal to create a society founded on tolerance, enlightenment, and liberty. To this effect, the medical research to eliminate malaria will benefit all races alike. For Herzl, it seems that Western values, such as enlightenment, progress, and freedom, were not the opposite of colonialism but rather its prerequisites.

Not by accident does Löwenberg's and Kingscourt's journey to *Altneuland* culminate in Jerusalem. What twenty years before had been "a gloomy, dilapidated city" is now "in splendor, youthful, alert, [and has] risen from death to life." The old part of town remained virtually untouched; only a magnificent Peace Palace had been added and the Temple had been renovated. But outside the historic district the picture was different. "Modern sections intersected by electric streetcar tracks; wide, tree-lined streets, homes, gardens, boulevards, parks; schools, hospitals, government buildings, pleasure resorts . . . Jerusalem was now a twentieth-century city."[94] Reading this triumphant description of urban modernism, one is reminded of fin-de-siècle Vienna: "The center of this urban reconstruction was the Ringstrasse. A vast complex of public buildings and private dwellings, it occupied a broad belt of land separating the old inner city from its suburbs."[95] Löwenberg sees the apparent similarities between the old and new cities as an opportunity, or as he puts it: "Old institutions need not go under at one blow in order that new may be born . . . Having seen here a new order composed of none but old institutions, I have come to believe neither in the complete destruction nor the complete renewal of a social order. I believe

... in the gradual reconstruction of society."[96] Löwenberg seems to refer to the simultaneity of different social states within the new society, but at the same time Herzl lets his character tackle the fundamental challenge of Zionism: *Altneuland* is not an imaginary *u-topia*, but a real *topos* consisting of multiple historical and religious layers.

Then again, Löwenberg's journey to Jerusalem also becomes a spiritual homecoming on a personal level. During a visit to the temple he finally comprehends and overcomes the reasons for his self-contempt in Vienna. The epiphany takes place while he listens to the song to the Sabbath bride from Heine's *Romanzero* (1851), specifically, as he contemplates the third part entitled "Hebrew Melodies": "Come beloved, / your bride is waiting to reveal, / her bashful face to you."[97] Heine's captivating lyrics prompt Löwenberg to remember the time in Vienna when Jews were ashamed of themselves and had to conceal their religion. Inspired by the atmosphere of a new beginning in Jerusalem, Löwenberg realizes that there is no longer any need for Jews to hide in the ghetto with self-contempt, since "[t]he strong, the free, the successful Jews had returned home, and received more than they gave."[98]

*

Herzl's utopian vision of Jerusalem is a better, freer version of Vienna and the margins of the Habsburg Empire. Herzl's Zionism attempts to overcome contemporary Viennese racism by envisioning a Jewish nation in Palestine. Within this vision, Jews have finally left the backwardness of the East European shtetl, as well as Vienna's new ghetto, which Herzl criticizes in his play by that same name. Finally, Jews will able to live without persecution or restriction, and, finally, they will be at home. In fact, there is no need to go back to Vienna because they never left Europe—only the state is now "made up of socialist and capitalist elements, and productive, clean, organized, and happily patriarchal: a non-decadent Europe created, mostly, by East European Jews."[99] If Herzl's Jerusalem in *Altneuland* is a new and improved image of Vienna, his conversion to Zionism was significantly shaped by his journalistic engagement in Paris. Herzl's Zionist advocacy would be inconceivable without his years in Paris and his extensive travels as the ambassador of the Zionist movement in Europe and in the Near East.

It was in Paris that Herzl conceived his "mighty dream" of a Zionist nation-state based on enlightened values and mutualist economic principles. Or, as Hillary Hope Herzog puts it: "It was Herzl's experience as a political correspondent in Paris that not only deepened his understanding of the political world, but also provided a new perspective from which to assess developments in his home city."[100] His visionary blueprint represents, in Ernst Bloch's less favorable assessment, no more than "private capitalism with land reform," rendering an "immediately attainable utopia with a capitalistic-democratic background."[101] Nevertheless, Herzl aimed to overcome the alienation and anti-Semitism he experienced in Vienna by following Bloch's paradoxical but quintessential description of utopia to the tee: "a homecoming to a place of childhood where no one has been before: 'heimat.'"[102] In this respect, *Altneuland* can be read as a utopian novel, despite Herzl's proclaimed anti-utopian intention. "In the genre utopia," writes Philip E. Wegner, "there has been a continuous exchange of energies between the imaginary communities of the narrative utopia and the imagined communities of the nation-state, the former providing one of the first spaces for working out the particular shapes and boundaries of the latter."[103] Arguably, Herzl's *Altneuland* provides such an imaginary space in the constitution of a future nation-state.

Notes

1. Hannah Arendt, *The Jew as Pariah: Jewish Identity and Politics in the Modern Age*, ed. Ron H. Feldman (New York, 1978), 166.
2. Erich Auerbach, "Philology and Weltliteratur," *Centennial Review* 13 (Winter 1969): 17.
3. Hans Christoph Buch, *Die Nähe und die Ferne: Bausteine zu einer Poetik des kolonialen Blicks* (Frankfurt, 1991), 14.
4. See Carl E. Schorske, *Fin-de-Siècle Vienna: Politics and Culture* (New York, 1981), 120.
5. Steven Beller, *Herzl* (London, 1991), xiii.
6. See Peter Loewenberg, "Theodor Herzl: Nationalism and Politics," in *Decoding the Past: The Psychohistorical Approach* (New Brunswick, 1996), 129.
7. "Introduction," in *The Cambridge Companion to the Fin de Siècle*, ed. Gail Marshall (Cambridge, 2007), 2.
8. Amos Elon, *Herzl* (New York, 1986), 32.
9. Theodor Herzl, "An Autobiography (1898)," in *The German-Jewish Dialogue: An Anthology of Literary Texts 1749–1993*, ed. Ritchie Robertson (Oxford, 1993), 149.
10. Two of Herzl's plays (*Die Wilddiebe* and *Der Flüchtling*) were preformed in the Burgtheater.
11. "Nicht als Dramatiker, sondern als Journalist wurde Herzl bekannt. Die literarischen Berichte von seiner Reise nach Italien 1889, die die *Wiener Allgemeine Zeitung* veröffentlichte, zeigen ihn als feinen Stilisten und subtilen Beobachter." Stefana Sabin, *Der Schriftsteller als Politiker: Theodor Herzl und das zionistische Engagement* (Göttingen, 2010), 13.
12. Herzl, "An Autobiography (1898)," 150.
13. "Einleitung," in *Theodor Herzl: oder der Moses des Fin de siècle*, ed. Klaus Dethloff, 7–58 (Vienna, 1986), 23.
14. Theodor Herzl, *The Complete Diaries of Theodor Herzl*, 5 vols., vol. 1, ed. Raphael Patai and trans. Harry Zohn (New York, 1960), 1:3.
15. Herzl, *Complete Diaries*, 1:13.
16. "A record of Herzl's unhappy marriage and of his melancholia exists in memoirs of his friends and colleagues. It is apparent that Julie Herzl had little insight into her husband. There is no indication of empathy with his fantasies, understanding of his emotional needs, or interest in his political ideas on the part of his wife." Loewenberg, *Decoding the Past*, 110.

17. Ibid., 113.
18. Stefan Zweig, *Die Welt von Gestern: Erinnerungen eines Europäers* (Frankfurt, 2000), 131.
19. Theodor Herzl, *Feuilletons*, 2 vols. (Berlin, 1911), 2:63–64.
20. John K. Noyes, *The Mastery of Submission: Inventions of Masochism* (Ithaca, NY, 1997), 53.
21. Ernest Pawel, *The Labyrinth of Exile: A Life of Theodor Herzl* (New York, 1989), 160.
22. Ibid.
23. In Herzl's words, mutualism is a "middle road between capitalism and collectivism. Producers' and consumers' cooperatives are only beginnings, suggestions of the mutual principal." Herzl, *Complete Diaries*, 3:852.
24. Gregory Claeys and Lyman Tower Sargent, eds., *The Utopia Reader* (New York, 1999), 199.
25. See Franz Oppenheimer, *Die Siedlungsgenossenschaft. Versuch einer positiven Überwindung des Kommunismus durch Lösung des Genossenschaftsproblems und der Agrarfrage* (Leipzig, 1896), 9.
26. "Herzl stated his interest in cooperatives as early as 1896, and there is no reason to believe that Oppenheimer influenced him in any fundamental way." Derek J. Penslar, *Zionism and Technology: The Engineering of Jewish Settlement in Palestine, 1870–1918* (Bloomington, IN, 1991), 56.
27. Beller, *Herzl*, 16.
28. Pawel, *Labyrinth of Exile*, 169–70.
29. Edda Ziegler, *Heinrich Heine: Leben-Werk-Wirkung* (Zurich, 1993), 127.
30. Ibid.
31. Klaus Dethloff, ed., *Theodor Herzl: oder der Moses des Fin de siècle* (Vienna, 1986), 19.
32. A situation Ernst Bloch describes as "die Ungleichzeitigkeit des Gleichzeitigen" [non-simultaneity of the simultaneous]. Bloch borrowed the term from art historian Wilhelm Pindar. *Das Problem der Generation in der Kunstgeschichte Europa* (Berlin, 1926), 11.
33. "Einleitung," *Theodor Herzl*, ed. Dethloff, 19.
34. "While . . . the degradation of Captain Dreyfus left a lasting impression on Herzl, it was his antecedent fantasies that provided the primary impulse for his political development." Loewenberg, *Decoding the Past*, 112. "Rather than the Dreyfus case, the timing of Herzl's conversion to the idea of a state for Jews points much more to a Viennese cause . . . It was the experience of Vienna, his hometown, as a centre of triumphant political anti-Semitism that drove him to think that the Jewish Question could no longer be solved at home." Steven Beller, *Theodor Herzl and Austria: A Century Later* (Vienna, 2004), 39.
35. "Das neue Ghetto," *Theodor Herzl*, ed. Dethloff, 155.
36. Gisela Brune-Firnau, "The Author, Feuilletonist, and Renowned Foreign Correspondent Theodor Herzl Turns Toward Zionism and Writes the Manifesto 'The Jewish State,'" *Yale Companion to Jewish Writing and Thought in German Culture 1096–1996*, ed. Sander L. Gilman and Jack Zipes (New Haven, CT, 1996), 222.
37. Karl Kraus did not agree with the ideas Herzl put forward in *Der Judenstaat*. He pointed out that Jews living in different nations were not alike, nor do they necessarily want to move to another country. See Karl Kraus, *Eine Krone für Zion* (Vienna, 1898), 3–5.
38. Kraus's review of *Das neue Ghetto* is reprinted in Karl Kraus, *Frühe Schriften: 1892–1900*, vol. 2, ed. Johannes J. Baakenburg (Munich, 1979), 156–57.

39. Qtd. in "Einleitung," *Theodor Herzl*, ed. Dethloff, 30.
40. See Pawel, *The Labyrinth of Exile*, 210; and Elon, *Herzl*, 125.
41. On the same day, 27 July 1895, he also commenced his well-known *Zionistisches Tagebuch*. Herzl's Zionist diary has been read as an autobiographical *Bildungsroman*; see Shlomo Avineri, "Theodor Herzl's Diaries as a Bildungsroman," *Jewish Social Studies* 5, no. 3 (Spring/Summer 1999): 1-47; and Peter Loewenberg, "Between Fantasy and Reality," in *Theodor Herzl: Visionary of the Jewish State*, ed. Gideon Shimoni and Robert S. Wistrich (Jerusalem, 1999), 3–14.
42. "Der Judenstaat," *Theodor Herzl*, ed. Dethloff, 207.
43. "Einleitung," *Theodor Herzl*, ed. Dethloff, 32.
44. The metaphor of a steerable airship originated when, during a visit with Herzl to the Hotel Castille, 37 Rue Cambon, shortly after the writing of *Der Judenstaat*, a friend and colleague, Emil Schiff, expressed amazement about Herzl's confused and unkempt appearance. Schiff, who was also a physician, ascertained that Herzl looked as though he had invented a steerable balloon. And the next day, after he had read the manuscript, Schiff broke out in tears because he thought that Herzl had gone mad. See "Einleitung," *Theodor Herzl*, ed. Dethloff, 65–66.
45. "Das lenkbare Luftschiff," *Theodor Herzl*, ed. Dethloff, 178.
46. In Goethe's *Unterhaltungen deutscher Ausgewanderten* (1795), a group of educated Germans seek diversion during the trying times of the French Revolution. In Stolberg's *Insel*, a group of friends develop a vision of a self-contained island in a pleasant climate in the course of philosophical conversations. For further discussion of Stolberg's island utopia, see Chapter 2.
47. "Das lenkbare Luftschiff," *Theodor Herzl*, ed. Dethloff, 178.
48. In Greek mythology, when Halcyone's husband drowned, she threw herself into the sea. Out of pity the Gods changed the pair into kingfishers or halcyons, and Zeus forbade the winds to blow for seven days before and after the winter solstice, the birds' breeding season.
49. "Das lenkbare Luftschiff," *Theodor Herzl*, ed. Dethloff, 184.
50. Ibid., 185.
51. Ibid.
52. Theodor Herzl, *Zionistisches Tagebuch 1895–1899, Briefe und Tagebücher*, ed. Johannes Wachen et al. (Berlin, 1984), 2:351–52.
53. Jeremy Stolow, "Utopia and Geopolitics in Theodor Herzl's 'Altneuland,'" *Utopian Studies* 8 (Winter 1997): 75.
54. Qtd. in Pawel, *The Labyrinth of Exile*, 438.
55. Na'ama Rokem, "Making Use of Prose: The Politics of Genre in Theodor Herzl and H. N. Bialik," in *Theodor Herzl: From Europe to Zion*, ed. Mark H. Gelber and Vivian Liska (Tübingen, 2007), 212.
56. Buch, *Nähe und Ferne*, 114.
57. Cabet's communal utopia *Voyage en Icarie* (The Voyage to Icaria) reflected the contemporary oppression of industrialization. *Altneuland*'s protagonist David Littwak praises the rationality of Cabet's utopia: "The 19th century, however, was a curious backward era. At the beginning of that era, muddle-headed visionaries were taken seriously, while sober, practical men were branded as lunatics. . . . Stephenson, the inventor of the railway, and Cabet, the dreamer of Icaria, were contemporaries." Theodor Herzl, *Old New Land*, trans. Lotta Levensohn (Princeton, 2004), 144–45.

58. Bellamy is also mentioned by Littwak: "Take the famous [utopia] of the American, Edward Bellamy, who outlined a noble communistic society in his *Looking Backward*. In that utopia, all may eat as much as they please from the common platter. The lamb and the wolf feed in the same pasture. Very fine. Only then, the wolves are no longer wolves, and human beings no longer human." Herzl, *Old New Land*, 145–46.
59. Like Herzl in *Der Judenstaat*, Littwak is critical when he discusses Hertzka's *Freiland*: "After Bellamy's book came *Freiland*, a utopia by the romantic philosopher Hertzka. *Freiland* is a brilliant bit of magic, which may well be compared with the juggler's inexhaustible hat. Beautiful dreams, indeed, or airships if you care to call them that, but not maneuverable." Herzl, *Old New Land*, 146.
60. It is again Littwak who explains: "Believe me, gentlemen, our mutualism has not made us the poorer in strong personalities, the richer, if anything. Here the individual is neither ground between the millstones of capitalism, nor decapitated by socialistic leveling." Herzl, *Old New Land*, 90.
61. After having introduced the historical situation in Ireland in 1830s, Littwak summarizes the achievements of the Ralahine community: "It was soon seen that the laborers of Ralahine worked twice as hard as any others in the district . . . yet it was the same soil; the people were the same. It was merely that they had discovered a saving principle: that of the agricultural producers' co-operative." Herzl, *Old New Land*, 150.
62. Robert Wistrich, "Theodor Herzl: Zionist Icon, Myth Maker and Social Utopian," in *The Shaping of the Israeli Identity: Myth, Memory and Trauma*, ed. Robert Wistrich and David Ohana (London, 1995), 25.
63. Several years before the publication of Herzl's *Judenstaat*, the Viennese academic Joseph Popper-Lynkeus concluded in his tract *Fürst Bismarck und der Antisemitismus* (1886) that the Jews could only be saved by the creation of their own state. Other early Zionist utopias are discussed by Miriam Eliav-Feldon in: "'If You Will It, It Is No Fairy Tale': The First Jewish Utopias," *The Jewish Journal of Sociology* 25, no. 2 (1983): 87–91.
64. Schorske, *Fin-de-Siècle Vienna*, 120.
65. See Ian Burama's essay on Herzl in *Anglomania: A European Love Affair* (New York, 1998), 176–98. Tellingly, the epigraph quotes Herzl in 1900 exclaiming: "England, great England, England the free, England commanding all the seas—She will understand us and our purpose" (176). See also Steven Beller, "Herzl's Anglophilia," in *Theodor Herzl and the Origins of Zionism*, ed. Ritchie Robertson and Edward Timms, (Edinburgh, 1997), 54–62.
66. Herzl wrote on 15 May 1897: "I urged Kellner to write a series of literary profiles of representative exponents of the Zionist idea: Disraeli, G. Eliot, Moses Hess etc." Herzl, *The Complete Diaries*, 2:548.
67. Edward Said, "Zionism from the Standpoint of Its Victims," in *The Edward Said Reader*, ed. Moustafa Bayoumi and Andrew Rubin (New York, 2000), 120.
68. Herzl, *Old New Land*, 4.
69. Ibid., 14–15.
70. Ibid., 15.
71. Ibid., 19.
72. Ibid., 26.
73. Herzl, *Briefe und Tagebücher*, 2:216.

74. "'Der Architekt Steineck hat uns e Red' gehalt'n. Me kann sag'n es war e scheene Red,' me kenn auch sag'n, es war e grobe Red. Ich sag,' es war e grobe Red.' Friedmann fiel ihm ins Wort: 'Du, Mendel, beleidigen wirst Du nicht! Das erlaub' ich nicht.' Aber Mendel entgegnete: 'Beleidigen? Wer beleidigt? Er hat uns beleidigt. Er hat gesagt, mir sein nit wert, dass uns bescheint de Sonn.' Worum sein mir es nit wert? Weil mir nit woll'n ereinlass'n e jed'n.'" Herzl, *Altneuland*, 159.
75. Muhammad Ali Khalidi, "Utopian Zionism or Zionist Proselytism?: A Reading of Herzl's *Altneuland*," *Journal of Palestine Studies* 30, no. 4 (Summer 2001): 66.
76. Pawel, *The Labyrinth of Exile*, 471–72.
77. Herzl, *Old New Land*, 42.
78. Herzl, *Complete Diaries*, 2:739.
79. Ibid., 2:746.
80. Walter Benjamin, "Rezension von Max von Boehns *Puppen und Puppenspiele* (1929)," in *Gesammelte Schriften*, vol. 3, ed. Rolf Tiedemann and Herrmann Schweppenhäuser (Frankfurt, 1972), 216.
81. Herzl, *Old New Land*, 61–62.
82. Ibid., 68–69.
83. Israel Zwangwill (1864–1926), a prominent English supporter of Herzl from 1895 and the leader of the "Western" wing of the Zionist movement, underscored the normalizing function of a Jewish state.
84. Sophie Perriaux and Daniel Steuer, "Zionism, the Shoa and the Foundation of Israeli Identity," in *Theodor Herzl and the Origins of Zionism*, ed. Ritchie Robertson and Edward Timms, (Edinburgh, 1997), 137.
85. Herzl's original text reads: "Will man heute ein Land gründen, darf man es nicht in der Weise machen, die vor tausend Jahren die einzig mögliche gewesen ware. Es ist töricht, auf alte Kulturstufen zurückzukehren, wie es manche Zionisten möchten. Kämen wir beispielsweise in die Lage, ein Land von wilden Tieren zu säubern, würden wir es nicht in der Art der Europäer aus dem fünften Jahrhundert tun. Wir würden nicht einzeln mit Speer und Lanze gegen Bären ausziehen, sondern eine grosse fröhliche Jagd veranstalten, die Bestien zusammentreiben und eine Melinitbombe unter sie werfen." "Der Judenstaat," *Theodor Herzl*, ed. Dethloff, 206.
86. Theodor Herzl, *The Jews' State*, trans. and intro. by Henk Overberg (Northvale, 1997), 141.
87. Herzl, *Old New Land*, 200.
88. However, a brief glance at a travel guide would have yielded a different picture: "The area of ancient Palestine is now occupied by about 650,000 souls or 62 persons per square mile." *Baedeker Palestine & Syria: Handbook for Travellers*, ed. Karl Baedeker (Leipzig, 1894), lviii.
89. Herzl, *Old New Land*, 169–70.
90. Ibid., 170.
91. Herzl's translator, Lotta Levensohn, whites out Herzl's apparent racial bias by translating the passage as "Menschen, wenn auch schwarze Menschen" [human beings, even black human beings] as: "human beings, because their skins are black." Ibid.
92. Ibid.
93. Derek J. Penslar and Ivan Davidson Kalmar, "An Introduction," in *Orientalism and the Jews*, ed. Derek J. Penslar and Ivan Davidson Kalmar (Lebanon, NH, 2005), xv.
94. Herzl, *Old New Land*, 247.

95. Schorske, *Fin-de-Siècle Vienna*, 24.
96. Herzl, *Old New Land*, 289.
97. "Komm, Geliebter, deiner harret / Schon die Braut, die dir entschleiert / Ihr verschämtes Angesicht." Quoted in Herzl, *Old New Land*, 251.
98. Ibid., 253.
99. Mikhal Dekel, *The Universal Jew: Masculinity, Modernity, and the Zionist Moment* (Evanston, IL, 2010), 111.
100. Hillary Hope Herzog, *"Vienna Is Different": Jewish Writers in Austria from the Fin de Siècle to the Present* (New York, 2011), 68.
101. Ernst Bloch, *Prinzip Hoffnung*. 3 vols. (Frankfurt, 1959), 2:704.
102. Bloch, *Prinzip Hoffnung*, 3:1628.
103. Phillip E. Wegner, *Imaginary Communities: Utopia, the Nation, and the Spatial Histories of Modernity* (Berkeley, 2002), xvi.

Bibliography

Arendt, Hannah. *The Jew as Pariah: Jewish Identity and Politics in the Modern Age*. Edited by Ron H. Feldman. New York: Grove Press, 1978.
Auerbach, Erich. "Philology and Weltliteratur." Translated by M. and E. W. Said. *Centennial Review* 13 (Winter 1969): 1–17.
Avineri, Shlomo. "Theodor Herzl's Diaries as a Bildungsroman." *Jewish Social Studies* 5, no. 3 (Spring/Summer 1999): 1–47.
Baedeker, Karl. *Baedeker Palestine & Syria: Handbook for Travellers*. 2nd ed. Leipzig: Karl Baedeker, 1894.
Beller, Steven. *Herzl*. London: Peter Halban, 1991.
———. *Theodor Herzl and Austria: A Century Later*. Vienna: Federal Ministry of Foreign Affairs, 2004.
Benjamin, Walter. "Rezension von Max von Boehns *Puppen und Puppenspiele* (1929)." In *Gesammelte Schriften*, Vol. 3, edited by Rolf Tiedemann and Herrmann Schweppenhäuser, 213–18. Frankfurt: Suhrkamp, 1972.
Bloch, Ernst. *Prinzip Hoffnung*. 3 vols. Frankfurt: Suhrkamp, 1959.
Brune-Firnau, Gisela. "The Author, Feuilletonist, and Renowned Foreign Correspondent Theodor Herzl Turns Toward Zionism and Writes the Manifesto 'The Jewish State.'" In *Yale Companion to Jewish Writing and Thought in German Culture 1096–1996*, edited by Sander L. Gilman and Jack Zipes, 219–27. New Haven, CT: Yale University Press, 1996.
Buch, Hans Christoph. *Die Nähe und die Ferne: Bausteine zu einer Poetik des kolonialen Blicks*. Frankfurt: Suhrkamp, 1991.
Burama, Ian. *Anglomania: A European Love Affair*. New York: Vintage, 1998.
Claeys, Gregory, and Lyman Tower Sargent, eds. *The Utopia Reader*. New York: New York University Press, 1999.
Dekel, Mikhal. *The Universal Jew: Masculinity, Modernity, and the Zionist Moment*. Evanston, IL: Northwestern University Press, 2010.
Dethloff, Klaus, ed. *Theodor Herzl: oder der Moses des Fin de siècle*. Vienna: Böhlau, 1986.
Eliav-Feldon, Miriam. "'If You Will It, It Is No Fairy Tale': The First Jewish Utopias." *The Jewish Journal of Sociology* 25, no. 2 (1983): 85–105.

Elon, Amos. *Herzl.* New York: Schoken, 1986.
Herzl, Theodor. *Altneuland.* Leipzig: Hermann Seemann, 1902.
———. *Feuilletons* II. Berlin: J. Singer, 1911.
———. *Old New Land.* Translated by Lotta Levensohn. Princeton, NJ: Markus Wiener, 2004.
———. *The Complete Diaries of Theodor Herzl.* Edited by Raphael Patai and translated by Harry Zohn. 5 vols. New York: Herzl Press, 1960.
———. *The Jews' State.* Translated and introduced by Henk Overberg. Northvale: Jason Aronson, 1997.
———. *Zionistisches Tagebuch, 1895–1899, Briefe und Tagebücher,* vol. 2. Edited by Johannes Wachen et al. Berlin: Propyläen, 1984.
Herzog, Hillary Hope. *"Vienna Is Different": Jewish Writers in Austria from the Fin de Siècle to the Present.* New York: Berghahn Books, 2011.
Khalidi, Muhammad Ali. "Utopian Zionism or Zionist Proselytism?: A Reading of Herzl's *Altneuland.*" *Journal of Palestine Studies* 30, no. 4 (Summer 2001): 55–75.
Kraus, Karl. *Eine Krone für Zion.* Vienna: Moriz Frisch, 1898.
———. *Frühe Schriften: 1892–1900.* 2 vols. Edited by Johannes J. Baakenburg. Munich: Kösel, 1979.
Loewenberg, Peter. "Between Fantasy and Reality." In *Theodor Herzl: Visionary of the Jewish State,* edited by Gideon Shimoni and Robert S. Wistrich, 3-14. Jerusalem: Magnes Press of the Hebrew University, 1999.
———. "Theodor Herzl: Nationalism and Politics." In *Decoding the Past: The Psychohistorical Approach,* 101–36. New Brunswick: Transaction Publishers, 1996.
Marshall, Gail, ed. *The Cambridge Companion to the Fin de Siècle.* Cambridge: Cambridge University Press, 2007.
Noyes, John K. *The Mastery of Submission: Inventions of Masochism.* Ithaca, NY: Cornell University Press, 1997.
Oppenheimer, Franz. *Die Siedlungsgenossenschaft. Versuch einer positiven Überwindung des Kommunismus durch Lösung des Genossenschaftsproblems und der Agrarfrage.* Leipzig: Duncker & Humblot, 1896.
Pawel, Ernest. *The Labyrinth of Exile: A Life of Theodor Herzl.* New York: Farrar, Straus & Giroux, 1989.
Penslar, Derek J. *Zionism and Technology: The Engineering of Jewish Settlement in Palestine, 1870–1918.* Bloomington: Indiana University Press, 1991.
Penslar, Derek J., and Ivan Davidson Kalmar, eds. *Orientalism and the Jews.* Lebanon, NH: Brandeis University Press, 2005.
Perriaux, Sophie, and Daniel Steuer. "Zionism, the Shoa and the Foundation of Israeli Identity." In *Theodor Herzl and the Origins of Zionism,* edited by Ritchie Robertson and Edward Timms, 131–51. Edinburgh: Edinburgh University Press, 1997.
Pindar, Wilhelm. *Das Problem der Generation in der Kunstgeschichte Europa.* Berlin: Frankfurter Verlags-Anstalt, 1926.
Robertson, Ritchie. "1918: This Year of the Dissolution of the Austro-Hungarian Empire Marks a Crucial Historical and Symbolic Change for Joseph Roth." In *Yale Companion to Jewish Writing and Thought in German Culture 1096–1996,* edited by Sander L. Gilman and Jack Zipes, 355–62. New Haven, CT: Yale University Press, 1996.
———. *The German-Jewish Dialogue: An Anthology of Literary Texts 1749–1993.* Oxford: Oxford University Press, 1993.

Rokem, Na'ama. "Making Use of Prose: The Politics of Genre in Theodor Herzl and H. N. Bialik." In *Theodor Herzl: From Europe to Zion*, edited by Mark H. Gelber and Vivian Liska, 201–20. Tübingen: Max Niemeyer, 2007.

Sabin, Stefana. *Der Schriftsteller als Politiker: Theodor Herzl und das zionistische Engagement.* Göttingen: Wallstein, 2010.

Said, Edward. "Zionism from the Standpoint of Its Victims." In *The Edward Said Reader*, edited by Moustafa Bayoumi and Andrew Rubin, 114–69. New York: Vintage, 2000.

Schorske, Carl E. *Fin-de-Siècle Vienna: Politics and Culture.* New York: Vintage, 1981.

Stolow, Jeremy. "Utopia and Geopolitics in Theodor Herzl's 'Altneuland.'" *Utopian Studies* 8 (Winter 1997): 55–77.

Wegner, Phillip E. *Imaginary Communities: Utopia, the Nation, and the Spatial Histories of Modernity.* Berkeley: University Press of California, 2002.

Wistrich, Robert, and David Ohana. *The Shaping of the Israeli Identity: Myth, Memory and Trauma.* London: Frank Cass, 1995.

Ziegler, Edda. *Heinrich Heine: Leben-Werk-Wirkung.* Zurich: Artemis & Winkler, 1993.

Zweig, Stefan. *Die Welt von Gestern: Erinnerungen eines Europäers.* Frankfurt: Fischer, 2000.

Chapter 5

ROBERT MÜLLER
Anti-Exoticism, and Joseph Roth: Finis Austriae

> Exoticism is defined as a nineteenth-century literary and existential practice that posited another space, the space of an Other, outside or beyond the confines of a "civilization" that, by virtue of its modernity, was perceived by many writers as being incompatible with certain essential values—or, indeed, the realm of value itself.
> —Chris Bongie, *Exotic Memories*¹

Anti-Exoticism in Robert Müller's *Tropen* (1915)

Although Theodor Herzl's fin-de-siècle utopia apparently applied European colonial policy to create his Zionist society *ex nihilo*, fundamental differences remain between the Viennese blueprint for a Zionist utopia and contemporary European imperialism. According to Derek J. Penslar: "[T]here was a qualitative difference between an imperialist power's system of controlling and exploiting colonies for the benefit of the metropolitan government, and the Zionist goal of using an international organization to create an autonomous homeland."² Thus, it is hard to believe that Herzl wanted to be the Austrian colonial vanguard in Africa, let alone that he wanted to strengthen the position of the Habsburg Empire in the world. On the contrary, he was looking for a safe haven from Vienna's anti-Semitism to make a new beginning. Nevertheless, the nexus of Austrian colonial utopias and German imperialist *realpolitik* was formed merely half a generation later. The new kind of colonial utopia aspired to establish a "German India Company" that would challenge the predominance of the British Empire. In order to do so, Germanic people would have to finally rid themselves of their "old slave soul" and escape their self-imposed "territorial confinement."³

At the beginning of World War I, the young Viennese expressionist writer Robert Müller developed this bold version of Austrian colonial utopia. Müller envisioned bringing about a global miscegenation of the human races. The impetus, I surmise, for his problematic fusion of races arose from his sensitivity to the confrontational but productive tensions among and within the ethnic groups comprising the Habsburg monarchy. On the one hand, Müller contradicted Claudio Magris's "Habsburg myth," which portrays Austria's emperor Franz Joseph I presiding over the harmonious Austrian peoples, too peaceful to participate in vicious European colonialism. On the other hand, he implicitly criticized the exoticist prose of Peter Altenberg's *Aschantee* (1897), which celebrated the "savage" as the excluded other of civilized modernity.[4] Hence, I argue that Müller's seminal novel *Tropen: Der Mythos der Reise* (1915) sheds a critical light on categories such as alterity and difference, and goes beyond the common understanding of exoticism.[5]

Even if some of the literary critics at the time considered Robert Müller an important modernist writer, he is today relegated to the margins of the Austrian literary canon.[6] The answer to this critical neglect can be found in Müller's provocative writings, as they often argue for Austria's aggressive colonial expansion fostered by a Nietzschean breed of new men who aimed to ruthlessly conquer the world on the eve of the twentieth century. As we will see, he never stated these literary ideas without ironies, paradoxes, and reversals, and his grandiosity never succeeded within the logic of his narratives. Notwithstanding this fictional failure, Müller's Nietzschean "Übermensch" bears too much resemblance to the Aryan ideology to have found appreciation in the aftermath of the holocaust.[7]

*

Müller grew up in Vienna as the son of a merchant from Bohemia, and—according to Müller's own family mythology—of a Swedish mother who gave him his "Viking" blood. At the age of twenty-two, and having studied philology for several semesters at Vienna University, he traveled to New York, where he worked as a reporter for the German-language newspaper *New Yorker Herold* to secure his subsistence. Although he returned to Vienna the following year, the mercantile world had made a lasting impression on the young journalist. In 1912, he organized the last public performance by Karl May, the celebrated author of countless adventure novels. Through his constant stream of publications Müller gradually became one of the most fascinating and controversial figures in Viennese cultural circles. Soon after the beginning of the war, he volunteered for the army and glorified the Habsburg Empire in his essays. Given his traumatic experiences in the trenches, however, he slowly and steadily turned into a pacifist. Although severely injured, in 1915 he published *Tropen: Der Mythos der Reise*. As we will see, *Tropen* marks a departure from his earlier belligerent position, subverting and refining his Manichean worldview.

In 1916, Müller was relegated to the War Press Office (*Kriegspressequartier*), where he cofounded the secret society "Die Katakombe," a group of activist intellectuals seeking to undermine the militaristic capitalism that ruled Europe at the time. After the war, on 21 August 1919, a new chapter in Müller's life began when he founded a Viennese publishing company (Literarische Vertriebs- und Propaganda-Gesellschaft), which became known as "Literaria." While Müller continued to tirelessly write novels, essays, and articles, he managed to build up a short-lived but powerful publishing empire. This ambitious publishing enterprise sought to combine European spirit (*Geist*) and American action, or deeds (*Tat*), and gave Müller an opportunity to pursue his dream to become a poet-publicist—a writer whose only duty would be to produce quality journalism and avant-garde literature. Unfortunately, the tidal wave of the 1923 hyperinflation swept away his grandiose business ventures. His aspirations thwarted, Müller committed suicide on 27 August 1924. He was only thirty-seven years old.[8]

Although his prolific career was eventually cut short, Müller had, even before World War I, been elevated—through a steady flow of critical essays in such well-known literary magazines as *Der Brenner* and *Der Ruf*—to a lofty position as one of the most revered publicists in Vienna.[9] Hence, the fact that Müller is not part of today's Austrian literary canon has little to do with a dearth of publications or with his books having limited availability.[10] As mentioned earlier, it is primarily a result of his controversial prewar ideology, in which he amalgamated thoughts by Nietzsche, Darwin, and Bergson into a belligerent, or rather racist, *Weltanschauung*. At several places in his rich collection of political and cultural essays, he is concerned with the possibility—if not necessity—of Austrian overseas colonies. The texts implicitly inform readers about the relationship between the cosmopolitan capital of Vienna and the Habsburg Empire's peripheral provinces. In essays with titles like "Österreichische Kolonien," "Der Kolonialmensch," "Die Internationalisierung der Kolonien," and "Der Kolonialmensch als Romantiker und Sozialist," Müller shows how Austria influenced—and was influenced by—exotic spaces beyond the confines of civilized Europe shortly before World War I. Already in 1912, Müller speaks of "a clash of cultures, which Europe, squeezed between Americanism and Asianism, will have to fight."[11] Central Europe—specifically the Habsburg Empire—is seen as the focal point at which cultures are to melt together in the future. On the one hand, Müller states that Europeans perceive Americans like Theodore Roosevelt as a paragon of the new human being, someone who represents a "modern, socially conscious and physically active psyche."[12] But Europeans are equally threatened by America's "desire to regress into the jungle,"[13] which is paradoxically coupled with an emphasis on technological progress and economic productivity. On the other hand, from Müller's European vantage point, he sees Asia's influence in its "ethical fatalism, idolatry of instinct, exoticism, condemnation of the intellect."[14] To be sure, Müller approves of both: American technology and Asian irrationality.

But he cautions Europeans to disdain their innate willpower and consciousness and urges them to avoid drifting unconditionally towards irrationality. While conjuring up these Manichean oppositions, Müller assumes a rather reactionary position at the beginning of the war.

In his polemical pamphlet "Karl Kraus oder Dalai Lama," he invokes the tropical zone as an untapped El Dorado: "In reality [the tropics] are only regions in which railway systems have to be built, malaria infested swamps have to be dried up, immensely rich prairies have to be harvested, the metal mines have to be exploited, and a couple of black and yellow folks have to be hanged."[15] In Müller's bifocal world order, Austrians are to cultivate the land and reign over their colonial subjects. But Müller does not stop with these general proclamations. In the same year, in an essay entitled "Was erwartet Österreich von seinem jungen Thronfolger?," he outlines his ostentatious geopolitical program for Austria's future colonies:

> It is the task of Austria-Hungary to transport *German thought to the Mediterranean Sea* ... When the Baghdad railroad is built, and when with its support the great *Arabian Empire of German signature*—like England's India today—is founded as the northeastern continuation of the central African Empire to amalgamate to a *German Colonial Belt at the Equator*, ... then when the great German deed, which we should all keep in mind, is in the process of becoming, then Austria will prove its usefulness.[16]

Unlike the fin-de-siècle narratives by Hertzka and Herzl, Müller's colonial utopia, conceived shortly before World War I, seeks to link the Habsburg Empire with Germany's overseas imperialism. To this effect, Müller proposes a cultural amalgamation, which he calls *Germantik*, "a category of character traits that share the emotions and tightening of experience of Romanticism, but remain more northern."[17] For Müller, the Habsburg Empire is predestined to take on this mediating role. It has precisely the right location and multiethnic population to synthesize "Germanic" and "Asian" lifestyles. Austria must create "through a strong economy [and] highly developed intuition, [and through] its art already generated through a mixture of cultures and its formative sensuality, ... a foreign-language-speaking, ethnologically shaded *Deutschtum*, a superior imperial being of the empire."[18] As the essay was published in 1916, it is apparent that Müller failed to take the sociopolitical realities of wartime into account.

Müller's colonialist project, which tends to border on the grandiose, if not supremacist, is more akin to a dystopia; it finds its best expression in his essay collection *Macht* (1915). The last chapter, entitled "Atlantis, ein deutscher Kontinent," is structured like a political fairy tale in which Atlantis bridges America and Europe. Critic Hans Heinz Hahnl detects a conservative trait in Müller's concept of Atlantis: "Atlantis, that signifies [for Müller] a return to a lost paradise, and—at the same time—a striving forward into an immeasurable continent. It is the myth of the conservative utopia."[19] But towards the end of the war, in his essay collection *Europäische Wege* (1917), Müller shows a surprising shift in his political convictions. His assessment of imperialism turned upside down, he argues: "The final goal in the development of all states is to get rid of the state.... In order to dissolve the state, it has been the best course of action to first promote the imperial state."[20] Perhaps his own traumatic experience in World War I, and its sobering consequences for the Habsburg Empire, had tempered his political views. As Günter Helmes puts it: "The elements of quasi-fascist thinking are no longer to be found in Müller's postwar writings. Racial and national stereotypes disappear to a certain extent."[21] Consequently, shortly after the armistice, Müller calls for an internationalization and socialization of all colonies worldwide. Nevertheless, he still upholds his claim to an Austrian piece of the colonial pie:

> All the successor states to the [Habsburg] monarchy under the control of the International League of Nations should take a share of product and settlement colonies. *African-Austrian* is the ideal solution to all social and economic questions regarding the countries bordering the Danube. A solution, together with a congress of diasporic peoples, enables a higher political form for the world altogether![22]

As hinted earlier, Müller softens his belligerent imperial fantasies and makes them more transparent in *Tropen: Mythos der Reise*. The novel features an American named Jack Slim, a Dutchman, van den Dusen, and a German narrator, Brandlberger. The three adventurers go on a treasure hunt in a South American jungle somewhere in Brazil and Venezuela, encountering an indigenous tribe in the Amazon delta. As the trip is fairly uneventful, the narrator focuses instead on the psychological impact of the tropics on himself and his fellow travelers. After a couple of peaceful weeks in a tribal village, an accident forces them to continue their search for El Dorado. Accompanied by an attractive priestess called Zana, they advance to the alleged hiding place of the loot. When it becomes apparent that there is no treasure to rescue, the adventurers compete for Zana's attention. While petty jealousy runs wild, they quickly deteriorate mentally and physically under the tropical sun. Slim and, shortly thereafter, van den Dusen mysteriously die, whereas Brandlberger, supposedly with Zana's assistance, is the only one who returns from the Amazon expedition. After several weeks in a feverish delirium in Rio de Janeiro, the young German engineer travels home to Europe. In the end, it remains unclear whether Brandlberger was responsible for the death of his travel companions.

The ruthless Brandlberger is the incarnation of Müller's new man: a synthesis of various qualities of all races, possessing the "characteristics of a modern culture, a cerebral tension, mixed with the peculiar relaxation of prehistoric man."[23] At the beginning of the jungle journey, Jack Slim, the American, appears to be the Nietzschean Übermensch as he is the one who masters both deeds and spirit alike. He is supposedly a close friend of Tolstoy, Gauguin, and Peter Altenberg.

Moreover, Slim has not only persuaded the German emperor Wilhelm II to dispatch the Kruger telegram but has also drafted plans for a colonial German empire in Arabia.[24] At the same time, Slim has vowed to work toward a closer alliance between the Habsburg monarchy and the Vatican. But toward the end of the expedition Slim sees Americans like himself in decline, and he encourages Brandlberger to overcome his shame of "his most beautiful violent drives."[25] Even if these hyperbolic statements in the novel are in tune with Müller's prewar political essays, the plot unfolds as a complex cacophony of narrative threats, and meanders like a tropical stream: "We still meandered along the river, whose banks—inarticulate as those of a swamp—never made the effort to become decently parallel. Lured out of the woods, some trees always stood in the water."[26] The narrative creates a murky zone between fictional reality and imagination, and produces a moment of uncanny dislocation: the Blue Danube is transposed into the muddy Amazon. The nation-state and its fixed borders give way to a boundless swamp. Müller's exotic jungle is foremost a site of metaphysical alteration and a threat to the European intruders, with the natives surviving the onslaught of the desperados through quiet defiance.

Furthermore, the Amazon delta exudes femininity: "I'm thinking of the woods, the primeval forest, the sensuality of this natural setting, its raw quality, its primordial élan, its terrible, confusing drive. I think of *the drive*, the tropics in the mind of the white man. Woman, for her part, has never left the tropics."[27] The tropical forest is figuratively a femme fatale with whom only the indigenous can maintain the integrity of their bodies. In the long run, the desired El Dorado becomes a deadly trap for the Western travelers. Their sense of superiority vanishes from day to day and is swiftly replaced by apathy. Sexual dissatisfaction increases their violent proclivities, while the communication between indigenous and civilized cultures breaks down. The impossibility of universal understanding becomes apparent. The exoticism of the Western travelers, marked by its dichotomies, becomes superfluous. Slowly, but steadily, Brandlberger's initial idea of the "fight of the races and senses"[28] is transformed into a utopian concept that sublates the difference between civilization and the jungle: "The step from Europe's center to the jungle is less adventurous than one had expected. Whatever one experiences, it is always the same adventure; it hardly matters if one ends up under a panther or an omnibus; but what matters least is whether *she* is called Zana or Miss So-and-so."[29] That Brandlberger undermines the universal creed of the progress of Western civilization becomes apparent when Vienna's topography is uncannily reproduced in the infrastructure of the jungle village:

> Now, I was my own boss, master of a new hut. It was located, like the first one, at the second ring . . . Slim had received a beautiful hut at the first ring, the Dutch fellow, like me, had his hut at the second. . . . Outside at the third ring, in the security belt zone by the proletarians, the unrefined, and the oppressed, who are the first who have

to believe it when an enemy tribe invades their nest, is where the remains of the male clan reside.[30]

Slim's beautiful residence could be located at the "Ringstrasse," Brandlberger's less attractive house might be at the "Gürtel," and the proletarian dwellings could be in neighborhoods such as "Ottakring" or perhaps "Leopoldsstadt." Analogies like these aim to dissolve the exotic strangeness of tribal villages. Paradoxically, Müller advances a notion of Austrian colonialism that destroys the idyllic gaze upon the exotic jungle and at the same time redirects criticism to "civilized" Vienna. In this respect, Brandlberger's gaze argues against the Habsburg myth and a romanticized notion of exoticism. For Müller, the journey into the tropics does not primarily entail alienation; the traveler is instead exposed to a process of "*re*-cognizing" his place of origin for the first time. The implicit shift of perspective devalues the belief in the universal applicability of Western progress. To highlight this inversion, Brandlberger allows Slim, van den Dusen, and himself to offer a surreal performance in the tribal village: "Today, the grand performance, Europe in Pomacco. For children, admission is free! The whitest Indians of the world. A tribe without feet, unique of its kind! The fattest man of the world, a special attraction for the female sex, small and large! Come on in!"[31] Hence, Vienna's Prater as the site "producing" exoticism is reversed by Pomacco's Occidentalist performance.

According to Brandlberger, exoticism is not only relative; it is ultimately an outdated theorem: "I was done with the exotic. This point of view was outmoded. Impressionism? It was wrong; it was a defect of observation. It was not deep, absolutely not deep."[32] In Müller's cultural relativism, exoticism is presented as an overcome paradigm since it idealizes the other, outside of the confines of Western civilization. As put by Angelika Jacobs: "The outside perspective onto the Western cultures of Müller's *Tropen* novel demonstrates, first and foremost, how threatening the so-called self can be, and demands the fantastic mode of the utopia."[33] Müller's utopia of racial mixture seeks to create a third space in which the jungle is reflected within the city. Müller's utopianism elegantly details the social dysfunction of the Habsburg society. From these dysfunctional roots, *Tropen* develops the fiction of an exotic utopia brought about by an envisioned global fusion of the human races. The impetus for this visionary amalgamation arose from Müller's sensitivity toward the tensions among and within the ethnic groups, and from his awareness of the strangeness and distance between the various nationalities, all comprising the polyglot Habsburg Empire.

When Müller finds fault with the Habsburg monarchy for failing to realize the benefits of its multicultural heterogeneity, he anticipates a modern-day rhetoric of empire. Michael Hardt and Antonio Negri articulate a critique similar to Müller's in *Multitude* (2004), when they call for a "social multiplicity to manage to communicate and act in common while remaining internally different."[34] An imaginary discourse between various colonies at the fringes, they aver, allows all participants to negotiate the conflict between the "social multiplicity" of a society and preserving their individual identities.

The imagined colonial communities within a larger heterogeneous empire are recurring tropes not only in the works of Müller but also in the colonial utopias of von Hellenbach, and von Sacher-Masoch. Even if Musil's narrator of *Man without Qualities* (1930) contends that "words such as colony and overseas sounded like something quite untried and remote,"[35] Austrian colonial utopias of the late nineteenth century were concerned with precisely these topics. The utopias either adhered to a grand universalizing scheme of colonialism (i.e., Herzl's Zionism), or—as in the case of Leopold von Sacher-Masoch—implicitly elevated colonial space to "a site of destabilization where cultural hierarchies and truth values lose their credibility."[36] Paradoxically, Müller puts forward a notion of exoticism in which "civilized" Vienna is criticized from the perspective of the jungle. As Michael C. Frank points out, Müller makes a great effort, in his "novel of disillusionment," to undermine the exotic imagery of native cultures by foregrounding the otherwise repressed violence of colonialism.[37] It is not the encounter with the natives that Müller's narrator Brandlberger finds uncanny but the recovery of his alienated self. Since the story of *Tropen* ends in disillusionment, it is noteworthy that Müller's last novel, *Flibustier* (1922), expresses the possibility of all Brandlberger had hoped for becoming reality. The pragmatic protagonist Krumka reads an adventure story in which this is the case:

> An English adventurer, half businessman, half pirate, founded a state in the style of Robert Clive's East India Company—a state of free shareholders of all races. It was a complete, liberal, established empire; the promiscuity of the pirates of white, yellow, and brown races and the bountiful output of the love of the kidnapped beauties from the Near East to Australia flowed together into a new racial formation.[38]

This story resonates with Lazar von Hellenbach's *Insel Mellonta* (1883); it shares not only the fantasy of promiscuity and racial mixing with Müller's exotic story but also realizes its utopian potential as a fiction within a fiction. Evidently, von Hellenbach's island utopia overlaps in terms of intertextual connections with Müller's *Flibustier*. But if von Hellenbach is Müller's creative soul mate, Theodor Hertzka could function as Müller's ideological antagonist in almost every respect.

As we have seen in Chapter 3, Hertzka's *Freiland* (1890) endeavors to resuscitate the positive aspect of technological progress by repressing the negative social implications of Viennese modernism. But Hertzka is oblivious to the downside of such speedy progress. The author still possesses the optimistic confidence originating in the nineteenth-century liberal ideal of the good society, which situates the individual at the center of the social world. Hertzka adheres to what Stefan Jonsson calls the expressivist paradigm of subjectivity—that is to say, to an identity that is grounded in subjective intrinsic dispositions: "A person's statements, behaviors and social positions are seen as expressions of his or her identity, the essence of which is taken to be an internal personal kernel."[39] Even if Hertzka's utopia *Freiland* addresses many of the uncertainties at the liminal moment of modernism in which he lived, his prescription for overcoming the critical condition fails to move forward but rather reinvigorates Enlightenment concepts of the free individual.

With the onset of modernism in Vienna, the expressivist paradigm of subjectivity is replaced by the idea that the primary markers (behaviors, memories, statements, etc.) of the social or symbolic order merely "constitute and consolidate the identity of the human subject."[40] Müller's preface to *Tropen* describes Brandlberger as a "type belonging to the early twentieth century before the war, a man without specific qualities or talents."[41] In dialectical opposition to the certainty Hertzka's characters possess in his enlightened nineteenth-century fictional universe, Müller's twentieth-century characters appear to have merely borrowed the content of their consciousness. In this scenario, the holistic individual is only a carrier of socially shared ideas. Or, as the Viennese philosopher Ernst Mach puts it: "Apart from insignificant, worthless personal memories, an individual remains even after his demise in *others*."[42] If such transcendentalism is foreign to Hertzka's one-dimensional characters, it suits von Hellenbach's theory of birth and death as mere experiential changes. Brandlberger exemplifies this when he—after Slim's demise—seamlessly takes on Slim's role for the rest of the narrative. To a certain degree, Müller's *Tropen* extends the discourse of Viennese colonial utopias into the twentieth century but continues the journey in uncomfortable ways. He excavates, inspects, discusses, and finally pushes all blindspots, oversights, and misperceptions of the colonial utopias to their dialectical limits. The only thing left for Joseph Roth to do is to arrange a funeral for Austria's utopias.

Finis Austriae: Joseph Roth's *Kapuzinergruft* (1938)

> Austria cannot be found in the Alps; chamois, edelweiss and gentians are there, but hardly a notion of a double-headed eagle. The substance of Austria is fed and continuously replenished by the Crown Lands.
> —Joseph Roth, *Die Kapuzinergruft*[43]

The myth of Austria resides in its supra-nationalism. Not that the Habsburg Empire's various religions and nationalities ever lived in perfect harmony, but the dream of a *Vielvölkerstaat* served Robert Müller as a political program for the "Austrification of the world."[44] Defying political realities, Müller thought that Austria's charm would eventually win over the rest of the world. Needless to say, with the loss of World War I and the dissolution of the Danube monarchy, this "charming" imperialism had to be adjusted. Writer Joseph Roth, slightly younger than Müller, came of age in the interwar period. Most of Roth's novels from the 1920s deal with the fate of Austria and Germany's lost generation, but in the 1930s novels, Roth intermittently shifts his focus to the demise of the Habsburg Empire. Two of his novels from this period portray the political realities in Vienna (his last novel, *Kapuzinergruft*, 1938), and in the margin of the empire (*Radetzkymarsch*, 1932) from the nineteenth century to the present.

The objective of this chapter, however, is not to portray Joseph Roth as an example of a "backward-facing" utopianist but instead to show the continuities between his work and the Austrian colonial utopias produced a generation earlier.[45] For example, Roth's essay collection *Juden auf der Wanderschaft* (The Wandering Jews, 1927) addresses the fate of contemporary Jewish migrants from Central Europe. In this collection, Roth rejects both Herzl's Zionism and the acceptance of Jewish migrants by the host culture as viable solutions to the plight of Central European Jews. Similar to von Sacher-Masoch, Roth regards the essence of the Habsburg Empire not as its center but its periphery—a place he populates with subaltern protagonists never quite coming to terms with the loss of the empire. Claudio Magris characterizes Roth and other Austrian intellectuals of the interwar period as having a tendency to recall the vanished Habsburg monarchy as a harmonious bygone time, in which Central Europe was orderly and secure. In the memoirs of these intellectuals, Austria becomes the gold standard of security.[46] In spite of Magris's assessment, I want to demonstrate here that Roth's late fiction is neither nostalgic for the Habsburg Empire nor an insipid portrait of Central Europe as a place of despotism and social injustice. Roth claims that his writings, rather than embellishing the past, "turn reality into a higher form of truth through the medium of language."[47] That is to say, he mediates the history of the empire's marginal communities through fiction. Roth presents an allegorical engagement with history that does not merely yearn for a lost paradise but asserts its relevance by critiquing the contemporary social situation.

To paraphrase Raymond Williams, "myth" has been held to be a deeper version of reality, a realistic report representing complex feelings and thereby analyzing human nature.[48] In this respect, mythical narratives are capable of legitimizing and solidifying contemporary social interaction. Roth's concept of myth resonates with Williams' definition and yet has little in common with Magris's thesis on the Habsburg myth. Magris argues that after the demise of the Habsburg Empire in 1918, writers such as Joseph Roth, Robert Musil, and Stefan Zweig could not cope with the new cultural and political situation in Austria. Bereft of the crown lands in Eastern Europe, they were enticed to remember the Habsburg Empire as an ideal nation in an almost timeless space. Diverging from Magris's thesis, I show in this chapter that Roth assumes an increasingly critical position and abandons hope for a viable future for the Habsburg Empire. His short story "Leviathan" (1934) still renders the cultural matrix of the lost Habsburg Empire in a reality of metaphysical dimensions. But only four years later, in *Kapuzinergruft*, Roth turns Vienna into a dystopia with death as the ubiquitous metaphor. Put differently, the colonial utopias of the Habsburg Empire that Hertzka, von Sacher-Masoch, von Hellenbach, and Herzl revered come full circle in the wake of the devastating World War I.

Perhaps Roth's early loss of his father prompted him to cloak his own biography in legends. Be that as it may, the following biographical facts can be established: Roth was born in Brody, Galicia, in 1894, near Lemberg at the eastern end of the Habsburg Empire. Jewish culture played an important role in the region. He grew up in the home of his maternal grandfather Jechiel Grübel, an orthodox Jewish businessman, and he attended a German-speaking gymnasium. By 1914, Roth had moved to Vienna to study philosophy and literature. Lemberg, the provincial capital, had come to seem too narrow to the young, ambitious Roth, who presumed that fortune awaited him in Vienna, the cultural center of the Habsburg Empire. Two years later, in 1916, he voluntarily served in the Austrian army. Like so many other young men of his generation, he was left with a feeling of existential homelessness after the war and the ensuing collapse of the Habsburg Empire. Soon after the war, he moved to the thriving metropolis of Berlin, where he embarked on a successful career as a journalist for several German newspapers. By 1923 he was already one of best-paid reporters in Germany, and traveled throughout Europe to write his celebrated travel reviews for the feuilleton of the prestigious *Frankfurter Zeitung*. The Viennese *Arbeiterzeitung* serialized his first novel *Das Spinnennetz* in 1923. His subsequent books often portray drifters and refugees who have lost their social moorings.[49] As a prominent journalist of Jewish descent, Roth himself became a refugee after Hitler's rise to power in 1933 and spent the remainder of his life in exile in Paris. After ultimately spiraling into alcoholism and despair, he died prematurely in 1939.

In his study *Schiffbruch mit Zuschauern* (1979), Hans Blumenberg posits that mythic narratives create an orientation in the everyday oppression of contingency and provide relief for individuals and society in general. Furthermore, the polyvalence of myth makes it rich and versatile in its applicability. Claude Levi-Strauss gives us a concrete example of how mythic narratives fulfill a societal relief function. If two family clans from the same aboriginal village in South America give completely different and contradictory accounts of their village history, this antinomy cannot be explained by a bird's eye view capturing reality. Instead, the split into two relative perceptions results not from the actual arrangement of buildings viewed objectively but rather from a fundamental antagonism the families were not able to symbolize. This antagonism, as Slavoj Zizek points out, demonstrates "an imbalance in social relations that prevented the community from stabilizing itself into a harmonious whole."[50] Hence, the problem-solving capacity of myth lies in its projection of an imaginary mediation between the fundamental antinomies of a given society.[51] Mythical narratives provide legitimation for contemporary social actions and actors. In what follows, I will show not only how Roth's mythology helps to uncover the deeply rooted conflicts underlying the history of the Habsburg Empire but also how his novels and reports seek to ameliorate the oppression of contingency identified by Blumenberg.

*

In Roth's short story "Leviathan," Galicia's mythic simplicity is threatened by the onslaught of modern capitalism. "Leviathan" features the well-liked coral dealer and storyteller, Nissen Piczenik. As a traditional Eastern Jew, Piczenik is trying to come to terms with the upheaval of modernism through his personal mythology. For him, the corals he sells are not only the financial bedrock of his existence but are imbued with mystical and erotic qualities:

> What the corals longed for was to be picked by divers and taken to the surface of the earth, to be cut, polished, and threaded, in order to fulfill the true purpose of their existence: namely, adorning beautiful peasant women.[52]

Piczenik desires to do more than merely embellish beautiful peasant women with precious coral jewelry. He dreams of his spiritual home, the ocean, and wants to become one with it, "the mighty, unknown sea with the immeasurable Leviathan on its bed and with all its sweet, bitter and salty mysteries."[53] Piczenik's Leviathan is not the classic sea monster; it resembles more a gatekeeper of a lost treasure, or Hobbes's incarnation of an ideal state, generating hope for the community in times of crisis. In the context of the story, the Leviathan is a ruthless businessman who sells cheaper artificial corals and eventually corrupts and ruins Piczenik. Personified in this businessman, the hegemonic structure of the Habsburg periphery becomes transparent. Modern capitalism destroys Piczenik on two levels: economically because the genuine corals become more expensive than the artificial ones, and spiritually because the corals are bereft of their mythic telos and erotic power. Having mixed fake corals with genuine ones, Piczenik loses his customers and starts to drink, and eventually decides to migrate to Canada. When the ocean liner sinks in the Atlantic, Piczenik finds his true home on the ocean bed—or, as the story's narrator puts it:

> As for Niessen Piczenik, who also drowned then and there, one cannot say that he simply drowned like the others. Rather—this can be stated with a good conscience—he went home to the corals, to the bed of the ocean, where the mighty Leviathan coils.[54]

Instead of dying, the coral dealer returns home, to the place where he belongs, although far away from the Habsburg monarchy. In other words, Roth lets Piczenik's homecoming to the corals coincide with his individual seafaring mythology.[55] Piczenik's fate holds—in Raymond Williams's definition of myth—a deeper version of human reality within its poetic realism, and thereby analyses human nature in general. One is reminded of Lazar von Hellenbach's hero Alexander in *Insel Mellonta*, whose inability to awaken from his dreamlike fantasy world represents his utopian aim to eliminate violence and suffering from any given society. Alexander's dream, just like Piczenik's homecoming, confirms the vision of a solitary seer whose only misfortune is to live before his time. Piczenik's final destination in the ocean's depths magically resolves the historic dilemma of East European Jews at the dawn of the Second World War. Ordinary human beings, like Roth's other characters, exist on terra firma, but their movements and motivations are equally well expressed, if not better depicted, in seafaring metaphors. We speak of comforting harbors, islands of happiness, but also dangerous reefs, tempests, and sea leviathans. The perils of the deep oceanic blue elevate the safety of the harbor to an appealing time and space of primordial substance. Reversing this reading, Roth uses a shipwreck, rather than the safe harbor, to produce a metaphorical homecoming. The irony of the metaphor is evident when Piczenik achieves his self-realization while drowning in these oceanic feelings.

That Roth was in fact less hopeful about the plight of the Jewish population living at the periphery of the Habsburg Empire is shown in his seminal essay collection *The Wandering Jews*, which was first published in 1927. The essayistic vignettes address their embattled situation in a nonfictional mode, as Roth's translator Michael Hofmann points out: "Roth wrote these evocative dispatches to warn against the false comfort of Jewish assimilation and to lay bare the schism between Western and Eastern Jews, reflected on the concept of Jewish identity, and looked with foreboding at Germany's future."[56] Instead of creating another mythological image, Roth's reporting literally demystifies the living condition of Jews in Eastern Europe. The first part of the book discusses the lives, mores, and religion of the Jewish communities in Galicia. The second part, however, portrays Jews in Western Europe and abroad. Needless to say, Roth touches upon the omnipresent anti-Semitism of the time, as well as how assimilated Western Jews distanced themselves from their Eastern European co-religionists. If their grandfathers still engaged in a desperate struggle with Jehovah, begging him for forgiveness, the prayers of their clean-shaven Western grandsons had become empty and formulaic.

Most interestingly for our purpose, Roth implicitly rejects Theodor Herzl's colonial utopia. In a nutshell, he does not see Zionism as a viable way out of the plight of East European Jewry. Zionism and Jewish nationhood represent for Roth enlightened idealism, which delivers at best "a partial solution to the Jewish question."[57] Hence, Roth opposes the motion towards a Jewish nationhood, since "Jews constitute a 'national minority' in many countries."[58] For him, such national minorities will only attain freedom and equality once their host countries achieve sufficient economic stability to allow for sympathy for the plight of others. The remarkable exception to this predicament is Paris, where Roth sees, in Hillary H. Herzog's words, a "possibility of a positive form of assimilation and acculturation being carried out across two generations."[59] Other than in Paris, Roth regards the general conditions for Jews in Europe as getting steadily worse, as he put in the preface of the second edition in 1937: "It is—failing some divine intervention—hardly possible to believe that the 'host nations' will find such freedom and such dignity."[60] Roth's sobering assessment of the prospects for Jews from Central Europe underscores that his (constant) dialogue with the past of the Habsburg Empire in his historical novels helps him to better comprehend present problems.

In his influential study *The Historical Novel* (1937), George Lukács demands of realist writers to portray societal forces that eventuate progress. For Lukács, Roth does not qualify as a historical novelist because he fails to portray the discontent of the oppressed as an important factor in the demise of the empire. Instead of following Lukács' Marxist reading of Roth's *Radetzkymarsch*, I suggest that Roth's marginal characters embody what Raymond Williams calls a social realism with its "lived dominance and subordination"[61] of the hegemonic society. Roth's mythological underpinning provides the reader with enough hope to bear with the oppression of contingency in the Habsburg monarchy. In "Leviathan," Roth's anti-modernism seeks to substantiate a cultural critique through the use of mythology. Suffice it to say, many left-liberal critics have criticized Roth's polemics against modernism and see in his prose a nostalgic longing for a clerical monarchy. More recently, Jörg Fauser delivered perhaps the best defense of Roth's political romanticism:

> The Jewish humanist didn't move his spiritual home and his human desire into the lost world of the Catholic monarchy because he was caught in the past, but for him the spiritual vision of an ancient kingdom—with its underlying dream of religious freedom, human tolerance, and the laissez vivre—promised more substance than bigwig democracy, fascism or communism, separately or together.[62]

Spiritual freedom and tolerance for Roth were apparently a higher good than democratic equality, and although he vehemently opposed war profiteering, nationalism, and human rights violations, he "seldom wrote about workers except to deplore their lack of cultural ambition."[63] Neither *The Wandering Jews* nor "Leviathan" offers an immediate answer to the dire social situation of Eastern European Jewry, since migration to the West comes at the cost of self-effacing assimilation. Hence, in "Leviathan," Piczenik's soul is spared from the spiritually empty existence in exile, when he finds his true home in the ocean. Assuming a mythical alternative space between the materialistic West and the desolate East saves his identity.

*

At the beginning of Roth's *Kapuzinergruft*, the character, a Polish count Chojnicki, states prophetically: "The essence of Austria is not the center, but the periphery."[64] As we have seen in Chapter 1, half a century earlier Leopold von Sacher-Masoch conveyed a similar sentiment in his novels, although he is best known for his ingenious portrayal of weak, subservient male characters at the fringe of the empire, who were subsequently denounced by the Viennese psychiatrist Richard von Krafft-Ebing as masochists. Less often, Roth's prose is characterized by his deployment of weak, subservient male protagonists at Habsburg's periphery. But just like any self-defeating protagonist in Sacher-Masoch's short stories, Roth's protagonist in *Kapuzinergruft*, Franz Ferdinand Trotta, renounces his sensual desires in a similar manner. Upon closer examination, it appears that Roth's elegies of the Habsburg Empire are populated with emasculated protagonists trying to tackle the windmills of modernity, never quite able to deal with the loss of Habsburg's glory. Crucial to Roth's narrative constellation is the interplay between disempowered men and female characters at the margins. If the periphery serves as a site of cultural critique of the metropolis and modernity, women are emblematic for the loss incurred by the relentless historical progress in Central Europe.

In *Kapuzinergruft*, Roth tells the story of Franz Ferdinand Trotta, in whose individual fate the downfall of the entire Habsburg monarchy is reflected. Up to the summer of 1914, Trotta and his friends are part of Vienna's *jeunesse dorée* (gilded youth), who enjoyed a decadent lifestyle, heedless of the urgency of the historical moment. When World War I finally breaks out, Trotta enlists as a lieutenant in the same infantry regiment that his Slovenian cousin, the farmer Branco, and his friend the coachman Manes Reisinger belong to. Instead of experiencing the excitement of battle alien to his everyday life in Vienna, the Russian army quickly captures Trotta, and he returns to Vienna only after the war is over. The civilian life in the new republic presents unforeseen challenges to Trotta, and personal and business affairs take a beating. In the end, in order to survive, Trotta is forced to open a boarding house in his heavily mortgaged family home. Most of his guests are his insolvent prewar friends. When his mother—an emblem of the bygone imperial past—dies, Trotta aimlessly cruises around Viennese coffee houses in pursuit of companionship. Finally, by March 1938, when Hitler annexes Austria to Germany, Franz Ferdinand sees no escape except to seek shelter in the emperor's crypt, the gravesite of the entire Habsburg dynasty, and raises the rhetorical, yet existential, question: "Where should I, a Trotta, now go?"

The novel *Kapuzinergruft* is a first-person narrative, and the narrator—the war veteran Franz Ferdinand—is, far from being omniscient or in control of the unfolding events, unreliable at several points in the story. Neither the subjective point of view, nor the past–present structure of the narrative invites comparison with the colonial utopias of von Sacher-Masoch, von Hellenbach, Hertzka, or

Herzl. Instead, the novel presents a situation in which all of Central Europe's erstwhile utopian potential has come to a shrieking halt. The general tone of the book is somber, if not morbid, since an image or reference to death appears on almost every other page. Without showing the aptitude or inclination to change the present situation, Roth's characters review Austria's missed chances for a better future. Ostensibly, the force of the historical circumstances paralyzes Franz Ferdinand Trotta. As mentioned earlier, at the end of the narrative, in March 1938, Franz Ferdinand is left with nowhere to go and nothing left to lose. In other words, Roth construes a teleology in which all the past opportunities to intervene on the political plane culminate in Austria's darkest hour. Franz Ferdinand's fatal passivity in the postwar period derives from the chic attitude of the pleasure-seeking and ennui-combating upper class youth before World War I. Their voluntary indifference to civic concerns and public politics opposes the mindset of civic leaders such as Hertzka and Herzl a generation earlier. Interestingly, Franz Ferdinand's introduction of his father aptly reflects the generational rift:

> And as his son, I should be allowed at this moment to say that I imagine that my father might have changed the course of history, if he had lived longer. But he died about one and a half years before Franz Ferdinand's assassination. I am his only son, and in his will he named me as the heir of his ideas. It was not for nothing that he had me baptized as Franz Ferdinand. But at that time, I was too young and foolish, if not to say careless. In any case, I was frivolous. I took, as they say, each day as it came.[65]

While his "rebellious and patriotic"[66] father conjures up a utopia to save the Habsburg monarchy, his son—and heir to his ideas—remains inward and idle. Carl E. Schorske explains the dynamics of generational tension in prewar Vienna: "Where the fathers had lived by naïve faith as the underpinning of social action, the sons, suffering from loss of control over life and destiny, can approach public life only as private option; hence they often withdraw to the life of art and instinct."[67]

The fictional Franz Ferdinand Trotta was born in 1891, which would make his father a contemporary of Hertzka's and Herzl's. That is to say, they were part of the generation that came of age in Vienna during the decline of liberalism and the surge of nationalism and anti-Semitism. As Schorske puts it: "For all these men the rise of anti-Semitism was not the first trauma, but the second of their short lives: as the liberal culture of their fathers had failed them in the 1880s. Having quested for a new, holistic cultural community as Germans, they found themselves threatened and abandoned to a new isolation as Jews."[68] It is not the traumas that have been inflicted that cause the generational difference between these fathers and sons, but while the latter remain fatally idle, the former were inspired to create blueprints for societal changes. Hence, both Hertzka and Herzl, of the older generation, were not only prominent journalists for the

Neue Freie Presse, the leading Viennese daily, but they founded powerful civic movements to combat the anti-Semitism of their day.

But in terms of blueprints for a utopia, *Kapuzinergruft* aligns itself more closely to von Sacher-Masoch's idea of a pan-Slavistic empire than to Hertzka's global community in East Africa, or Herzl's Zionist haven in Palestine. The clearest expression of this is found at the beginning of the novel, when Franz Ferdinand introduces his father: "My father dreamt of a Slavic kingdom under the governance of the Habsburgs. He dreamt of a monarchy comprised of Austrians, Hungarians, and Slavs."[69] Later in the text, Franz Ferdinand remembers his father saying: "The colorful contentment of the capital and residential city Vienna nourished itself quite obviously . . . from the crown countries' tragic love of Austria: tragic, because it remained unreciprocated."[70] Franz Ferdinand's father clearly provides the general direction of criticism of the empire, although his fatherly friend Count Chojnicki ultimately names the culprit for the k. & k. monarchy's demise: "Not our Czechs, not our Serbs, not our Poles, not our Ruthenians betrayed us, but our Germans, the state's folk."[71] Count Chojnicki, and through him Joseph Roth, condemns the *Nibelungentreue* of Vienna's ethnically German ruling class, which always aligned itself with German art and culture rather than venturing out and exploring what the crown lands of the monarchy in the east had to offer. Unfortunately, the creative generation of Franz Ferdinand's father was too old or had deceased by the interwar period; and the younger generation, who had lost their world in the course of the war, turned out to be ill-equipped to engage with politics at a productive level. As mentioned earlier, Roth's *Kapuzinergruft* has often been criticized as a backward-facing utopia, and while it is true that it gives ample expression to its author's existential anguish and loss of homeland, one should not overlook its abundant critiques of Austria's past and present political failures.[72]

Conclusion

Tropics of Vienna has brought together three related discourses: utopianism, postcolonialism, and exoticism in late nineteenth- and, to a lesser extent, early twentieth-century narratives, which are filled with conscious and unconscious aspirations for an alternative social and spatial organization. Through the design of colonial utopias, Austrian liberal writers Leopold von Sacher-Masoch, Lazar von Hellenbach, Theodor Hertzka, and Theodor Herzl contributed to the contemporary debates on topics such as the nation-state, sex and gender relations, and anti-Semitism. These authors addressed issues pertinent to Viennese society, but by doing so, raised far more substantial questions and concerns about Austrian national identity, cultural traditions, and values. While these colonial utopias tend to employ different rhetorical and narrative strategies, each text creates a unique visionary space. Moreover, the symbolic enactment of colonial communities reinforces—and at the same time negates—a peaceful Habsburg Empire, which was allegedly bypassed by vicious European colonial practices.

The authors in *Tropics of Vienna* consistently imagined what an overseas Habsburg Empire might have looked like. As it turns out, their blueprints were counter-images of contemporary Vienna. In reaction to the great economic depression between 1873 and 1896, nationalism and chauvinism were on the rise while the waves of immigrants from the margins of the Habsburg Empire to Vienna in the 1880s challenged the dominance of liberalism in the politics of the monarchy. Nonetheless, not all colonial utopias discussed in *Tropics of Vienna* propose the same economic or social remedies to rescue Austria from the impending crisis. While Hertzka's Freeland amendment and von Hellenbach's communal inheritance idea recommend economic reforms, von Sacher-Masoch's German-speaking pan-Slavism and Herzl's Zionism offer wide-ranging sociopolitical changes.

A closer look at the utopias that became more widely available has revealed the influence of less-known utopian narratives. For one thing, we have seen that Herzl's Zionist manifesto *Altneuland*, which has become one of the most successful utopias, was greatly inspired by Hertzka's novel *Freiland*, which was largely forgotten in the twentieth century. For another, von Sacher-Masoch, who is today primarily known for his novella *Venus in Furs*, turns out to have been profoundly concerned with the emancipation of the Eastern margins of the Habsburg Empire, as expressed in his colonial utopia *Paradies am Dniester*. Ironically, the para-psychologist von Hellenbach produces by far the most intriguing and complex utopian narrative of these Viennese fin-de-siècle writers. His *Insel Mellonta* depicts an unprejudiced tropical society in a style that is readily reminiscent of Jules Verne and Charles Fourier.

The colonial utopias of *Tropics of Vienna*, when taken together, produce a cohesive picture of Austria viewed from afar. The distant places overseas may indeed have remained for the most part unexplored and uncontested, but the displacement clearly awakened a consuming interest in an elusive ideal. Moreover, as mentioned earlier, these utopian schemas address the decisive conflicts in the Vienna of their day. In addition to the enormous economic crisis and mass immigration from Eastern Europe, these problems included fear of and anxiety about the proletarian masses, anti-Semitism, a restrained libidinal economy, and power issues between the genders. Thus, these utopias employ a notion of the otherness of space as a literary device to compensate for the critical situation in Vienna by projecting blueprints for utopian societies elsewhere. The relationship between the foreign and the familiar in these texts is dialectical, so that what is distant and what is close collapse into each other. Nevertheless, the redemptive quality of another space neither takes the realities of the other area into account, nor does it reflect on European economic exploitation of the respective colonies in Africa, East Asia, and South America.

My critical reading of these utopian narratives has sought to tease out moments in which they produce, rather than reflect, the colonial and utopian discourse of their time. These narratives may not have altered the historical course of the Habsburg monarchy, but they certainly attest to active civic and political engagement. Moreover, they served as an inspiration to Viennese writers of the twentieth century; one might argue, for example, that Arthur Schnitzler and Sigmund Freud developed a modernist mode of utopia: a colonization of the mind. Put differently, while the utopian narratives discussed in *Tropics of Vienna* may have created unrealized political programs and social alternatives to the contemporary condition of the Habsburg Empire in the late nineteenth century, they also contested and subverted the idea of a homogeneous empire, and thereby continue to resonate in the twenty-first century.

Notes

1. Chris Bongie, *Exotic Memories: Literature, Colonialism, and the Fin de Siècle* (Stanford, 1991), 4–5.
2. Derek J. Penslar, *Zionism and Technology: The Engineering of Jewish Settlement in Palestine, 1870–1918* (Bloomington, 1991), 3.
3. Robert Müller, *Tropen: Der Mythos der Reise. Urkunden eines deutschen Ingenieurs* (Munich, 1915), 195.
4. See Angelika Jacobs, "'Wildnis' als Wunschtraum westlicher 'Zivilisation': Zur Kritik des Exotismus in Peter Altenbergs *Ashantee* und Robert Müllers *Tropen*," *Kakanien revisited* 3 (2002): 1–12.
5. "The exoticist produces pictures, which as a projection of his inner being are intended to compensate for his alienated view of self and reality." Wolfgang Reif, *Zivilisationsflucht und literarische Wunschträume: Der exotistische Roman im ersten Viertel des 20. Jahrhunderts* (Stuttgart, 1975), 11.
6. At the time, writers such as Robert Musil, Hermann Hesse, and Alfred Döblin, among others, wrote favorable reviews of Müller's novel *Tropen*. See *Expressionismus—Aktivismus—Exotismus. Studien zum literarischen Werk Robert Müllers 1887–1924*, ed. Helmut Kreuzer and Günter Helmes (Göttingen, 1981). Interestingly, Jennifer Anna Gosetti-Ferencei does not even mention Müller's novel in her *Exotic Spaces in German Modernism* (Oxford, 2011).
7. See Michael C. Frank's insightful essay on Müller's "forgotten" text. "Die Exotik von Robert Müllers *Tropen* (1915): Begegnung mit einem fremden Roman," in *Vergessene Texte*, ed. Aleida Assmann and Michael C. Frank (Konstanz, 2004), 187–206.
8. For further biographical information, consult Thomas Schwarz, *Robert Müllers Tropen: Ein Reiseführer in den imperialen Exotismus* (Heidelberg, 2006), 33–45.
9. Most prominently, in his pamphlet "Karl Kraus oder Dalai Lama" (1914), Müller claims that Kraus's hatred of the media was triggered by his exclusion from mainstream publications. Although some of Müller's claims are closer to fantasy than fact, the virtuosity of Müller's style suits its subject Kraus.
10. Günter Helmes edited Robert Müller's complete works in thirteen volumes (*Werkausgabe in Einzelbänden*, 1992–1997).

11. "[Ein] Kulturkrieg, den Europa, zwischen Amerikanismus und Asiatismus ... eingeklemmt, wird zu führen haben." Qtd. in Günter Helmes, *Robert Müller: Themen und Tendenzen seiner publizistischen Schriften* (Frankfurt, 1986), 121.
12. "moderne, sozial interessierte und physisch executiv gewordene Psyche." Ibid., 122.
13. "eine Lust zum Rückfall in den Djungel." Ibid.
14. "ethischer Fatalismus, Götzendienst vorm Instinkte, Exotismus, Verketzung des Intellekts." Ibid.
15. "Tropen ... In Wirklichkeit sind das nur Landstriche, in denen Eisenbahnen gebaut, Malariasümpfe trockengelegt, ungeheure erträgnisreiche Prärien kultiviert, Metalladern exploitiert und ein paar Schwarze und Gelbe gehenkt werden müssen." Robert Müller, *Kritische Schriften I*, ed. Jürgen Berners (Paderborn, 1993), 167.
16. "Die Aufgabe Österreich-Ungarns ist es, den *deutschen Gedanken ins Mittelmeer zu tragen*. ... Wenn die Bagdad-Bahn gebaut ist und wenn mit ihrer Hilfe das grosse *arabische Reich deutscher Signatur*—wie heute das Indien Englands—gegründet wird, als nordöstliche Fortsetzung des zentralafrikanischen Reiches zu einem *deutschen Kolonisationsgürtel am Äquator*, ... dann wenn dieses grosse deutsche Werk, das wir alle im Sinn tragen sollen, im Werden ist, wird sich der Nutzen Österreichs erweisen." Robert Müller, *Gesammelte Essays*, ed. Michael Matthias Schardt (Paderborn, 1995), 22–23. (Italics in the original).
17. "[E]iner Kategorie von Wesenszügen, die mit der Romantik das Emotionelle und Schraubung eines Erlebnisses gemeinsam haben, aber nördlicher bleiben." Qtd. in Helmes, *Robert Müller*, 124.
18. "[Österreich müsse] durch Wirtschaft im grossen Stil [durch seine] hohe ausgebildete Intuition, [durch seine] schon aus Mischung entstandene Kunst und seine formende Sinnlichkeit ... ein fremdsprachiges, ethnologisch schattiertes Deutschtum, einen überlegenen imperialen Reichsmenschen erschliessen." Müller, *Gesammelte Essays*, 191.
19. "Atlantis, das bedeutet [für Müller] Heimkehr ins verlorene Paradies und Vorwärtsstürmen in einen unermesslichen Kontinent. Es ist der Mythos der konservativen Utopie." Hans Heinz Hahnl, "Atlantische Verlockungen (Nachwort)." Müller, *Gesammelte Essays*, 302.
20. "Das Endziel aller Staatsentwicklung ist die Staatslosigkeit. ... Um den Staat loszuwerden, war gewiss der beste Weg, den imperialen Staat zu fördern." Ibid., 202.
21. "Die Elemente quasi faschistischen Gedankenguts finden sich nicht mehr in Müllers Nachkriegsschriften. Rassische und nationale Vorurteile verschwinden zu einem gewissen Grad." Helmes, *Robert Müller*, 69.
22. "So mögen denn die Sukzessionsstaaten der [Habsburger] Monarchie unter der Kontrolle der Internationalen Liga sowohl mit Produkten- als auch Siedlungskolonien beteiligt werden. *Afrikanisch-Österreichisch* ist geradezu die ideale Lösung aller donaustaatlichen sozialen und wirtschaftlichen Fragen. Die Lösung zusammen mit der Kongressidee der diasporierten Völker bereitet auch eine höhere politische Form des Erdballes überhaupt vor!" Robert Müller, *Kritische Schriften II*, ed. Ernst Fischer (Paderborn, 1993), 343. (Italics in the original).
23. "Eigenschaften aus einer modernen Kultur, eine zerebrale *Spannung*, gemischt mit der eigentümlichen *Relaxation* des Urmenschen." Müller, *Tropen: Der Mythos der Reise*, 36. (Italics in the original).
24. A message German emperor Wilhelm II sent to Paul Kruger, the president of the Transvaal Republic in 1896. Müller's fictional character Slim is not only a friend of Wilhelm II, but teaches him how to execute colonial might.
25. "seiner schönsten gewalttätigen Triebe." Müller, *Tropen: Der Mythos der Reise*, 195.

26. "Nach wie vor schlängelten wir uns dem Fluss entlang, dessen Ufer, so unausgesprochen wie die eines Sumpfes, sich nie und niemals zu einer schönen Parallelität bequemen wollten. Aus dem Reich des Waldes gelockt, standen immer ein paar der Bäume im Wasser." Ibid., 19.
27. "Ich denke an den Wald, den Urwald, an die Sinnlichkeit dieser Natur, ihre Rohheit, ihren ursprünglichen Elan, ihren schrecklichen, verwirrenden Trieb, ich denke an *den Trieb*, die Tropen im Gemüt des weissen Mannes. Die Frau nämlich ist ihrerseits nie aus den Tropen herauskommen." Ibid., 29. (Italics in the original).
28. "Kampf der Rassen und Sinne." Ibid., 70.
29. "So gewiss ist es aber auch, dass die weibliche Natur der Tropen in jener weiblichen einer modernen Grossstadt wiederkehrt, und, dass der Schritt vom europäischesten Europa mitten in den Djungle hinein nicht so abenteuerlich ausfällt, als man es sich erwartet hat. Denn was immer man erlebt, es ist stets dasselbe Abenteuer, es ist gleichgültig, ob man unter einen Panter oder einen Autobus gerät, das Gleichgültigste aber ist, ob *sie* Zana oder Fräulein Soundso heisst." Ibid., 29. (Italics in the original).
30. "Da war ich nun mein eigener Herr, Herr einer neuen Hütte. Sie lag, wie die erste, am zweiten Ring. . . . Slim hatte eine schöne Hütte am ersten Ring erhalten, der Holländer gleich mir die seine am zweiten. . . . Draußen am dritten Kreis, in der Vorschanze bei den Proleten, Unedlen und Unterdrückten, die am ersten daran glauben müssen, wenn ein feindlicher Stamm das Nest berennt, wohnen noch die Überbleibsel des männlichen [Clans]." Ibid., 83–84.
31. "Heute große Vorstellung 'Europa in Pomacco.' Kinder haben freien Zutritt! Die weißesten Indianer der Welt! Ein Stamm ohne Füße, einzig in seiner Art! Der dickste Mann der Welt, besondere Attraktion für das weibliche Geschlecht, klein und groß! Hereinspaziert!" Ibid., 80.
32. "Mit der Exotik war ich fertig. Dies war ein veralteter Standpunkt. Impressionismus? Er war falsch; er war ein Defekt der Beobachtung. Er war nicht tief, absolut nicht tief." Ibid., 96.
33. "Die Aussenperspektive auf die westlichen Kulturen in Müllers *Tropen*-Roman demonstriert in erster Linie, wie bedrohlich das vermeintlich Eigene sein kann und fordert den phantastischen Modus der Utopie." Angelika Jacobs, "Wildnis," 11.
34. Michael Hardt and Antonio Negri, *Multitude* (New York, 2004), xiv.
35. Robert Musil, *Der Mann ohne Eigenschaften*, vol. 1 (Reinbek, 2005), 32.
36. Russell A. Berman, *Enlightenment or Empire: Colonial Discourse in German Culture* (Lincoln, NE and London, 1998), 225.
37. Frank, "Die Exotik," 196.
38. "Ein englischer Abenteurer, halb Kaufmann, halb Pirat, hatte dort nach dem Muster der Robert Cliveschen ostindischen Kompagnie einen Staat von freien Unternehmern aller Rassen begründet. Es war ein vollständiges, freihändiges gegründetes Reich; die Promiskuität unter den Kapernfahrern weisser, gelber und brauner Rassen und die üppige Liebesproduktion der geraubten schönsten Weiber von Vorderindien bis Australien schwemmte ein ganz neues Rassengebilde zusammen." Qtd. in Bettina Pflaum, *Politischer Expressionismus: Aktivismus im fiktionalen Werk Robert Müllers* (Paderborn, 2008), 119.
39. Stefan Jonsson, *Subject without Nation: Robert Musil and the History of Identity* (Durham, NC, 2000), 6.
40. Ibid., 7.
41. "Typus des beginnenden 20. Jahrhunderts vor dem grossen Kriege, ein Mann ohne eigentliche Begabung und ohne Character." Müller, *Tropen: Der Mythos der Reise*, 7.

Suffice it to say, the "intertextual" similarities to the title of Robert Musil's novel *Mann ohne Eigenschaften* (1930–43) are hard to overlook.

42. "Bis auf geringfügige wertlose persönliche Erinnerungen bleibt er auch nach dem Tode des Individuums in *anderen* erhalten." Qtd. in Frank, "Die Exotik," 203.
43. "Österreich ist nicht in den Alpen zu finden, Gemsen gibt es dort und Edelweiss und Enzian, aber kaum eine Ahnung von einem Doppeladler. Die österreichische Substanz wird genährt und immer wieder aufgefüllt von den Kronländern." Joseph Roth, *Die Kapuzinergruft* (Munich, 2003), 17.
44. See Hans Heinz Hahnl's essay, "Atlantische Verlockungen," in Müller, *Gesammelte Essays* 304–5.
45. Roth's critics routinely employ the expression *rückwärts gewandte Utopie* (backward-facing utopia) to describe his alleged *gegenwartsfremden Monarchismus* (monarchism alienated from the present) (Hilde Spiel). For further examples of this line of criticism, consult Kati Tonkin's *Joseph Roth's March into History: From the Early Novels to Radetzkymarsch and Die Kapuzinergruft* (Rochester, 2008), 6.
46. Tellingly, the first chapter of Stefan Zweig's *Die Welt von Gestern: Erinnerungen eines Europäers* (1944) is entitled "Die Welt der Sicherheit."
47. Following Roth reportage as an art form, "ist niemals von der Realität gelöst, sondern in Wahrheit—durch das Mittel der Sprache—umgewandelte Realität." Qtd. in Joseph Roth, *Das journalistische Werk 1929–1939*, ed. by Klaus Westermann (Cologne, 1991), 157.
48. Raymond Williams, *Keywords: A Vocabulary of Culture and Society* (Oxford, 1983), 210–12.
49. *Hotel Savoy* (1924), *Die Rebellion* (1924), *Die Flucht ohne Ende* (1927), and *Zipper und sein Vater* (1928) all portray drifters and refugees fighting against the windmills of modernity in postwar Europe.
50. *The Zizek Reader*, ed. Elizabeth and Edmond Wright (Oxford, 1999), 78.
51. See Phillip E. Wegner, *Imaginary Communities: Utopia, the Nation, and the Spatial Histories of Modernity* (Berkeley, 2002), 36.
52. "Es war die Sehnsucht der Korallen, von den Tauchern gepflückt und an die Oberfläche gebracht, geschnitten, geschliffen und aufgefädelt zu werden, um endlich ihrem eigentlichen Daseinszweck zu dienen: nämlich der Schmuck schöner Bäuerinnen zu werden." Joseph Roth, *Romane und Erzählungen 1936–1940*, ed. Fritz Hackert (Cologne, 1991), 546.
53. "[D]as mächtige, unerforschte Meer mit dem unermesslichen Leviathan auf dem Grund mit all seinen süßen, bitteren und salzigen Geheimnissen." Ibid., 575.
54. "Was aber Piczenik betrifft, der ebenfalls damals unterging, so kann man nicht sagen, er sei einfach ertrunken wie die anderen. Er war vielmehr—dies kann man mit gutem Gewissen erzählen—zu den Korallen heimgekehrt, auf den Grund des Ozeans, wo der gewaltige Leviathan sich ringelt." Ibid., 574.
55. See Wolfgang Müller-Funk, "Landnahme und Schiffsbruch: Carl Schmitt, Theodor Herzl, Joseph Roth. Eine Forschungsskizze," in *Judentum und Antisemitismus: Studien zur Literatur und Germanistik in Österreich*, ed. Anne Betten and Konstanze Fliedl (Berlin, 2003), 44–45.
56. Joseph Roth, *The Wandering Jews*, trans. Michael Hofmann (New York, 2001), back cover.
57. Ibid., 136.
58. Ibid., 17.

59. Hillary Hope Herzog, *"Vienna Is Different": Jewish Writers in Austria from the Fin de Siècle to the Present* (New York, 2011), 138.
60. Roth, *Wandering Jews*, 137.
61. Raymond Williams, *Marxism and Literature* (Oxford, 1977), 110.
62. "Der jüdische Humanist verlegte seine geistige Heimat und seine menschliche Sehnsucht nicht deshalb in die versunkene Welt der katholischen Monarchie, weil er ein spintisierender Vorgestriger war, sondern weil für ihn allein schon die geistige Vision des alten Reichs, der ihm zugrunde liegende Traum von religiöser Freiheit, menschenrespektierender Toleranz, Laissez-vivre mehr Substanz enthielt als Bonzen-Demokratie, Faschismus, Kommunismus einzeln und zusammen." Jörg Fauser, *Lesestoff. Von Joseph Roth bis Eric Ambler* (Frankfurt, 2003), 66.
63. Ritchie Robertson, "1918," in *Yale Companion to Jewish Writing and Thought in German Culture 1096–1996*, ed. Sander L. Gilman and Jack Zipes, 355–62 (New Haven, CT, 1996), 356.
64. The entire passage reads: "Ich will damit sagen, dass nur diesem verrückten Europa der Nationalstaaten und der Nationalismen das Selbstverständliche sonderbar erscheint. Freilich sind es die Slowenen, die polnischen und ruthenischen Galizianer, die Kaftanjuden aus Boryslaw, die Pferdehändler aus der Bacska, die Moslems aus Sarajevo, die Maronibrater aus Mostar, die 'Gott erhalte' singen. Aber die deutschen Studenten aus Brünn und Eger, die Zahnärzte, Apotheker, Friseurgehilfen, Kunstphotographen aus Linz, Graz, Knittelfeld, die Kröpfe aus den Alpentälern, sie alle singen 'Die Wacht am Rhein.' Österreich wird an dieser Nibelungentreue zugrunde gehn, meine Herren! Das Wesen Österreichs ist nicht Zentrum, sondern Peripherie." Roth, *Die Kapuzinergruft*, 17.
65. "Und mir, der ich sein Sohn bin, möge an dieser Stelle gestattet sein, zu sagen, dass ich mir einbilde, mein Vater hätte vielleicht den Gang der Geschichte verändern können, wenn er länger gelebt hätte. Aber er starb, etwa anderthalb Jahre vor der Ermordung Franz Ferdinands. Ich bin sein einziger Sohn. In seinem Testament hatte er mich zum Erben seiner Ideen bestimmt. Nicht umsonst hatte er mich auf den Namen Franz Ferdinand taufen lassen. Aber ich war damals zu jung und töricht, um nicht zu sagen leichtsinnig. Leichtfertig war ich auf jeden Fall. Ich lebte damals, wie man so sagt: in den Tag hinein." Ibid., 7.
66. "Er war ein Rebell und ein Patriot, mein Vater—eine Spezies, die es nur im alten Österreich-Ungarn gegeben hat." Ibid., 6.
67. Carl E. Schorske, *Thinking with History: Explorations in the Passage to Modernism* (Princeton, NJ, 2001), 148.
68. Ibid., 145.
69. "Mein Vater träumte von einem slawischen Königreich unter der Herrschaft der Habsburger. Er träumte von einer Monarchie der Österreicher, Ungarn und Slawen." Roth, *Kapuzinergruft*, 7.
70. "Die bunte Heiterkeit der Reichs-, Haupt- und Residenzstadt nährte sich ganz deutlich ... von der tragischen Liebe der Kronländer zu Österreich: der tragischen, weil ewig unerwiderten." Ibid., 72.
71. "Nicht unsere Tschechen, nicht unsere Serben, nicht unsere Polen, nicht unsere Ruthenen haben [uns] verraten, sondern nur unsere Deutschen, das Staatsvolk." Ibid., 140.
72. Kati Tonkin rightfully suggests that it was "not Roth who has been searching vainly for his fatherland in the lost world of the Habsburg monarchy but the narrator." Tonkin, *Joseph Roth*, 191.

Bibliography

Berman, Russell A. *Enlightenment or Empire: Colonial Discourse in German Culture*. Lincoln, NE and London: University of Nebraska Press, 1998.
Bongie, Chris. *Exotic Memories: Literature, Colonialism, and the Fin de Siècle*. Stanford, CA: Stanford University Press, 1991.
Buch, Hans Christoph. *Die Nähe und die Ferne: Bausteine zu einer Poetik des kolonialen Blicks*. Frankfurt: Suhrkamp, 1991.
Fauser, Jörg. *Lesestoff. Von Joseph Roth bis Eric Ambler*. Frankfurt: Neue Kritik, 2003.
Frank, Michael C. "Die Exotik von Robert Müllers *Tropen* (1915): Begegnung mit einem fremden Roman." In *Vergessene Texte*, edited by Aleida Assmann and Michael C. Frank, 187–206. Konstanz: Universitätsverlag, 2004.
Gosetti-Ferencei, Jennifer Anna. *Exotic Spaces in German Modernism*. Oxford: Oxford University Press, 2011.
Hardt, Michael, and Antonio Negri. *Multitude*. New York: Penguin, 2004.
Helmes, Günter. *Robert Müller: Themen und Tendenzen seiner publizistischen Schriften*. Frankfurt: Peter Lang, 1986.
Herzog, Hillary Hope. *"Vienna Is Different": Jewish Writers in Austria from the Fin de Siècle to the Present*. New York: Berghahn Books, 2011.
Jacobs, Angelika. "'Wildnis' als Wunschtraum westlicher 'Zivilisation': Zur Kritik des Exotismus in Peter Altenbergs *Ashantee* und Robert Müllers *Tropen*." *Kakanien revisited* 3 (2002): 1–12.
Jonsson, Stefan. *Subject without Nation: Robert Musil and the History of Modern Identity*. Durham, NC: Duke University Press, 2000.
Kreuzer, Helmut and Günter Helmes, ed. *Expressionismus—Aktivismus—Exotismus. Studien zum literarischen Werk Robert Müllers 1887–1924*. Göttingen: Vandenhoeck & Ruprecht, 1981.
Mayer, Michael. *'Tropen gibt es nicht': Dekonstruktion des Exotismus*. Bielefeld: Aisthesis, 2010.
Müller-Funk, Wolfgang. "Dystopien im Kontext des habsburgischen Mythos: Joseph Roth, Ludwig Winder." In *Vom Zweck des Systems: Beiträge zur Geschichte literarischer Utopien*, edited by Árpád Bernáth, Endre Hárs, and Peter Plener, 107–24. Tübingen: Franke, 2006.
———. "Landnahme und Schiffsbruch: Carl Schmitt, Theodor Herzl, Joseph Roth." In *Judentum und Antisemitismus: Studien zur Literatur und Germanistik in Österreich*, edited by Anne Betten and Konstanze Fliedl, 32–47. Berlin: Erich Schmidt, 2003.
Müller, Robert. *Gesammelte Essays*. Edited by Michael Matthias Schardt. Paderborn: Igel, 1995.
———. *Kritische Schriften I*. Edited by Jürgen Berners. Paderborn: Igel, 1993.
———. *Kritische Schriften II*. Edited by Ernst Fischer. Paderborn: Igel, 1993.
———. *Tropen: Der Mythos der Reise. Urkunden eines deutschen Ingenieurs*. Munich: Hugo Schmidt, 1915.
Musil, Robert. *Der Mann ohne Eigenschaften*. Edited by Adolf Frise. 2 vols. 20th edition. Reinbek: Rowohlt, 2005.
Penslar, Derek J. *Zionism and Technology: The Engineering of Jewish Settlement in Palestine, 1870–1918*. Bloomington: Indiana University Press, 1991.

Pflaum, Bettina. *Politischer Expressionismus: Aktivismus im fiktionalen Werk Robert Müllers.* Paderborn: Igel, 2008.
Reif, Wolfgang. *Zivilisationsflucht und literarische Wunschträume: Der exotistische Roman im ersten Viertel des 20. Jahrhunderts.* Stuttgart: Metzler, 1975.
Robertson, Ritchie. "1918." In *Yale Companion to Jewish Writing and Thought in German Culture 1096–1996,* edited by Sander L. Gilman and Jack Zipes, 355–62. New Haven, CT: Yale University Press, 1996.
Roth, Joseph. *Die Kapuzinergruft.* Munich: dtv, 2003.
———. *Das journalistische Werk 1929–1939.* Edited by Klaus Westermann. Cologne: Kiepenheuer & Witsch, 1991.
———. *Romane und Erzählungen 1936–1940.* Edited by Fritz Hackert. Cologne: Kiepenheuer & Witsch, 1991.
———. *The Wandering Jews.* Translated by Michael Hofmann. New York: W. W. Norton, 2001.
Schorske, Carl E. *Thinking with History: Explorations in the Passage to Modernism.* Princeton, NJ: Princeton University Press, 2001.
Schwarz, Thomas. *Robert Müllers Tropen: Ein Reiseführer in den imperialen Exotismus.* Heidelberg: Synchron, 2006.
Tonkin, Katie. *Joseph Roth's March into History: From the Early Novels to* Radetzkymarsch *and* Die Kapuzinergruft. Rochester: Camden House, 2008.
Wegner, Phillip E. *Imaginary Communities: Utopia, the Nation, and the Spatial Histories of Modernity.* Berkeley: University Press of California, 2002.
Williams, Raymond. *Keywords: A Vocabulary of Culture and Society.* Oxford: Oxford University Press, 1983.
———. *Marxism and Literature.* Oxford: Oxford University Press, 1977.
Zizek, Slavoj. "Fantasy as a Political Category: A Lacanian Approach." In *The Zizek Reader,* edited by Elizabeth and Edmund Wright, 87–101. Oxford: Blackwell, 1999.

INDEX

Adorno, Theodor W., 10, 41, 62, 78, 82; *Dialectic of Enlightenment*, 10n9
Africa, 2, 3, 7, 44, 53, 54, 58, 68–70, 74–79, 93, 100, 101, 111, 114–115, 127, 128; see also Kenya, Transvaal Republic, Uganda, Zanzibar
alienation effect, 51
Altenberg, Peter, 9n3, 115, 129n4; *Aschantee*, 64n48, 112
Altneuland (Herzl), 4, 7–8, 68, 80, 84, 85, 92–103
America, 42, 113, 114
Americanism, 113
anarchy, 23, 30, 87–88, 98
Antigone (Sophocles), 48
anti-Semitism, 5, 7, 41, 42, 68, 69, 71, 72, 85, 88, 89, 90, 95, 100, 101, 102, 104, 112, 123, 126, 127, 128
Anzengruber, Ludwig, 44
Arabian Empire, 114
Arbeiterzeitung, Die, 121
Arendt, Hannah, 84
Aryan ideology, 112
Aschantee (Altenberg), 112
Asia, 21, 58, 113, 114
Asianism, 113
assimilation (Jewish), 43, 91, 123
Aus Halb-Asien (Franzos), 20
Australia, 118
Austria, 1, 2, 4, 5, 8, 17, 18, 19–22, 27, 31, 43, 50–51, 69, 70, 89, 112–114, 119–121, 125–128
Austrification (of the world), 119
Austro-Hungarian Empire, 6, 13

Bacon, Francis, 45, 79; *New Atlantis*, 45
Baghdad, 62n5, 114
Baumann, Oscar, 11
Bellamy, Edward, 39, 44, 94, 106n58; *Looking Backward: 2000–1887*, 39, 44, 94
Benjamin, Walter, 72, 81n16, 98, 107n80
Berlin, 21, 99, 121
Berman, Nina, 10n9
Berman, Russell A., 2–3, 9n5, 10n9, 10n10, 15, 21–22, 27, 33n13, 34n37, 35n60, 51, 64n51, 77, 78, 82n30, 131n36
Bildungsroman, 60, 105
Blavatsky, Helena Petrowna, 40
Bloch, Ernst, 1, 9n4, 39, 60, 62n2, 82n37, 102, 103, 104n32, 108n101
Bloch, Joseph Samuel, 5, 11n25, 71
Bongie, Chris, 111; *Exotic Memories*, 111
Bosnia-Herzegovina, 6
bourgeoisie, 39, 47, 49, 56, 57, 61, 71, 95, 96
Brazil, 52, 54, 58, 115
Brecht, Bertolt, 51
Brenner, Der, 113
Brody (Galicia), 121
Buch, Hans Christoph, 5, 10n21, 51, 58, 64n53, 103n3, 105n56
Budapest (Hungary), 69, 70

Cabet, Etienne, *Voyage en Icarie*, 94, 105n57
Cain's Legacy, see *Vermächtnis Kains* (Sacher-Masoch)
Campanella, Tomasso, *City under the Sun*, 45
capitalism, 3, 102, 104n23, 106n60, 113, 122

Central Europe, 1, 4, 6, 7, 13, 16, 18, 21, 100, 113, 120, 124, 125, 126
Chamberlain, Joseph, 80
chauvinism, 43, 49, 53, 69, 128
Christianity, 47, 54, 71, 72, 95
City under the Sun (Campanella), 45
civilization (European), 7, 20, 21, 26, 30, 44, 47, 48, 54, 56, 57, 58, 59, 68, 77, 100, 111, 116, 117
class, 4, 15, 16, 17, 24, 26, 29, 30, 39, 40, 41, 49, 50, 56, 57, 61, 65n71, 69, 79, 126, 127
collectivism, 80, 104n23
colonial discourse, 2, 3, 8, 15, 21, 51, 52, 54, 101
colonialism, vi, 2–3, 6, 7, 16, 22–23, 28, 31, 40, 51, 62, 68, 77, 82n30, 101, 112, 117–118; internal, 16, 33
community, 6, 7, 18, 19, 30, 31, 41, 43, 44, 45, 46, 47, 51, 52, 54, 55, 56, 58, 61, 88, 94, 106n61, 121, 122, 126, 127
cosmopolitanism, 8, 43, 101
Croatia, 40
cross-cultural encounter, 77, 78

Daniel Deronda (Eliot), 95
Defoe, Daniel, *Robinson Crusoe*, 46
Deleuze, Gilles, 31, 36n72
Dialectic of Enlightenment (Adorno and Horkheimer), 10n9
diaspora, 91
discourse (dominant), 7, 40, 62
Disraeli, Benjamin, 78, 106n66; *Tancred*, 95
Dniester (river), 25, 29, 35n66
Döblin, Alfred, 129n6
dominance, 18, 22, 54, 59, 111, 124, 128
Don Juan von Kolomea (von Sacher-Masoch), 15, 20, 22
Dreyfus, Alfred, 89, 104n34
dual monarchy, 49, 50
Dühring, Eugen, *Die Judenfrage als Racen-, Sitten-, und Kulturfrage*, 42

East Asia, 1, 128
economic freedom, 72
economy, 5, 7, 42, 49, 59, 61, 88, 94, 114
Eigenthum, Das (von Sacher-Masoch), 14, 29, 30, 33n33

Eliot, George, *Daniel Deronda*, 95
England, 1, 8, 42, 77, 106n65, 114, 130n16
enlightenment, 2, 8, 10n9, 70, 72, 74, 101, 119, 134
Entdeckungsreise nach Tahiti und in die Südsee (Forster), 53
Europe (Europa), 9n1, 50, 130n11, 131n29, 133n64
ethnicity, 2, 16, 24
Exotic Memories (Bongie), 111
exoticism, 8, 17, 51, 52, 111, 112, 113, 116, 117, 118, 127

Far East, 2, 29
fin-de-siècle, vi, 4, 7, 8, 41, 68, 71, 85, 92, 95, 96, 101, 111, 114, 128
Fischhof, Adolf, 8, 11n29
Forster, Georg, 2; *Entdeckungsreise nach Tahiti und in die Südsee*, 53
Fourier, Charles, 47–48
Frankfurt, 5, 88, 92
Frankfurter Zeitung, 121
Franzos, Karl Emil, *Aus Halb-Asien*, 20
free market, 72, 80
Freeland, see *Freiland*
Freiland (Hertzka), vi, 7, 11n28, 39, 68–71, 73–80, 80n1, 94, 106n59, 118, 119, 128
French Revolution, 44, 52, 56, 57, 105n46
Freud, Sigmund, 24, 129
Friss Újság, 70

Galicia, 9, 14–17, 20, 24, 25, 27, 28–30, 121–123
Gartenlaube für Österreich, 18, 19
Gauguin, Paul, 115
Gellner, Ernest, 9n7
gender, 2, 5, 13, 14, 15, 16, 22, 24, 26, 28, 30, 40, 53, 59, 87, 127
Germanization, 20, 21
Germantik, 114
Goethe, Johann Wolfgang von, 64n64, *Unterhaltungen deutscher Ausgewanderten*, 91, 105n46
Gratzke, Michael, 14, 32n3
Graz (Austria), 17, 33n19, 133n64
Greece, 53
Greek mythology, 54, 75, 105n48
Gründerkrise, 5, 49

Habermas, Jürgen, 10n22
Habsburg Empire, 2–6, 7, 8, 11n29, 13–18, 26, 27, 28, 31, 40, 41, 43, 45, 49, 51, 80, 91, 102, 111, 112, 113, 114, 117, 120–125, 128–129
Habsburg myth, *see* myth (Habsburg)
Hamburg, 62n5
Hechter, Michael, 16
hegemony, 4, 14, 19, 22
Heine, Heinrich, 88–89; *Romanzero*, 102
Hellenbach, Lazar von, v, vi, 4, 7, 39–67, 69, 118, 119, 121, 123, 125, 127, 128; works by: *Das neunzehnte und zwanzigste Jahrhundert*, 40, 41, 60; *Der ungarisch-kroatische Konflikt*, 40; *Die antisemitische Bewegung*, 42, 43, 57–58; *Die Insel Mellonta*, vi, vii, 39, 40–49, 51–62, 118, 123, 128; *Die öffentliche Meinung und die Nordbahnfrage*, 40; *Die Okkupation Bosniens und deren Folgen*, 40
Hermand, Jost, vi, 41, 57, 62n11, 65n84
Hertzka, Theodor, v, vi, 2, 4, 5, 7, 9, 11n28, 39, 68–83, 94, 106n59, 114, 118, 119, 121, 125–128; works by: "Arischer und semitischer Geist," 71; *Das sociale Problem*, 70; *Die Gesetze der sozialen Gerechtigkeit*, 69; *Eine Reise nach Freiland*, 70; *Entrückt in die Zukunft*, 70; *Freiland*, vi, 7, 11n28, 39, 68–71, 73–80, 80n1, 94, 106n59, 118, 119, 128
Herzl, Julie, 86, 103n16
Herzl, Theodor, v, vi, 4, 5, 7–9, 11n23, 11n28, 11n30, 34n37, 42, 68, 79–80, 84–110, 111, 114, 118, 120, 121, 123, 126–128; works by: *Altneuland*, 4, 7–8, 68, 80, 84, 85, 92–103; "Das lenkbare Luftschiff," 91, 92; *Das neue Ghetto*, 89–91, 104n38; *Das Palais Bourbon: Bilder aus dem französischen Parlamentsleben*, 86; *Der Flüchtling*, 103n10; *Der Judenstaat*, 11n28, 34n37, 42, 68, 80n1, 88–92, 95, 99, 100, 104n37, 105n44, 106n59; *Die Wilddiebe*, 103n10; *Zionistisches Tagebuch*, 105n41
Hess, Moses, 106n66
Hesse, Hermann, 129n6
Himalayan mountain range, 45
historical materialism, 39

history, 6, 9, 21, 30, 48, 72, 80, 89, 91, 120, 126
Hitler, Adolf, 121, 125
Hobbes, Thomas, 122
Hofmannsthal, Hugo von, 4; "Die österreichische Idee," 21
Höhnel, Ludwig Ritter von, 11
homosexuality, 15
Honold, Alexander, 6, 9n3, 11n27, 50, 64n48
Horkheimer, Max, 10; *Dialectic of Enlightenment*, 10n9
Hungary, 42, 85, 114,
hybridization, 5, 7, 27, 40, 54, 55
hyperinflation of 1923, 113

ideology, 2, 17, 18, 27, 41, 60, 113
île mystérieuse, L' (Verne), 46
imperialism, 3, 4, 5, 6, 22, 101, 111, 114, 115, 119
India, 111, 114, 118
individualism, 69, 79, 80
industrialization, 95, 105n57
Insel Mellonta, Die (von Hellenbach), vi, vii, 39, 40–49, 51–62, 118, 123, 128
Intermere (Taylor), 62
inversion, 5, 7, 21, 26, 31, 40, 52, 59, 62, 94, 117
Ireland, Ralahine community, 94, 106n61
Italy, 86

Jerusalem, 72, 93, 98, 101, 102
Jewish Question, 8, 84, 88, 89, 91, 104n34, 123
Jewish State, The, see *Judenstaat, Der* (Herzl)
Judaism, 71, 95
Juden auf der Wanderschaft (Roth), 9, 120, 123
Judenstaat, Der (Herzl), 11n28, 34n37, 42, 68, 80n1, 88–92, 95, 99, 100, 104n37, 105n44, 106n59

Kafka, Franz, *Das Schloss*, 4
Kakania (Kakanien), 1, 2, 6
Kapitulant, Der (von Sacher-Masoch), 6, 22, 24–28
Kauffmann, Kai, 14, 17, 18, 21, 32n7, 33n21, 34n38
Kenya, 5, 70, 73, 76

Koschorke, Albrecht, 14, 22, 32n5
Kraus, Karl, 90, 104n37, 114, 129n9
Kropotkin, Peter, 88
Kruger, Paul, 130n24
Kubin, Alfred, *Die andere Seite*, 4
Kürnberger, Ferdinand, 20–23, 25, 33n30, 44

land ownership, 70
Laube, Heinrich, 44
Lemberg (Galicia), 16, 33n19
Lemon, Robert, 4, 10n14
Levensohn, Lotta, 105n57, 107n91
Levi-Strauss, Claude, 55, 65, 121
liberalism, 43, 49, 69, 70, 71, 72, 85, 90, 126, 128
Libre Parole, 86
liminality, 27, 52
Lohmüller, Torben, 14, 32n7
London, 18, 85
Looking Backward: 2000–1887 (Bellamy), 39, 44, 94
Lueger, Karl, 71, 85
Lukács, George, *The Historical Novel*, 124

Magris, Claudio, 9n6, 27, 35n59, 112, 120
Magyar Hírlap, 70
Malta, 62n5
Man without Qualities, see *Mann ohne Eigenschaften* (Musil)
Mann ohne Eigenschaften (Musil), 1, 50, 118, 131–132n41
Mann, Thomas, *Tod in Venedig*, 21
Mannheim, Karl, 17, 29, 33n22
Marin, Louis, 4, 10n19–20, 48–49, 52, 63n39
Marx, Karl, 39
Masai, 70, 73, 74–76, 79
masochism, 14, 15, 22, 28, 59
mauscheln, 97
May, Karl, 75, 112
Mediterranean (Sea), 52, 62n5, 91, 93, 97
Mellonta Tauta (Poe), 48
Mennel, Barbara, 14, 32n3
Messianic holes, 72
metropolis (modern), 2, 98, 121, 125
modernism, 5, 21, 71, 79, 95, 101, 118, 119, 122; anti-Modernism, 124; reactionary, 30

More, Thomas, 49; *Utopia*, 45
Müller, Robert, v, 4, 8, 82n33, 111–119, 120, 129n10, 130, 131; works by: *Europäische Wege*, 115; *Flibustier*, 118; "Karl Kraus oder Dalai Lama," 114, 129n9; *Macht*, 114; *Tropen: Der Mythos der Reise*, 4, 8, 82n33, 111–112, 115, 117–119, 129n6, 131n33
Müller-Funk, Wolfgang, 4, 10n12, 10n17, 11n27, 33n16, 132n55
multiethnic (state), 1, 6, 7, 14, 17, 18, 19, 26, 28, 40, 49, 53, 114
Munich, 41
Musarion: oder die Philosophie der Grazien (Wieland), 53
Muselmännchen, 99
Musil, Robert, 1, 2, 4, 9n1–2, 50, 51, 64n49–50, 118, 120, 129n6, 131n35, 131n41; *Mann ohne Eigenschaften*, 1, 50, 118, 131–32n41
mutualism, 79, 88, 94, 104n23, 106n60
myth, 17, 29, 31, 54–55, 75, 105n48, 114, 120, 121–123
myth (Habsburg), 2, 9n6, 31, 112, 117, 119, 120

nationalism, 5–8, 9n7, 40, 42, 43, 49, 50, 62, 65n71, 85, 99, 119, 124, 126, 128, 133n64
natural history, 23, 52
nature, 23–25, 28, 40, 41, 54, 61, 75, 76, 77, 120, 123
Naturzustand, 30
Near East, 40, 61, 79, 85, 100, 102, 118
Neue Freie Presse, 44, 69, 86, 90, 127
New York, 112
New Yorker Herold, 112
Nietzsche, Friedrich, 113; concept of Übermensch, 112, 115
Nordau, Max, *Entartung*, 95
Noyes, John K., 14, 15, 24, 32n3, 32n7–8, 32n10, 33n14, 34n49, 87, 104n20

Oppenheimer, Franz, 70, 81n5, 88, 104n25–26
Orientalism, 4, 20, 78
Österreichische Gartenlaube, see *Gartenlaube für Österreich*
Österreichische Wochenschrift, 5, 71

Pacific (Ocean), 3, 53, 62, 93, 94, 97, 98
Palestine, 5, 8, 34n37, 68, 84, 91–102, 107n88, 127
pan-European empire, 78; democracy, 23; fantasies, 50
pan-Slavism, 6, 13, 19, 20, 23, 28, 30, 31, 84, 127, 128
paracolonial space, 6, 16, 22, 24, 27, 28, 31, 84
Paradies am Dniester (Sacher-Masoch), 6, 7, 24, 28–31, 32n4, 128
parapsychology, 40–41
Paris, 8, 18, 33n19, 55, 84–92, 102, 121, 124
Pascha, Emin, 11n25, 77
peripeteia, 45
periphery; peripheral, 1, 6, 8, 13–18, 22, 24, 26–28, 31, 113, 120, 122, 123, 125, 133n64
Pindar, Wilhelm, 104n32
Poe, Edgar Allen, *Mellonta Tauta*, 48
Popper-Lynkeus, Joseph, *Fürst Bismarck und der Antisemitismus*, 106n63
postcolonialism; postcolonial, 3–4, 10n9, 16, 127
Prague, 17, 33, 40, 49
Prel, Carl du, 39–41, 62n1, 62n9
Presse, Die, 19
progress (technological), 10n9, 69, 71, 73, 77, 79, 80, 95, 101, 113, 118
Proudhon, Pierre-Joseph, 79, 88; *Qu'est-ce que la propriéte?*, 30

race, 3, 8, 15, 22, 23, 31, 34n46, 36n71, 40, 42, 52–54, 71, 79, 95, 96, 101, 112, 115–118
Ralahine community (Ireland), 106n61
rationality, 2, 7, 20, 24, 25, 41, 64, 85, 105n57
Realpolitik, 111
reform, 5, 7, 26, 71, 95, 102, 128
Reifowitz, Ian, 5; *Imagining an Austrian Nation*, 5, 11n23
Renan, Ernest, 55, 65n71, 65n73
Rio de Janeiro, 52, 115
Robinson Crusoe (Defoe), 46
romanticism (political), 95, 114, 124
Romanzero (Heine), 102
Rosner, Carl Leopold, 44

Roth, Joseph, v, 4, 8, 111, 119–127, 132–133; works by: *Das Spinnennetz*, 121; *Juden auf der Wanderschaft*, 9, 120, 123; *Kapuzinergruft*, 119, 120, 121, 125, 127; "Leviathan," 120, 122–123; *Radetzkymarsch*, 8, 120, 124
Rousseau, Jean Jacques, 52, 59
Ruf, Der, 113
Ruskin, John, "Cestus of Aglaia," 65n66
Ruthner, Clemens, vi, 3, 10n12–13, 11n26, 11n27, 16, 33n16

Sacher-Masoch, Leopold von, v, vi, 6–7, 13–38, 50, 59, 64, 84, 87, 118, 120, 121, 125, 127, 128; editorship of *Gartenlaube für Österreich*, 18; works by: *Afrikas Semiramis*, 15; *Das Eigenthum*, 14, 29, 30, 33n33; *Der Kapitulant*, 6, 22, 24–28; *Der Hajdamak*, 20; *Der Staat*, 50; *Don Juan von Kolomea*, 15, 20, 22; *Iluj*, 22; *Judenraffael*, 22; *Jüdisches Leben*, 21; *Liebe*, 25; *Marzella oder das Märchen vom Glück*, 24, 34n48; *Paradies am Dniester*, 6, 24, 32n4, 128; *Souvenirs: Autobiographische Prosa*, 17; *Über den Werth der Kritik*, 13, 32n1; *Venus im Pelz*, 6, 13, 22, 128; *Vermächtnis Kains*, 14, 15, 22, 24, 25, 29, 50
Said, Edward, 3–4, 20, 78, 95–96, 106n67
Schiff, Emil, 105n44
Schloss, Das (Kafka), 4
Schnabel, Johann Gottfried, *Insel Felsenburg*, 46–47
Schnitzler, Arthur, 90, 129
Schönerer, Georg von, 71, 85
Schopenhauer, Arthur, 23, 42
science, 8, 10n9, 18, 41, 72, 82, 101
science fiction, 46, 48
Sebald, W. G., 21–22, 34n39
sexuality, 5, 14, 24, 26
Simmel, Georg, 43, 63n23
Slovakia, 1, 40
social conditions, 39
social injustice, 9, 120
society, 10n7, 16, 106n58, 118, 121, 123, 124; Austrian Society, 2, 8, 71, 72, 87, 90, 117, 127; multi-ethnic society, 14; society in Hertzka, 7, 68, 69, 73, 74, 78–79,

society (*continued*)
118; society in von Hellenbach, 7, 39, 43, 47, 48, 53–55, 57, 58, 61, 65n71, 128; society in Herzl, 8, 88, 89, 91, 94–96, 101–102, 111; society in von Sacher-Masoch, 14, 18, 23, 25, 27, 29; critique of society, 9, 59
Sophocles, *Antigone*, 48
South America, 1, 3, 115, 121, 128
space (empty), 3, 5, 7, 8, 15, 68, 74, 77
space (paracolonial), *see* paracolonial space
Spain, 16, 86
spiritualism, 41, 46
Spitzer, Daniel, 44
Sternberger, Dolf, 10n22
Stifter, Adalbert, 18, 33n15
Stolberg, Friedrich Leopold Graf zu, 47; *Insel*, 47, 63n35, 91, 105n46
subordination, 124
superiority (moral), 27, 54, 74, 79, 116
supremacy (cultural), 15
suspension in fantasy, 14, 31

Tahiti, 52, 53
Tancred (Disraeli), 95
Taylor, William Alexander, *Intermere*, 62
technology, 8, 77, 94, 95, 113
Thaler, Karl von, 18
theosophy, v, 7, 39, 40–41, 54, 60, 62
Tolstoy, Leo, 14, 115
transgression, 5, 7, 13, 15, 40, 52, 62, 75
transnationalism, 2, 7, 80
Transvaal Republic, 130n24
travelogue, 51, 53
Triebverzicht, 24
Tropen: Der Mythos der Reise (Müller), 4, 8, 82n33, 111–112, 115, 117–119, 129n6, 131n33
tropics, 77–78, 82n33, 100, 114–117, 128
Turgeniev, Ivan, 20

Übermensch (Nietzschean), 112, 115
Uganda, 80
Unterhaltungen deutscher Ausgewanderten (Goethe), 91, 105n46
Utopia (More), 45
utopianism, 6, 13, 69, 117, 127

utopias, vi, 1–9, 13, 14, 16–19, 22–23, 28–31, 39–62, 65n71, 68–74, 77, 79–80, 84–85, 93–95, 97, 99–100, 102–103, 105n57, 106n58, 111–112, 114, 117–119, 120–123, 127–129, 132n45; blind spots of, 48, 56, 69

Venezuela, 115
Venus im Pelz (von Sacher-Masoch), 6, 13, 22, 128
Venus in Furs, see *Venus im Pelz* (von Sacher-Masoch)
Verfassungspatriotismus, 5, 10
Verne, Jules, 46, 128; *L'île mystérieuse*, 46
Vielvölkerstaat, 119
Vienna, 62, 85–87, 90, 92, 112–113, 125, 126; anti-Semitism, 5, 7, 8, 42, 68, 69, 71–73, 77, 85, 90, 93, 96, 99, 102–103, 104n34, 111; bourgeoisie, 26, 49; coffee houses, 51, 96, 125; critique of Vienna, 7, 68, 95, 97, 117, 118, 121, 127; fin-de-siècle and modernism, 21, 71, 85, 95, 101, 119; image of Vienna, 5, 79, 84, 93, 94, 102, 116, 127, 128; philosophical circles, 41; population, 49–50, 69; press and publishing, 18, 19, 69, 90, 113; socio-economic conditions, 2, 43, 49, 61, 98, 101, 120
Volk, 18, 21, 34, 35, 41, 42, 58, 63n35, 87, 130n22, 133n71
völkisch, 41, 42
Volksgemeinschaft, 41
Voltaire, 42, 52
Voyage en Icarie (Cabet), 94, 105n57

Wandering Jews, The, see *Juden auf der Wanderschaft* (Roth)
Weber, Max, *Protestantische Ethik und der Geist des Kapitalismus*, 21
Weltanschauung (racist), 113
Wieland, Christoph Martin, *Musarion: oder die Philosophie der Grazien*, 53
Wiener Allgemeine Zeitung, 69, 103n11
Wiesbaden (Hesse), 70
Wilhelm II (German emperor), 92, 98, 116, 130n24
Williams, Raymond, 120, 122, 124
Winckelmann, Johann J., 76
working class, 26, 49, 50, 56, 61, 69

xenophobia, 72, 77, 99

Zantop, Susanne, 3, 10n10, 10n11
Zanzibar, 73
Zeitschrift für Staats- und Volkswirtschaft, 70

Zionism, 8–9, 11n30, 68, 72, 84–86, 88–89, 91–92, 94–97, 99–101, 102, 105n41, 106n63, 106n66, 107n83, 107n85, 111, 118, 120, 123, 128
Zöllner, Friedrich, 40

www.ingramcontent.com/pod-product-compliance
Lightning Source LLC
Chambersburg PA
CBHW070044120526
44589CB00035B/2310